Expanding Horizons
In Business Education

NATIONAL BUSINESS EDUCATION YEARBOOK, NO. 32

1994

Editor:
ARTHUR MC ENTEE
University of Maine at Machias
Machias, Maine

Published by:
National Business Education Association
1914 Association Drive
Reston, Virginia 22091

EXPANDING HORIZONS IN BUSINESS EDUCATION

Copyright 1994 by

NATIONAL BUSINESS EDUCATION ASSOCIATION
1914 ASSOCIATION DRIVE
RESTON, VIRGINIA

$15.00

ISBN 0-933964-42-0

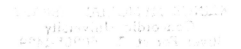

Preface

The one fact in business education that everyone seems to agree on is that it is not business education as usual in 1994.

National studies indicate that 85 percent of high school students will need additional training beyond high school to secure the jobs available by the year 2000. This fact alone demands that we alter the way we deliver business education.

The authors in this 1994 NBEA Yearbook present a number of avenues business educators can take to expand their programs to meet the needs of today's more efficient, quality-driven, high performance work places. In the K-8 schools, we see the infusion of keyboarding and desktop publishing skills. High school programming now includes curriculum integration, Tech Prep, and youth apprenticeship programs. Today's new global economy has encouraged the expansion of business education programs.

At the postsecondary level we see a continued emphasis on a technological-based world economy. Now, more than ever, opportunities for students are based on a meshing of academic and vocational skills. In addition, many business educators have reached out to special populations and have been successful in helping students attain minimum job-entry skills.

A special thank you goes out to Dr. Roberta Stearns, vice president, Casco Bay College, Portland, Maine, and Ms. Eleanor Lambertson, recently retired business education department chair, Beverly High School, Beverly, Massachusetts, who assisted me in reading and editing the 17 articles in this yearbook. These writings represent the collective works of 22 authors from 13 states.

This yearbook closes with a professional challenge—"Use It or Lose It!" Educators must use all of their professional know-how to keep up to date with economic and social changes in order to provide for the students an education that will prepare them for a future full of hope and opportunity.

> "The real magic of education is finding an approach
> that motivates and engages students to learn. . ."
>
> *John Fitzsimmons, President*
> *Maine Technical College System*

Arthur McEntee, Editor

Contents

PART III
EXPANDING HORIZONS IN BUSINESS EDUCATION: POSTSECONDARY EDUCATION

PART IV
EXPANDING HORIZONS IN BUSINESS EDUCATION:
MEETING THE CHALLENGE

Part I

EXPANDING HORIZONS IN BUSINESS EDUCATION: ELEMENTARY AND MIDDLE LEVEL EDUCATION

CHAPTER 1

TEACHING KEYBOARDING TO ELEMENTARY CHILDREN

ROWENA RUSSELL

Elementary Keyboarding Consultant, Corinna, Maine

Computers have ushered in an advanced technology age which has transformed the manner in which business education is delivered. One of the major areas to be affected is "typewriting," as it was commonly known for many years.

Computer users have been primarily interested in a practical skill which would enable them to get around the keyboard quickly and efficiently. Skill building, production skills, and many other peripheral skills are largely ignored by this new generation of keyboard users. Business educators have responded by providing courses emphasizing inputting skills and changing the title from "typewriting" to "keyboarding." The additional areas essential to developing outputting skills associated with typewriting have become known as formatting, word processing, or by other appropriate titles. Course content also has been altered to take advantage of available technology.

While business educators were becoming involved in the exciting new technology, another major change was occurring which would also drastically change keyboarding instruction at the secondary level. When computers were introduced and became popular as a writing tool in elementary schools, students developed their own keyboarding skills, often "hunt and peck." When keyboarding software was used, elementary teachers were not familiar with correct methods to assist students in developing proper keyboarding techniques. As a result, students have entered keyboarding classes in middle school or high school with many poor keyboarding habits already established.

ROLE OF BUSINESS EDUCATORS IN ELEMENTARY KEYBOARDING

Thus, elementary keyboarding skills have become an important issue. What should be the role of the business educator in this ongoing process? The keyboard is no longer the exclusive domain of the business teacher. However, it is the business educator who possesses the knowledge and skill to help correct a situation which neglects an important aspect of every child's education. It is extremely important that business educators recognize this responsibility and be convinced that they can be the child's advocate and can make a difference.

WHY TEACH KEYBOARDING TO ELEMENTARY CHILDREN?

Elementary students frequently use computers for writing, especially since the "writing to read" or the "whole language" approach has become popular. A variety of methods are utilized in acquainting them with the keyboard. Some states require keyboarding instruction for elementary students at a specific grade level. However, many states do not include the requirement that a certified keyboarding instructor be employed. Therefore, the instructor may be a qualified keyboarding teacher, or it may be any teacher, secretary, or aide who can type but who has no training in teaching keyboarding. In many cases, students are primarily self-taught, either with keyboarding software or by "trial and error." Invariably, students develop poor techniques in these situations. Individuals who are trained to teach keyboarding recognize that it is very difficult and often almost impossible to correct these bad habits.

In addition, students develop the attitude that they already can keyboard so it is not necessary to enroll in keyboarding courses again during their educational careers.

Research does confirm that students who have become proficient in touch keyboarding complete work faster and are more efficient in their use of the keyboard. Computer usage reinforces effective writing and editing skills, and students take a more active role in the learning process. Calhoun (1992) emphasizes the importance of keyboarding in motivating students and in improving their attitudes toward their work.

Currently, many workers must use a computer in their daily work. It is predicted that very soon nearly everyone will be required to use a computer in the performance of his/her duties. Also, home usage of computers is increasing dramatically. Economically, it is important that every student in our schools become a proficient keyboard user. Therefore, it is imperative that correct methods of keyboarding be administered when students begin to use the computer.

WHEN SHOULD KEYBOARDING BE INTRODUCED?

Authorities are in general agreement that students should be taught touch keyboarding just before they are required to utilize the skill for composition or sentence typing. Third or fourth grade has become a common placement of formal keyboarding instruction. Research indicates that fourth-grade students are developmentally ready to master keyboarding.

Another school of thought suggests that instruction on the keyboard begin in kindergarten and continue in stages throughout the elementary grades. Requirements may vary from state to state or from one school system to another.

ELEMENTARY KEYBOARDING CURRICULUM

When the plan includes instruction for kindergarten through elementary grades, kindergarten students are encouraged to use fingers on the left hand for the regular left hand keys and fingers on the right hand for keys on the right side of the keyboard. For example, a marker such as a piece of colored yarn may be placed in the center of the keyboard so that students can visualize the keys that each hand controls. Thus, they become conditioned to the fact that there are correct and incorrect ways to use the keyboard.

First graders may be introduced to the home keys. Some form of color coding is often used to help them place correct fingers on the keys.

Many plans permit first and second graders to look at the keys because their hands are too small to make the reaches and maintain contact with home keys. This type of instruction is generally followed by formal touch instruction on the alpha keys in third or fourth grade.

Numbers and symbols may be formally introduced at about fourth or fifth grade, or they may be introduced as the student needs to use them. Just as secondary students need a great deal of reinforcement in the learning stages, so do the elementary students. If students are taught correct procedures in a special keyboarding class and then return to the regular classroom to use computers, regular classroom teachers should be trained to monitor and reinforce proper techniques.

As soon as students have mastered the alpha keys and begin to write with the computer, a simple word processing program is introduced in some school systems.

When the computer education curriculum begins instruction at third grade or later, formal touch instruction should be started immediately so that students are utilizing touch keyboarding. It then should be continued in stages throughout the elementary years.

Unfortunately, many students are not receiving this type of formalized instruction. Therefore, it is evident that business educators must carry the torch and make certain that students receive keyboarding instruction at the appropriate time. Students are the people who suffer the consequences if an educational system fails to recognize this very vital need.

ELEMENTARY KEYBOARDING INSTRUCTION

Ideally, keyboarding instruction is offered in a room with a keyboard provided for each child. Instruction is also most effective when it is provided on a daily basis for an adequate period of time. Funding and physical facilities often are not available to provide such instruction.

Should elementary keyboarding then be forgotten and students allowed to flounder along on their own? The answer is a resounding "No." Let's be innovative and find ways to deliver keyboarding training in a manner which will help these students.

Some districts have purchased inexpensive electronic typewriters on which to provide keyboarding instruction. With the demands which are currently placed on teachers and schools, time is at a premium. This may mean that students do not have a half hour daily for 10, 12, or 15 weeks to devote to keyboarding instruction. It then becomes necessary to review scheduling carefully to determine the most favorable time for providing this training. In some instances, blocks of time may be available only once or twice a week and perhaps for only a few weeks.

Keyboarding instruction must begin with whatever facilities and time are available. An awareness of correct techniques and a respect for the keyboard must be developed. It is also of utmost importance that educators make concrete plans for the introduction of the keyboard, reinforcement activities, and some skill building over a period of years in the elementary grades. The curriculum should include material to be taught at each grade level, making certain that all teachers involved with the students are trained to reinforce that which students have already been taught.

There are innumerable examples of teachers who were concerned about student usage of the keyboard and who used creative ideas to make equipment, time, and instruction available. Some have salvaged typewriters being discarded by secondary schools and colleges or even by businesses. Some have used funds budgeted for language arts, libraries, or other areas to purchase inexpensive keyboards. A variety of plans for centralizing all computers in one school has been developed. Likewise, instruction is sometimes integrated into one or more subject areas in order to provide for keyboarding training. Computer education instructors often modify their curriculums to include keyboarding instruction once they have been convinced of its importance.

The use of paper keyboards, memorization of the keyboard, and other ineffective methods should be discouraged.

Physical facilities and room design and layout have often been overlooked. Little, if any, consideration is given to the proper height of desks and chairs, the correct position of the operator in front of the equipment, and finger placement on the keys. Proper position and correct techniques eliminate many errors and injuries caused by continuous computer use.

Again, it is the business educator who has the expertise in correct methods and techniques and who must furnish the leadership to ensure that students are being given the foundation in keyboarding that is very essential in the age of computers.

WHO SHOULD TEACH KEYBOARDING TO ELEMENTARY CHILDREN?

Certainly, only persons who have been trained in methods of teaching keyboarding should be administering keyboarding instruction to any student at any level, kindergarten through postsecondary. Such training should include not only the mechanics of teaching touch keyboarding but also methods of skill building, proofreading, simple formatting, and the other peripheral skills associated with typewriting instruction.

Before issuing a blanket statement that only middle school or high school business teachers should be teaching elementary keyboarding, it is important to realize that techniques of teaching elementary children are even more complex than teaching keyboarding. It would seem reasonable that business teachers should obtain some training in working with elementary children before starting keyboarding instruction with them. These factors lead us to the conclusion that both elementary and regular keyboarding teachers must receive the proper training to be effective in teaching keyboarding.

Another solution may be a cooperative arrangement with a keyboarding teacher and an elementary teacher working together to produce the desired results. In some states where funding does permit hiring keyboarding or computer instructors, methods courses have been offered to regular elementary classroom teachers so that they can at least supervise and reinforce correct methods being learned from keyboarding software.

Should keyboarding software be used? Many good computer software programs and accompanying textbooks are available. Keyboarding software programs represent another means of providing keyboarding instruction and additional motivation when it is not practical to have an instructor do so. Nevertheless, elementary teachers confirm the importance of supervision and reinforcement from the classroom teacher when utilizing keyboarding software. Instructors must evaluate the software carefully to make certain that it meets the instructional needs of students.

VARIATIONS IN TEACHING ELEMENTARY/SECONDARY KEYBOARDING

The attention span of younger children is much shorter. Activities must be varied frequently. Elementary children need a more relaxed approach when presenting the keyboard than secondary students do. Only one or two keys can be presented during a session with short drills and more reinforcement being necessary.

Elementary teachers use very different teaching methods when presenting new material. Suggestions from elementary teachers include using letters on a magnetic board or placing an outline of fingers and letters on a flannelgraph board rather than presenting a full keyboard with all letters of the alphabet. A second-grade teacher used a prop for each letter as it was being introduced. For example, she gave everyone a false nose to wear while learning the "n" key. The teacher wore a witch costume when introducing the "w." She explained that this is a type of reinforcement frequently utilized in teaching young children. Many teachers emphasized the use of color coding or other aids that help children learn key location more effectively. Evaluation should be conducted informally. Certificates of completion are recommended rather than formal grades.

TEACHING KEYBOARDING TO DISABLED CHILDREN

Disabled children are using the keyboard successfully as a means of communication. Students who are identified as learning disabled, mentally retarded, physically handicapped, visually impaired, and hearing impaired often benefit from keyboarding instruction. Nonverbal children are enabled to communicate with others and to participate in regular classes through a method called "facilitated communication."

The computer keyboard is an exciting communication tool for these children. Business educators can serve as an important resource for special needs students as well as providing keyboarding instruction.

SUMMARY

Because elementary students are using keyboards and because computers will be an important tool in their adult lives, it is essential that keyboarding instruction be included in the elementary school curriculum. Even when voice-activated computers become commonly used, predictions are that keyboarding skills will still be used for making corrections and for a variety of activities associated with the computer.

Many educators, administrators, and school boards do not understand the importance of correct keyboarding skills and the manner in which they must be developed. Business educators must assume the responsibility of ensuring that this important skill becomes a requirement in every school curriculum. It should not be a partisan effort in protecting turf but rather arise from a true concern for the proper education of our children.

REFERENCES

Calhoun, C. C., and Robinson, B. W. (1992). *Managing the learning process in business education.* Colonial Press.

Bureau of Adult & Secondary Vocational Education Task Force on Keyboarding. (1987). Guidelines for teaching keyboarding. Augusta, ME.

Eiser, L. (1987, April). No more hunt-and-peck. *Classroom Computer Learning,* pp. 52-56.

Headley, P. L. (1984, November). Keyboarding instruction in elementary school. *Business Education Forum,* pp. 18, 19.

Jackson, T. H. (1991, Winter). Building keyboarding skills at the elementary level. *The Balance Sheet,* pp. 19-22.

Keyboarding—An interview with Keith Wetzel. (1986, November). *The Writing Notebook,* pp. 10, 11.

Klopping, I. M. (1993, April). Don't lose control! *Business Education Forum. 47:*4, pp. 41, 42.

Lavin, J. (July 30 – August 1, 1993). The brilliant boy inside. *USA Weekend,* pp. 6-8.

Policies Commission for Business and Economic Education. (1984, October). This we believe about keyboarding. *Business Education Forum. 39:*1, p. 8.

Waner, K.; Behymer, J.; McCrary, S. (1992, October). Two points of view on elementary school keyboarding. *Business Education Forum,* pp. 27-29.

CHAPTER 2

KEYBOARDING TO DESKTOP PUBLISHING IN MIDDLE SCHOOL

SHARON ANDELORA

Woodcliff School, Woodcliff Lake, NJ 07675

FROM KEYBOARDING TO DESKTOP PUBLISHING IN MIDDLE SCHOOL LEVEL EDUCATION

The middle school is the best place to teach all students a formal computer applications course. Why? Since children are introduced to computers at the beginning of their educational life, they must learn the correct method to keyboard, enter information into the computer, manipulate the information, and create attractive reports using the information. Students can no longer wait until high school for a formal course in keyboarding and computer applications. With increasing graduation requirements and a demanding course load in high school, today most students, if they do not major in business education, no longer have the option of selecting such electives as keyboarding, word processing, and computer applications to complete their schedules.

KEYBOARDING

There has been a great deal of controversy in the past several years regarding when keyboarding lessons should begin in the educational process. Should it begin when the computer is first taught to the student (that could be as early as kindergarten)? Should it be later in elementary school? Should it be in the middle school? Should students wait until high school?

Keyboarding awareness. Students should become aware of the keyboarding process as soon as they are asked to input information into the computer. Students should learn the correct position of their fingers on the keys and the correct posture as they learn the computer. If this learning process takes place in the elementary school, a keyboarding awareness should be taught. However, a formal keyboarding course should be delayed until the students have matured in their finger dexterity and eye-hand coordination.

Finger dexterity. Most students do not have the finger dexterity to master the keyboard until the age of ten to twelve. For many young students, their fingers are not large enough to reach all the keys from the home row keys. Although a teacher can teach keyboarding at an early age, many students will not be able to do well due to the lack of finger dexterity.

Eye-hand coordination. It is a known fact that many students at a young age have limited eye-hand coordination. As students mature, their eye-hand coordination becomes more adaptable to many situations. Since keyboarding depends upon the student's eye-hand coordination, teaching keyboarding at too early an age will keep some students from successfully learning the keyboard.

For these two reasons, it is important that any keyboarding course taught to students at an early age be known as keyboarding awareness, not a formal keyboarding course. One major problem with giving a keyboarding course at a very early age is that children and parents believe that once they have had such a course, they do not need another keyboarding course. This is absolutely false. If students have a French course in third grade, they still need to continue taking lessons throughout their education. It is presumed that once a student knows the keys, the student has mastered the keyboard and no further lessons are needed. As educators, we must work together to change this perception. Since most students do not have the finger dexterity and/or the eye-hand coordination they need to master the keyboard at an early age, they need to take a formal keyboarding course when they mature.

Formal keyboarding course. The middle school is the perfect place to add that formal keyboarding course needed by all students today. Most students have developed their finger dexterity and eye-hand coordination sufficiently to be able to succeed in learning the keyboard. There are always some students who will be exceptions to this rule.

Ideally the course should be given to the students when they will be able to learn the skill on a daily basis for several weeks at a time. The ideal time schedule is a nine- to twelve-week block of time. Students should learn the keyboard at a pace that reinforces the skill before learning new keys. Learning the keyboard well but at a slower pace will save time in the long term.

Who should teach this course? The course should be taught by an educator who has been trained in keyboarding methods. Like any skill, learning keyboarding is like learning a musical instrument, and there are certain methods that must be taught and reinforced during this process. If the students are allowed to use poor techniques when keyboarding, it is very difficult to break these habits. Ever try to help a student who has keyboarded with two fingers for many years and can't break the habit? Business educators are ideal for this task as they have been trained to be that "drill sergeant" and are used to reinforcing the correct techniques over and over again. Teachers who do not insist on good techniques are not helping their students; actually they are failing to give their students the best education they deserve. One needs to be strict and forceful in training students in a skill subject and adhere to the rules and regulations of keyboarding. It does take time and patience, but the success of the students is well worth it.

Computer-instructed training vs. teacher-instructed training. Although the teacher is an important part of the teaching process of keyboarding, individual computer-instructed learning is ideal. Allowing the students to learn the keyboard at their own pace is much better than trying to keep the students at the same pace. Some students will learn faster than others, and it is important that they are allowed to go faster than other students. In the middle school, many students are pulled out of classes for various reasons such as band lessons, speech lessons, and gifted and talented courses. To keep students together is almost impossible with this kind of class schedule.

From experience this instructor has found that computer-instructed training has been ideal and has allowed the students to succeed at their own level and ability. It has also allowed the teacher to supervise the students to make sure the students are using the correct techniques at all times.

COMPUTER APPLICATIONS

Once the students have learned how to keyboard, it is important that they learn how to use this skill in various computer applications, such as word processing, databases, and spreadsheets.

Word processing. Every teacher has been taught to teach a concept from the known to the unknown. Since most students use the computer to write a school report or composition, learning the correct placement and procedure to keying a report should be the first word processing project. Once the student understands how to key a report; keying a title page, bibliography or reference page, and footnotes should be taught. Book reviews, class notes, and other school papers should also be part of the curriculum. As many students write letters to gather additional information for their school reports, personal business letters and envelopes are important word processing items that need also to be taught at this age. Learning to key outlines, tables, and columns of information will depend upon the word processing computer program being used in the classroom.

Databases. Since all students know how to use a phone directory, creating a phone book database using information about their friends is an easy way to explain the database concept and start the database unit. Other database projects that students enjoy include creating databases for their baseball card collection, tape or compact disk collection, computer program inventory, and video game cartridges collection.

Spreadsheets. Students are always keeping track of grades and their average in each of their subjects. Therefore, creating a spreadsheet of their grades is easy for the students to understand. Other spreadsheet projects include the statistics for a baseball team, basketball team, hockey team, or football team, sales accounting for a school club or business, and personal budgets. A very popular project that this instructor started with eighth-grade students is using the spreadsheet to keep track of weekly gains or losses in the stock market. A student is allowed to theoretically invest $10,000 in three different stocks. Each week the students log on to the Prodigy network to find out the latest closing price for their stock. The students record these prices in their spreadsheet to find out the up-to-date value of their stock portfolio.

The students also enjoy using the spreadsheet to create pie charts and bar graphs. An easy way for students to gather data for their graphs is to conduct polls on various topics. Students love to poll their friends on what kind of soda they like or what is their favorite baseball team. Once the students learn this concept, they can create graphs using the data from other spreadsheets they previously completed.

Telecommunications. In many schools students are taught how to use a modem and on-line services in the computer applications course or in the library. There are various telecommunications programs that are available for the middle school. The kind of telecommunications services that can be selected for the students basically depends upon the school's budget.

Integrated problems. Once the students have learned the major areas of computer applications—word processing, databases, and spreadsheets—students should be taught how to integrate these techniques while working on interesting projects. Depending upon the computer programs available to the students, integrated problems can also include desktop publishing projects. One of the projects this instructor's students enjoy working on is a newsletter that they can work on alone or with a friend. The student selects the topic, names the newsletter, and writes the articles. Graphics and graphs are imported from other programs.

Other exciting projects include creating promotional advertising flyers, travel brochures, and merging information from data bases into letters, invitations, and various reports.

Multi-media presentations. Students love to create multi-media presentations if the computer program is available. Students enjoy developing a script and putting the information into motion on the computer. With the use of CD-ROM technology, it is amazing the kind of presentations that the students can produce. Today the students can take color pictures and have them developed onto CD-ROMs to incorporate these pictures in their presentations. The students can also use a scanner to input their own photos into a multi-media presentation. These projects will become increasingly more popular when multi-media software and hardware are available in more classrooms.

Scheduling the course. Ideally the course should be required for all students in all grades in the middle school. Depending upon the time available in the school year, it should be divided equally by grade.

Several different configurations have been used for scheduling a business applications course at Woodcliff School. It was first started as a required course for all eighth-grade students every day for a full year. To allow seventh graders to learn the computer, the schedule was changed to teach the seventh graders two days a week and eighth graders three days a week. However, the instructor was not happy with the results caused by the time lapse between classes. It is difficult for some middle school students to remember what they did yesterday, let alone two and three days ago. To meet the needs of the sixth graders, the schedule was finally changed to a required trimester course meeting every day for 12 weeks for all three grades. This has worked best for this school as it has allowed the students to be taught every day for a period of 12 weeks annually. When the students are not in the course, they still use their computer knowledge to write their reports and assignments for other classes. This gives the students additional practice with the computer and reinforces their learning skills throughout the year.

The progress of the students has been outstanding using this schedule configuration. Although scheduling courses is never an easy task, a daily class would be a top priority, then as many weeks as possible to be divided between the grades, preferably between six to 12 weeks per grade.

Scope and sequence of units in computer applications. A plan should be developed to incorporate the learning of all the computer applications in the schedule time available in the middle school. Starting with the learning of the keyboard, the teacher should develop a sequence of units that reviews and reinforces the learning of one unit to another. The scope and sequence chart used in Woodcliff School is shown in Figure 1.

Figure 1
COMPUTER APPLICATIONS CURRICULUM
GRADES SIX, SEVEN AND EIGHT

CONTENT	GRADE 6	GRADE 7	GRADE 8
Proper Techniques at the Computer	Review, reinforce concepts/skills	Review, reinforce concepts/skills	Review, reinforce concepts/skills
Parts of the Computer	Macintosh computer	Review/reinforce concepts/skills	Review, reinforce concepts/skills
Keyboarding	Correct fingering (touch) system Continuity practice, one-minute writings, class assignments, etc.	Review, reinforce concepts/skills	Review, reinforce concepts/skills
Word Processing	Introduce word processing concepts Extend word processing practice to include: themes reports title page bibliography graphics book reviews class notes outlines	Review, reinforce concepts and extend skills to include: reports with footnotes letters and envelopes tables	Review, reinforce concepts/skills
Databases	Introduce concepts of databases	Review, reinforce concepts/skills	Review, reinforce concepts/skills
Spreadsheets		Introduce concepts of spreadsheets	Review, reinforce concepts/skills
Desktop Publishing		Introduce concepts of desktop publishing	Review, reinforce concepts/skills
Telecommunications	Introduce concepts of telecommunications	Review, reinforce concepts/skills	Review, reinforce concepts/skills
HyperCard		Introduce concepts	Develop stacks for presentations

Proper planning is a necessity to a computer applications program. Once you start teaching students computer applications, the same instructor should continue to teach them in all the consecutive grades in the school. Figure 1 shows that once a skill is taught, it is reviewed grade after grade.

Objectives. As with any curriculum, a teacher must develop course objectives appropriate to the age group and the prior computer education of the students. Therefore, each school will have different objectives. To help teachers create their own objectives, the objectives for the computer applications course at Woodcliff School are listed in Figure 2.

Figure 2

INTEGRATING COMPUTER SKILLS
WITH OTHER SUBJECT AREAS

TOPICS	OBJECTIVES
Techniques and Parts of the Computer	By the end of Grade 8, all students will be able to locate and use correctly the manipulative parts of the computer using the correct techniques as observed by the teacher and recorded on a checklist.
Keyboarding	By the end of Grade 8, all students will type using the correct fingering system with good techniques and form as observed by the teacher and recorded on a checklist.
Word Processing	By the end of Grade 6, all students will be able to type on the computer short reports/themes, title page, table of contents, bibliography, book reviews, class notes, report covers, and personalized stationery with graphics as measured by teacher review of classwork and recorded on a checklist.
	By the end of Grade 7, all students will be able to type on the computer letters/envelopes, short reports with footnotes, outlines, and tables as measured by teacher review of classwork and recorded on a checklist.
	By the end of Grade 8, all students will be able to type on the computer a complete report with footnotes as measured by teacher review of classwork and recorded on a checklist.
Databases	By the end of Grade 8, all students will be able to create a record form, and enter, sort, retrieve, and report data using a database as measured by teacher review and recorded on a checklist.
Spreadsheets	By the end of Grade 8, all students will be able to create a simple spreadsheet, be able to manipulate figures by simple formulas, and create bar graphs and pie charts using the figures from the spreadsheet.
Desktop Publishing	By the end of Grade 8, all students will be able to create and edit a document in a desktop publishing program importing the data from a word processing program and/or graphics program as measured by teacher review of classwork and recorded on a checklist.
Telecommunications	By the end of Grade 8, all students will be able to communicate via a modem to another computer outside of school as observed by the teacher and recorded on a checklist.
HyperCard	By the end of Grade 8, all students will be able to create a HyperCard stack for use in a classroom presentation.

It is important that once students learn various computer skills, they use this skill in all their other subjects. The more the students use their skills in other class projects, the more they appreciate their ability to use the computer. Students should be able to create databases for various parts in history; research papers in language arts, history, health, and science; spreadsheets in math; book reviews in reading, English, and language arts; and integrated projects in all subjects.

History. Computer skills can be used in many ways in a history class. Students can use word processing to write their history research papers, reports, class notes, timelines, and outlines. The students can use their computer skills to research history problems using a variety of data bases obtained using CD-ROMs and on-line services. In addition, there are many excellent history computer software packages that may be available in the schools.

English. Word processing is a necessity in English and writing classes. Research indicates that students produce better papers when using a computer as they can correct and change their compositions easily. All students in writing courses should have access to computer time.

Science. Students in science classes can use word processing to write science reports, bibliographies, outlines, and laboratory reports. They can use their training to create various data bases on a wide selection of science topics. In addition, there are outstanding computer software programs for science, some of which incorporate multi-media presentations using the computer, CD-ROMs, and video discs.

Health and Physical Education. Students use word processing to do various reports for health and physical education. Spreadsheets can be used to keep track of different physical activities, such as running times, situps, etc. There are some superb computer programs that will simulate various health areas, such as learning about the heart, lungs, hearing, and vision.

Math. Spreadsheets can be used quite often in a variety of math exercises. Math computer software programs are popular in giving additional math practice to students.

Reading. Word processing is used often in reading to write book reviews and compositions. The data base is used effectively in keeping track of the books read by the students.

These are just some suggestions of how computer skills can be used in various classes. If teachers use their imagination, there are many more ways for students to use their computer skills.

USING COMPUTER SKILLS IN EXTRA-CURRICULAR ACTIVITIES

There are many extra-curricular activities the students can participate in that would allow them to use their newly acquired skills. The school newspaper is one good example. The students can certainly use the computer to write their articles and lay out the newspaper. In addition, students can learn other computer equipment such as a scanner. Learning good desktop publishing techniques is a definite asset to any student.

The school yearbook is another good example of where the students can use their computer skills. In order to produce an outstanding yearbook at the lowest cost, the students can typeset the entire yearbook using the various computer fonts. This allows the students to try different fonts, font styles, and borders that add to their desktop publishing skills.

The Future Business Leaders of America organization is another example of extra-curricular activities available to the middle school student. In the past, this school has had several students place in the state competition; one student even placed in the national competition. The FBLA encourages the participation of middle school students.

Students can also create activities that can incorporate their computer skills. For several years, the students created a service club in which they volunteered to type for various teachers. They would type study sheets, review sheets, class exercises, and other materials that the teacher could use in the classroom. The students enjoyed being the special assistant to the teacher.

From time to time, students might be asked to help design a special flyer or school program. It gives the student recognition and shows off the student's expertise in computer skills.

OFTEN ASKED QUESTIONS

How does a teacher grade students in this course? One question that always comes up when discussing middle school computer applications is how does the teacher grade students in this course? Grading should be based more on quality than on quantity. The teacher should set high standards for this course and students should strive for perfection. It is important that students thoroughly complete an assignment and that the teacher check it for format, placement, and content. If there are errors, students should be required to correct them. Unless students understand their mistakes and correct them, they will not fully learn the basics of the application.

Grading should be based on each individual class since some classes might meet more than others due to assemblies, school-wide testing programs, and other interruptions. Set the standards based on the accomplishments by the majority of the students in the class.

How does the teacher check the student's progress? The best way for the teacher to monitor the progress of the students is by methodical records. All students should maintain a folder with pockets to hold their work, assignments, directions, and data disk. Each day the students come into the classroom, the folders are given out, and each student proceeds with the work. At the end of the class period, each student is required to record progress on a calendar in the folder. In this way, the student reviews what was completed during the class period and will know exactly where to start the next day. It also helps the teacher to monitor the progress of all students at all times. The folders are collected and stored until the next class period.

As students complete an assignment, the teacher checks the work for errors in content, format, and placement. If there are errors, the teacher should make notations on the assignment, and the student should correct it. When corrected, the student hands in both assignments in order for the teacher to double check and make sure all corrections have been made. If possible the student explains the mistake to the teacher and how it was corrected.

What about letting the students play computer games? This question is always asked when working with children at this age. The students would love to play games instead of learning about word processing, databases, and spreadsheets. Games can be used as a reward for students who have completed a unit and have exhibited good behavior. At the end of each unit, a fun day is given that allows the students to use any of the software programs that they want to use. A few students will use Print Shop; some will use Sim City (a simulated program that allows the students to design their own city); some will use Life and Death (a simulated program that allows the students to perform various surgical procedures); some will work on a keyboarding program to improve their keyboarding speed; and others will use the Carmen Sandiego programs. Since the students enjoy these fun days, they seem to work extra hard to complete their assignments in the required time, and they behave well in class. If students have not finished their assignments, they must complete their assignments before they can enjoy the fun day. This fun day could also be considered a make-up day for students who have been absent from the class during the unit.

What about the behavior of the students at this age? It seems that the students at this age are known to be disruptive, outspoken, and hard to manage. If students are not interested in the subject matter, this could be the case. A teacher must inform students what behavior is expected of them. The fun day has also been a great reward for good behavior, and since the class works as a unit, a student would not want to keep the class from having this reward.

Students at this age are in between the elementary student and the high school student. Most of the students are lovable and really want to learn about the computer. For some students, a teacher needs to work harder and give some tender loving care to modify their behavior. If you work with the students and show them that you are concerned about them and want them to succeed, you will have a wonderful experience as a teacher of the middle school student.

How do the students like the course? Most of the students love the course. There are always some students who do not like any course they take in school. The students are so proud of their work when they finish an assignment that they can't wait to show it to the teacher. Even when the students are not taking the computer course, they love to show the computer teacher reports they have finished at home.

The computer room is open before and after school for the students to have more time with the computers. This allows the students to use the computers for their other classes as well as to explore new software that is available in the computer room. During the school day, students often come into the computer room from another class to key an English composition, science bibliography, or other assignments, if there are extra computers available in the classroom. Students also love to come to the computer room during their free time after they finish eating lunch. Whenever possible, the computers should be available to the students. For some students, the computer room is their home away from home.

What do the parents think about the course? The parents are amazed at what the students know about the computer and how easily they can use the computer for their school work, school reports, and other school activities. The comments received from the parents are all complimentary. They are thrilled at the progress of their children. The students often tell their parents how they can do a household task much easier on the computer, such as making up an invitation list or a greeting card list on a database, designing a party invitation or personalized stationery on the computer, or writing letters or reports with a word processing program.

The students love to show off their newly acquired skill to their parents. They love to demonstrate new techniques and software to the family. For many students, using the computer is a family activity. Many parents have remarked that computer time must be scheduled among the family members and that they need more than one computer in the home. For some parents, this is the first time they have seen their child enthusiastic about a class in school.

If I am a high school business education teacher, can I teach in the middle school? In most states, secondary education is considered grades 7-12. You would need to check your particular state requirements for certification, but many states allow you to teach a business course at any grade level.

The major problem for most high school business teachers is their lack of desire to teach in the middle school. They are simply afraid to make that move downward. In addition, the myths of the junior high student being unmanageable, uncontrollable, and the worse student to teach does not help the situation. A teacher must experience the joys of teaching in the middle school to be convinced that the middle school is really a wonderful place to teach. Every day is a new experience. Every day is exciting. The enthusiasm of the middle school child makes teaching a remarkable experience.

TIPS AND TECHNIQUES
FOR THE MIDDLE SCHOOL COMPUTER TEACHER

1. Be fun, but firm.

2. Set high standards for your class. The students will strive to reach the goal you set for them.

3. Structure the class so that students know what is expected of them, what they are to do, how to behave, how to treat the computer equipment.

4. Be organized and instruct your students to be organized. Have the students keep all their work in a folder, maintain good records of their progress, and know exactly where to begin each day.

5. Have the students always review their progress at the end of each day. It is important that students know what they have learned and what they have done during a class period.

6. Cherish each day as a wonderful experience. The more you enjoy your work, the more the students will enjoy being with you. One of the greatest joys of teaching is to watch their eyes open wide and their mouths open with comments like "wow" or "awesome."

SUMMARY

All students need to know computer applications, and the middle school is the ideal place for them to learn how to apply these techniques in all their subject-matter courses. It should be a required course for all students and include the basic computer applications of keyboarding, word processing, databases, spreadsheets, telecommunications, desktop publishing, and if possible, multimedia presentations. Since time may be a limitation, the course may be given in parts, starting with keyboarding in the sixth grade, word processing and data bases in the seventh grade, and spreadsheets and other areas in the eighth grade. The existing curriculum should be studied, and any configuration that can be worked out with the other required courses should be tried. Although it may not be an ideal situation, any training that can be given in the middle school is a good beginning. Students can no longer wait until high school for this training.

Teaching computer applications in the middle school is a most rewarding experience for a teacher. Every day is exciting. The students are so eager to learn more and more about the computer that the class is never boring and dull; it is demanding and stimulating. It seems that there is never enough time in class to cover everything you want to teach; the time goes by so quickly that you cannot wait until the next day to see the class. You cannot really appreciate teaching in the middle school until you try it. Try it, you will love it!

Part II

EXPANDING HORIZONS IN BUSINESS EDUCATION: SECONDARY EDUCATION

CHAPTER 3

YOUTH APPRENTICESHIP PROGRAMS—BUSINESS AND SCHOOL PARTNERSHIPS

WILLIAM H. CASSIDY

Center for Youth Apprenticeship, South Portland, Maine

Business educators have a long and distinguished history of successfully preparing their students for America's businesses. As much as a decade ago, when many educational reformers and scathing reports were prolifically appearing on every front, business education programs were recognized as one of the few shining lights of our American educational system. Even with this endorsement, business educators recognize that new and innovative approaches must be invoked within their programs if they are to provide their students with the enhanced skills and knowledge they will require to participate in a global marketplace.

Youth apprenticeship programs are a bold new approach that links education with businesses in such a way that they collaborate in a partnership using the schoolplace and the workplace as a learning place. The student has the opportunity to apply core-subject knowledge, develop work readiness skills, and experience adult relationships in the business world through interaction with the workplace meister (mentor/trainer).

The business educator may be the moving force behind the establishment of a youth apprenticeship experience within the educational community; but it needs to be clearly stated that the establishment of this offering, as a component of the mainframe educational system, will require broad coalitions, as this option is not a stand-alone-program—it is part of an "emergent system." New approaches within both the schoolplace and the workplace must occur if the true systemic change is to bring a significant number of our secondary youth as responsible citizens and skilled workers into the "Third American Century."

THE PROGRAM COMPONENTS

The youth apprenticeship wave currently sweeping across America finds its origin in several European nations such as Germany and Denmark. Although none of the developing youth apprenticeship initiatives in the various states is lock-stepped to these, one will find certain fundamental components within virtually any program that shadows the European experience.

Although a youth apprenticeship program may adopt any number of configurations, there are common strands.

- Students are made aware of life and career opportunities in their elementary years, especially in grades seven and eight, as they plan their secondary education pursuits directed by information and knowledge of their own interests, aptitudes, and career aspirations.

- During the ninth and 10th grades, students are given the opportunity to expand career exploration, including job shadowing or site visitations for the youth apprenticeships available to them.

- Students often begin the combined school and workplace component of the program in the last two years of high school.

- Core subject instruction is directly related to the apprentice cluster and is taught in an applied fashion incorporating competency-based standards and authentic performance assessments.

- Youth apprenticeship experiences are built around occupational clusters, pursuing employment growth areas providing transferable skills to same.

- The workplace is used as a learning place rather than a training place, in that core academic experiences are performed in the workplace in cooperation with the supervisor/meister.

- Upon the successful completion of the youth apprenticeship program, the participant receives a certificate of initial mastery, matriculation towards a higher education credential, or advanced placement in a registered apprentice program.

It should be noted that youth apprenticeship should not be considered as another program, e.g. cooperative education, or work experience component of a vocational magnet school. Rather, youth apprenticeship programs must be a component of a comprehensive "system," for school-to-work/life transition. "Programs" tend to stand alone and, in doing so, merely contribute to the compartmentalized, departmentalized educational system which has proven so ineffective in addressing the needs of so many of America's youth.

Also, by its very nature, the youth apprenticeship program requires significant change in many other elements of the secondary school, particularly in the subject content and instructional applications. Desired outcomes are identified, and school and workplace activities are well coordinated and embody these identified outcomes.

The assessment aspects of the program exemplify the redirection required of the mainstream educational system we have known:

- Pre-entrance criteria call for a gateway assessment which assures that the student has mastered certain basic core skills and knowledge which will reasonably assure success in the youth apprenticeship experience;

- For those students completing the program, there is a need to assess skill mastery, and this assessment will be more crucial as more and more occupations move to portable credentials.

The youth apprenticeship program may serve as the beacon to which true systemic change may be drawn in any given local educational agency. Who better to tend the lantern's oil than the business educator?

ISSUES TO PROGRAM IMPLEMENTATION

Endeavors into educational reform driven by the Taylor Industrial Model, which is management driven, are doomed to failure. In this endeavor, a true

Demings philosophy is imperative. Educators, in harmony with others, must initiate this systemic change. Given the national and state dialogue on this educational option, the timing is most appropriate to move quickly, seizing the moment for advancement.

In the spirit of participatory management, we all are stakeholders in the event; thus, it is perfectly appropriate that the business educator be the moving force to introduce the youth apprenticeship concept and lead the initiative as it develops within the educational and business community.

There are, however, certain protocols one might incorporate in one's work to assure acceptance and implementation. The following are offered as suggested strategies toward that end. It should be noted that no implementation strategy is without need of modification to accommodate those specific idiosyncrasies that make up the local environment.

Research the topic. Prepare for the presentation of the concept by considering the various audiences in which the discussion will be advanced. It will be necessary to develop variations of the presentation in order to accommodate the particular needs of the individual(s) or groups. In order for one to receive acceptance by the listener, it is imperative to assure that one is informed on the intricacies of the topic.

As was noted earlier in this chapter, the establishment of strong coalitions will be crucial if this endeavor into new educational frontiers is to prevail. All stakeholders must become stockholders.

Advancing on the stakeholders. Initial discussions as to with whom, and what format they may take, will vary with the local education system driven by the policies established by the governing board. It is important to recognize how change occurs within the educational setting, for it would not do to scuttle a good idea merely because one went against the local cultural norms for innovation and change. It may be necessary to seek new and different power brokers and introduce them into the school culture. Let it be recognized that they, representing the community served by the school, desired this innovation.

Concept discussions should involve a broad area of participants. Traditionally, education has made educational decisions somewhat in a void guided by very limited input from a part-time board of directors. Even within the context of reform, we have, at best, made a feeble effort in providing for, or even welcoming, participation from outsiders.

This will not do. It will be necessary to bring together more factions than ever previously known to develop a consensus on what we expect students to know, and be able to do, upon completion of their youth apprenticeship experience.

This cohort will broaden its base, inclusive of such individuals, beyond the administrative/management types, as line-educators, workers, students, and parents/guardians.

Convening the Design Team. Upon gaining consensus on the youth apprenticeship concept, it will be necessary to convene a program design and implementation team. This group will serve as the steering committee to provide the necessary leadership in identifying the program implementors and mission.

The membership will mirror the individuals and organizations who were targeted in the introductory information phase. In the organization of this group, it is imperative that those who serve, or are asked to serve in this capacity, possess a fundamental belief in the basic premises of the program and have a desire to serve. Certainly, we have ample research in both the public and private sector to verify that unwilling participants will virtually assure a fall short of the mark.

The steering committee will address such matters in their program design as:

- Program awareness, both internal and external
- Program operations and management structure
- Internal and external awareness strategies
- Identification of potential occupational clusters and participating businesses
- Direction on entrance criteria and processes
- Research and development of:

    Applied academic subject matter

    Workplace standards inclusive of position, accountabilities, and worker behaviors
- Student assessment and the certificate of initial mastery
- System monitoring and evaluation
- Resetting the model to assure maximum stake/stockholder benefit.

Commencing Development. There are an infinite number of matters to be addressed in the establishment of an endeavor of this magnitude. However, there are certain components that are essential to the primary fabric. Any venture void of these components will lose the essence of the youth apprenticeship and merely replicate what already exists in work-experience programs, which fail to meet the needs of many learners, as they do not truly integrate the happenings of school and work. The following will highlight certain primary components of a comprehensive youth apprenticeship initiative. It should be noted that it is a given that through each of these, there is a broad based representative group designing or developing the program components.

- Identify the school/workplace coordinator who will head the local initiative— possibly the business educator who has knowledge of the school and business world and thus can operate within both environments effectively.

- Establish school/business partnership, identifying specific youth apprenticeship stations.

- Develop entrance criteria inclusive of such components as applications and portfolio protocols. The portfolio will be essential to the students in providing them information on their interest, abilities, and aptitudes, which help them self-select their pursuit of this option. To the business, this material will be invaluable in making their selection. They will have more comprehensive information than they previously had in hiring employees, whether school-aged youth or adults.

- Convene curriculum/standards craft committees, charging them to audit the stations, identify the accountabilities, and then identify appropriate school and workplace curriculum which would teach/train to those standards. These materials should also address work readiness and behavior development inclusive of self-esteem and stewardship.

- Train the trainers. Significant efforts will have to be made to prepare both the school-based educators and the workplace meisters in their roles within the program. Educators will require assistance in developing and delivering applied academic courses. Likewise, the workplace meister will require assistance in addressing such issues as interacting with adolescents, monitoring worker behaviors, and core academic experiences.

- Begin the creation of articulation agreements with the postsecondary institutions or registered apprenticeship programs which may serve as the capstone for an initial phase of lifelong learning.

- Develop strategies for program monitoring and evaluation.

SUMMARY

The preceding narrative offers only a scant overview of the multitude of issues that have to be addressed to invoke a true systemic educational change of this magnitude. Although the task is great, it is not insurmountable, and there are few educators better positioned to initiate the discussion and lead the endeavor than the business educator.

The youth apprenticeship program is not the "silver bullet," nor is it intended for all students, nor should it lead to the demise of beneficial education and training programs, such as business education. Youth apprenticeship is another option on the menu of offerings which may better serve 10 to 15 percent of our secondary students. The gap grows daily in our world of emerging technological wizardry, between those who have the necessary skills to succeed and those who do not. It is a world which requires workers who not only possess manipulative skills, but can critically think, solve problems, and show themselves as highly moral individuals who can work with others in the diverse culture of America and the global marketplace.

Although this writing addressed the issue on a very personal and local level, there is momentum building in many states and at the national level to develop a comprehensive youth apprenticeship system across America over the next three to five years. With this will come networks, coalitions, and various other resources for the local initiative to align with and benefit from.

In closing, it is imperative to recognize a singular common theme and validated fact from those scathing reports on America's education system of several years ago . . . what we have been doing has not worked for too many of our youth. We all—educators, businesses, students, parents, and public agencies—must unite as partners in concept-and-implementation, behind common initiatives, such as a youth apprenticeship, if we are to prepare our children to live and work in this global environment of today and the intergalactic environment of tomorrow.

CHAPTER 4

THE ADMINISTRATIVE STEPS FOR IMPLEMENTING APPLIED ACADEMICS

MARI C. SHAW

Southern Illinois University at Carbondale
McChord AFB Campus, Tacoma, Washington

Although making the shift from teaching to learning seems simple in concept, it is exceedingly difficult in implementation. Educational environments have been established, nearly since inception, on the assumption that teachers teach and students learn. Further, if certain students do not learn within a reasonable amount of time and with reasonable effort on the part of the teacher, then the students are at fault and typically fail. New paradigms of teaching and learning counter this model and do not focus on teaching and test-taking techniques. Rather, they consider how students learn and then decide how to organize the instruction so that students arrive at answers and are able to tell exactly how they did it. It is of no consequence whether one student gets it one way over a certain period of time and another student gets it another way over a different period of time. The important factor is that they "get it." Therefore, there is no doubt currently that when educators make a key decision about curriculum, there will be vocational and academic cooperative planning in the same room; not only that, but it will not seem the least bit remarkable. This exciting, changing paradigm for teaching and learning in an applied, interdisciplinary context follows.

HISTORICAL PERSPECTIVE

In the spring of 1989 the State of Washington accepted membership in the Agency for Instructional Technology's (AIT's) Consortium as an opportunity to deliver applied communication course work in its high schools. The state supervisors of Business Education and Language Arts/Reading met to work through an implementation plan that would best meet the needs of students, business/industry leaders, educators, and educational systems. They also developed guidelines to address funding and staffing models for districts utilizing the courseware. This initial and ongoing cooperation of the state academic and vocational staffs (the "WE" approach) is, by most definitions, the key component to the success of all the Applied Academic Projects. This "WE" (academic and vocational cooperative venture) approach to the deliverer of instruction is believed to be why the state has been so successful in the implementation, administration, and funding of applied programs— Principles of Technology, 1986; Applied Math, 1987; Applied Communication, 1989; and Applied Biology/Chemistry, 1992.

Putting aside the "THEM-vs-US" traditional delivery to education found in many districts, the basic model for implementation of all the applied academics projects in the state of Washington was similar; however, because this writer served as the state supervisor of Business Education in 1989 and is most familiar with the processes for implementing Applied Communication, this specific courseware will serve as discussion for the administrative steps necessary to integrate applied academics.

In the spring of 1989, through a nomination process, three English and three business education instructors were selected by the state program supervisors to serve as members of the implementation team for the Applied Communication Project. Along with the state supervisors of Business Education and Language Arts/Reading, the group attended a four day meeting in Memphis, Tennessee, sponsored by AIT. They were funded by state vocational dollars.

In addition to learning background information, working with national educators, and developing strategies for enhancement of units of instruction, the team was able to become better acquainted and develop the framework for statewide training of colleagues. The team's efforts culminated in an implementation plan that would ensure integrity of the project.

After returning to Washington, two additional team meetings were convened. Meetings were made possible because of the Division of Vocational-Technical Education's continued funding commitment for vocational and academic curriculum integration. The meetings lasted a full day and provided a forum for refining initial implementation guidelines. There was team consensus that this project would only be implemented as an integrated model. No stand-alone classes would be funded. As a result, the following application, including assurance statements, was recommended for adoption. The state directors of Vocational-Technical Education and Curriculum/Instruction approved the plan, and the application was sent to all secondary districts.*

Application for the Applied Communication Program – 1992-1993

School District: _____

Superintendent: _____
                               (Signature)

Vocational Director/Administrator: _____
                                            (Signature)

Vocational Area(s) in which program will be delivered: _____

_____

- -

I.   <u>Circle One Answer</u>

   A. Will the district purchase courseware and the   Yes   No
       equipment for the Applied Communication
       Program? (15 Modules = $438.75—ordered
       through AIT.)

   B. Will the district fund the in-service fee for   Yes   No
       instructor(s) to participate in state-sponsored
       in-services? (Anticipated four (4) days initial
       and three (3) days of follow-up training during
       the school year.)

   C. Will the district designate an instructor(s)   Yes   No
       to in-service other vocational staff on the
       integration of Applied communication in
       all appropriate program areas?

*D. List the name(s) of the vocational instructor(s)
       responsible for delivering instruction in Applied
       Communication:

_____   _____
Name and Certificate Number   Program Area

_____   _____
Name and Certificate Number   Program Area

OPTIONAL/ENCOURAGED LINKAGE OF VOCATIONAL/ GENERAL ACADEMIC COMPONENT

II.   List the name(s) of the academic instructor(s) team teaching the Applied
      Communication Program with vocational colleagues:

_____   _____
Name and Certificate Number   Program Area

_____   _____
Name and Certificate Number   Program Area

List the name of the district's contract person   _____
who will respond to requests for data on the   Name
program.

                                                          _____
                                                               Address

                                                          _____
                                                              Telephone

III. **Participation Assurances: By signing Page 1 of the application, the district assures that:**

   A. Vocational Applied Communication is an integrated component of a planned vocational program sequence for students with a vocational career objective. **Classes will not be funded as stand-alone offerings.**

   B. There will be coordination and articulation among the vocational programs integrating Applied Communication courseware and the Language Arts (English) programs.

C. During the second year of implementation, the trained, vocationally-certified instructor(s) is responsible for providing in-service training to vocational instructors within the district on how to integrate Applied Communication courseware into their vocational programs. The district will be responsible for all costs for providing this inservice activity.*

D. Instructor(s) attending the 30-hour initial training WILL attend the two (2) follow-up training sessions during the 1992-93 school year.**

* The 1992-93, 30-hour initial training session could be substituted for "C" above. Therefore, districts having already implemented the program are encouraged to send additional vocational/academic staff to this training.

** The registration materials following may be used for first-time districts implementing during the 1992-93 school year or by districts wishing to send additional staff if they have implemented since 1989. These are valuable sharing sessions intended to strengthen the delivery of your program. All districts are encouraged to send representatives.

Implementation Procedure – Applied Communication Courseware

1. The instructor(s) must be vocationally certified for the class to generate vocational FTEs. If the class is team taught, at least one instructor **MUST BE** vocationally certified.

2. Instructor(s) **MUST** attend the state in-service—if team will be teaching, team **MUST** attend the state in-service.
   Districts will pay all instructor costs for attending an initial four day in-service session and two follow-up in-service sessions held during the school year: January and May—1.5 days each.

3. Districts **MUST** provide materials, supplies and equipment to deliver Applied Communication. The minimum cost of modules is $438.75 plus postage. There may be additional costs incurred in delivering the program to the district contingent on existing equipment (VCRs, monitors, overheads) and supplies.

4. The district will provide extended contract time to all instructors responsible for delivering the program in addition to existing extended days. These extended days are designed to establish and organize the Applied Communication courseware.

5. Applied Communication materials may be integrated into either a 90- or 180-hour vocationally-approved class. **Applied Communication is not a stand-alone class.***

6. The Applied Communication courseware needs to be approved by the district's Advisory Committee (either general or program committee), and documentation of the approval **MUST BE** submitted with the application form to the state office. Typically, this approval would take the form of minutes of a meeting or a letter, either of which should be signed by the committee's chair.

7. The district will submit an annual report of the program, listing the objectives accompanied and recommendations for the next year. This report shall also include: data relative to students served, a summary of how in-service relative to Applied Communication will be delivered within the district, and the completion of a state office self-valuation form.

* **Other applied academic programs (Principles of Technology, Applied Math, or Applied Biology/Chemistry) may be either integrated or stand-alone offerings. Applied Communication is an integrated model only.**

APPLIED COMMUNICATION GENERAL INFORMATION

Materials/Courseware:

1. All 15 modules are available for purchase individually or as a package price. Because of the state contract with AIT, only districts approved for implementation will be able to purchase materials from AIT. Each module has 10 lessons. There are 150 total lessons in the program. Each lesson could consume one class period (50 minutes); however, some instructors may spend more or less time on selected lessons.

2. Each module includes: a video, instructor's guide, student worktext, and the notebook in which the materials are stored. Additional guides, worktexts and videos may be purchased separately.

Reporting:

1. Because the Applied Communication courseware will be integrated into existing vocational programs, there will be no change in reporting from what is currently being done.

In-service and Training:

1. There will be an initial four-day workshop to be held in May for 30 hours. Teachers participating would be identified as Level II trainers. Level I trainers were the State Training Team.

2. There will be two one-and-a-half-day follow-up workshops held during the school year.

3. Both college graduate credit and clock hour continuing education renewal units will be available for the training. Those instructors needing credit will be able to register for three quarter credits at the regular graduate credit rate. The cost for the credit is in addition to the workshop registration. The 30-hour training session registration fee will be approximately $200.

Equivalency/Cross Crediting:

1. Equivalency or cross crediting for classes integrating the Applied Communication courseware to meet a general education credit is a local district decision.

Follow-Up Evaluation:

1. Each district will be asked to submit an annual report. One of the components will be the completion of an evaluation form developed by the state office and a listing of recommendations for the second and ongoing years.

Advisory Committee Interaction:

1. Accompanying the application form, each district will be asked to submit documentation from the general or program Advisory Committee indicating that they approve the implementation of the Applied Communication courseware into the existing vocational program (integrated model) (Shaw, Application, 1992).

*I believe the application form represents important foundational information for states implementing any applied academics program. There **must** be evidence of administrative commitment and support from the onset and representation of an academic vocational cooperative partnership to establish ownership before implementation attempts.

Given that a major component of implementation is training, State Level I trainers agreed that a minimum 30-hour training course with two 1.5-day follow-up sessions needed to be required. The state's commitment to in-service did not waiver, and support for this training was approved. The following provides the elements of the 30-hour training course for instructors initially integrating the Applied Communication courseware. The last two days of the training, instructors (veteran Level II trainers) from the previous year's implementation return to "share the good news." This information attempts to share with the reader the necessity of integrating education, business, industry, and state support for the program.

APPLIED COMMUNICATION 30-HOUR TRAINING SESSION AGENDA

Wednesday:

4:00 - 6:00 p.m.	Registration	
6:00 - 7:30 p.m.	Opening Session/Introductions Review of District Assurances	Business Education -and- Language Arts/Reading State Supervisors
	Welcome Presentations	State Director of Curriculum/Instruction -and- State Director of Vocational-Technical Education
	Dinner: "Communication Skills in the Workplace"	Robert M. McKenzie Corporate Training Manager – The Boeing Company
7:30 - 8:00 p.m.	"Getting to Know You" Module 6 – Lesson 1	State Level I Trainer
8:00 - 8:30 p.m.	Workshop Overview	State Supervisors
8:30 - 8:45 p.m.	Admit Slip 1 (Input)	
8:45 - 9:00 p.m.	Applied Communication Implementation Video/Applied Popcorn	State Level I Trainer

Thursday:

7:15 - 8:00 a.m.	Continental Breakfast	
8:00 - 8:15 a.m.	Admit Slip Review and Architecture of a Module – Video 1A – Module 1	State Supervisors
8:15 - 10:15 a.m.	Break-out Work Sessions/Review of Modules – Objective: Develop Philosophy/Mission Statements	State Level I Trainers
10:15 - 10:30 a.m.	Break	
10:30 - 11:30 a.m.	General Session – Share the Good News – Reach Group Consensus on Philosophy/Mission – Recap Break-out Sessions	State Supervisors
11:30 - 11:45 a.m.	Break	
11:45 - 1:15 a.m.	Luncheon: "Essential Skills and Attributes for Service Occupation Employees"	Business/Industry Representative
1:15 - 1:45 p.m.	Break	

1:45 - 3:45 p.m.	Break-out Work Sessions/Review Modules – Objective: Develop Academic/Vocational SLOs	State Level I Trainers
3:45 - 4:00 p.m.	Break	
4:00 - 5:00 p.m.	General Session – Share the Good News – Reach Consensus on Student Learning Objectives	State Supervisors
5:00 - 5:30 p.m.	Admit Slip and Wrap-Up of Day's Activities	State Supervisors
5:30 - 8:00 p.m.	Dinner on Your Own	
8:00+	Hot Buttered Video (Participants spend time viewing and discussing videos rather than those introduced thus far.)	State Level I Trainers

Friday:

7:15 - 8:00 a.m.	Continental Breakfast	
8:00 - 9:00 a.m.	General Session – Catch Up/ Respond to Admit Slips – Redefine Agenda	State Supervisors
9:00 - 10:00 a.m.	Cooperative Learning	Curriculum Coordinator
10:00 - Noon	Thinking skills: Models of How Students Think/Applications to Teaching	Curriculum Director
Noon - 1:30 p.m.	Luncheon: "What's New and What Works?	Hardware/Software Representative
1:30 - 2:00 p.m.	Break	
2:00 - 4:00 p.m.	Break-Out Work Sessions Objective: Develop Materials for Presentations to Groups (Administrators, School Boards, Parents—PTA—Faculty, Advisory Committees, Students)	State Level I Trainers
4:00 - 4:15 p.m.	Break	
4:15 - 5:15 p.m.	General Session – Share the Good News – Reach Group Consensus on Presentations to Groups	State Supervisors
5:15 - 6:15 p.m.	Break	
6:15 - 7:45 p.m.	Dinner: "Good Morning," and other Oxymorons: The Very Fine Art of Communication" Welcome Level II Trainers (last year's trainees)	Business/Industry Communication Specialist
8:00 - 9:00 p.m.	Break-out Work Sessions—Novices and Veterans – Objective: Develop Evaluation Materials for Testing/ Grading and Supplementary	State Level I Trainers

10-Hour Veteran Level II Trainers have been requested to bring for Friday evening and Saturday sessions the following materials:

a. Extended Learnings and Materials
b. Grading Suggestions
c. Sample Supplemental Projects
d. Sample Video Tapes—(Homemade)
e. Suggestions for Organization of Materials

Saturday:

7:15 - 8:00 a.m.	Continental Breakfast	
8:00 - 9:45 a.m.	General Session – Share the Good News – Reach Group Consensus on Evaluation Materials – Admit Slip II	State Supervisors
9:45 - 10:00 a.m.	Break	
10:00 - Noon	Break-out Work Sessions – Objective: Implementation Activities for Modules	State Level I -and- Veteran Level II Trainers
Noon - 1:30 p.m.	Luncheon: "Motivation for Change"	Business/Industry or Education Representative
1:30 - 3:00 p.m.	Wrap-up/Evaluation for Veteran Level II Trainers	State Supervisors

THE BOEING INTERFACE

Since inception, the interdisciplinary approach to integrating applied academic course work has grown substantially in the state of Washington. Some of the programs—Applied Math and Principles of Technology—support two-year programs. Through the Carl D. Perkins legislation, secondary districts working in concert with Tech Prep provisions under the law now enjoy additional funding to articulate with community colleges in the Principles of Technology program. Enough curriculum has been developed for "PT" to support a three-year program.

Because the citizens of the state of Washington are very generous supporters of education, and business requires an educated workforce, the Boeing Company pledged its support to the applied academic programs. Boeing's Foundation in 1990 established an unprecedented partnership with schools. Through the foundation, over two million dollars was contributed in grants for equipment, in-service of instructional staff, materials, and instructional industry internships. Boeing felt strongly that these programs were designed to make learning meaningful within the context of work and that the curricula stressed application of subject matter. There was strong consensus that the programs delivered the same concepts found in academic disciplines and continue on to deliver the subject matter relative to real-life tasks.

Boeing's understandable definition of Applied Academics is: " . . . a part of an effort to make high school curriculum relevant to all students, a goal of both educators and business/industry leaders. The aim is to make learning meaningful within the specific context of work." (Owens, Evaluation Report,

1991). In order to pursue the intent of Boeing's definition, educational leaders of the state of Washington set out to continue their mission to ensure that vocational and academic curricula stressed applications of subject matter and the interdisciplinary nature of the workplace. Therefore, the focus of the curriculum has been and continues to be, not only theory, but the application and problem-solving methodologies of instructional efforts to assist students with becoming contributing members of society.

The Northwest Regional Educational Laboratory in Portland, Oregon, conducted follow-up studies for Boeing and found that the Boeing-funded projects had an impact beyond student achievement. In three of the four sites studied, the applied academics classes were team taught and provided students with an important model for the teamwork skills they need as they enter the workplace. In one case, the language arts teacher learned computer skills while the business education instructor learned more about small group work (cooperative learning). Two sites mentioned the prestige of the Boeing Company in helping their local community to value the need to improve education for nonbaccalaureate bound students.

Other areas of influence included: the use of the applied academics courses as part of a new business academy; the integration of Applied Communication into a workforce preparation curriculum; the establishment of a new technology education advisory committee; and the integration of applied academics into the Washington's Schools for the 21st Century and other educational reform efforts. (Owens, Survey Results, 1992).

Teacher Internships. The Boeing Company sponsored an internship program for teachers who use applied academics curriculum packages. Nine teacher interns from school districts throughout Washington explored the company's operations areas for a six-week period. Workplace skills such as problem solving, teamwork, acquiring new information, and keeping up with emerging technologies were emphasized. Teachers were expected to transfer those skills to their students with intentions of better preparing the students for the workplace. Interns overwhelmingly reported having positive experiences that could be shared with students in their classes (Owens, Teacher Internships, 1992).

Applied Communication Teachers' Survey. Through a follow-up study, the Northwest Regional Educational Laboratory surveyed teachers delivering applied academics courseware. The Applied Communication survey was completed by 16 teachers. They had an average teaching experience of 15 years. Ten of the teachers were certified in vocational education (four in Business Education); five in English; one in Language Arts. Thirteen teachers taught Applied Communication as a response to a request from their principal, curriculum director, or vocational director. Eleven teachers indicated that they would recommend Applied Communication materials to other teachers; four teachers were not sure. Almost all teachers agreed that Applied Communication units had a positive impact on students in academic achievement, understanding of subject content, and relevance of the subject matter to the world of work (Owens, Teacher Internships, 1992).

The majority of teachers agreed that Applied Communication units also had a positive impact on themselves in classroom performance, teaching ability, skills in handling student small-group work, use of varied materials in teaching, incorporation of job-related instruction into teaching, and integration of basic employability skills.

Unfamiliarity with all components of Applied Communication materials and time conflicts with regular classes were identified by teachers as the major problems in teaching Applied Communication or any applied course.

Boeing summary. The Boeing Company invested nearly $2 million from 1990-1992 in 51 Washington State high schools to develop or expand applied academics programs. State data show that during the 1991-92 school year, 3,368 students were served in Principles of Technology classes; 3,398 in Applied Math (stand-alone) classes; and 2,276 students in Applied Communication classes (Crossman, 1993).

Almost all of the schools using the Boeing company funds for program startup continued or expanded their programs the year following the Boeing funding. Therefore, the corporate investment served as seed money to expand the use of applied academics in Washington. Perhaps the fact that the Boeing funds were often used for one-time equipment purchases and teacher training enabled the school districts to continue funding the programs after the Boeing investment. The fact that most participating students and teachers in the applied academics courses felt quite positive toward the curriculum and were willing to recommend them to their friends, as indicated on Boeing and state evaluation instruments, undoubtedly also contributes to their widespread continued use and expansion.

THE EXCITING/STARTLING PILOT

Prior to statewide implementation, a pilot project was established to test the results of the delivery methodology, student interest, and student retention of the Applied Communication courseware. One of the Level I state trainers, Chuck Snyder, tested the materials in a class of at-risk students in the Tacoma School District. These students had all been through various court systems and were offered one last chance with the educational system before being incarcerated. The class was delivered cooperatively with a business education instructor, Sharon Calloway.

The outcome was astonishing! I observed the class and found there to be a 99 percent engagement rate during the eight-hour pilot. Students asked if they could return to class to learn more. They enjoyed working in groups, and their productivity level surpassed Chuck's traditional English classes for the same period of time. Yes, the students were really learning! It was exciting to see initially unmotivated youngsters excited about learning through problem-solving and group interaction.

SUMMARY

The challenges currently being posed to American society and, moreover, to its educational institutions are complex and overwhelming in many communities. With the space shuttle crossing the Atlantic in a matter of minutes; with the breakthrough in genetic engineering; with the development and manufacture of computer chips constituting the world's fourth largest industry; yes, even with McDonald's being bigger than United States Steel, it is clear that not only is change imperative, but that change requires skills and knowledge different from and greater than ever before. Quality training and appropriate equipment are essential if we are to continue the experience of total quality control. It is, therefore, incumbent upon the educational delivery systems to provide opportunities for students to acquire these new skills in an applied context and to enhance their levels of technological competencies. The economic future of Washington is directly correlated with the linkage between education and industry and the continued development of the most important component in our economy—a highly skilled and qualified work force, which is employed. There is no higher priority at this time than improving that linkage that will provide direct benefits to the quality of life for the people of Washington.

Education must be ready and able to alter its service deliverer as needed, not only in what it teaches but also in how and when it teaches. Incumbent upon education is the flexibility and willingness to undertake thoughtful and comprehensive, interdisciplinary curricular development and modification. It is evident that Washington State is ready and well on its way to achieving the success necessary to produce a quality, trained workforce for the Boeing Company and other businesses/industries.

Policy makers, state department staff, administrators, and teachers have made a sustained commitment to staff development and renewal activities so that education can better prepare students to enter, re-enter, and remain in the work force. The leadership provided by the Office of the Superintendent of Public Instruction is, by all indicators, responsible for initiating and supporting this commitment. State supervisors, like Bill Crossman, the state supervisor of Applied Academics and Marketing Education, in spite of heavy work schedules continue to work cooperatively on yet another project—applied academics—to ensure that all students have the opportunity to enhance and retain general education skills as they relate to workforce training.

Happy is the day when instructors are able to tell students good-bye at graduation saying, "Go feed yourself," and feeling confident that they had a positive influence in making sure this will happen.

Professional educators have realized that with the increased knowledge of how humans learn and of how to organize learning, they are already able to provide opportunities so all students can learn what they need to learn. Further, they can develop a joy of learning and ability to learn on their own for as long as they live. We already know how. There are no excuses. It is now a matter of commitment. **So what? Who cares? We all care!**

REFERENCES

Applied communication – Florida teaching supplement. (1991, September). Curriculum Guide. Tallahassee, Florida: Department of Education, Division of Vocational, Adult and Community Education, September 1991.

Applied communication inservice guide. (1991). Charleston, Illinois: Illinois State Board of Education, Department of Adult, Vocational and Technical Education.

Crossman, William. (1993, February). Interview with the State Supervisor of Marketing Education/Coordinator of Applied Academic Programs, Office of the Superintendent of Public Instruction, Olympia, Washington.

Implementation guide for applied communication in Oregon. (1990, Spring). Salem, Oregon: Oregon Department of Education.

Instructional design for applied communication – A curriculum and learning materials for high school vocational students. (1987, March). Bloomington, Indiana: Agency for Instructional Technology.

Kester, Dr. R. J. (1993, Winter). A new paradigm for teaching. *Continuing Edge,* 4:3. Newsletter. Seattle: Seattle Pacific University.

Owens, T. R. (1992). *Applied Communication Survey Results for the Boeing Company.* Portland, Oregon: Northwest Regional Educational Laboratory.

Owens, T. R. (1992). *Applied Communication Teacher Internships for the Boeing Company.* Portland, Oregon: Northwest Regional Educational Laboratory.

Owens, T. R. (1991). *The Boeing Company Applied Academics – Year 1 Evaluation Report – Executive Summary.* Portland, Oregon: Northwest Regional Educational Laboratory.

Shaw, M. C., and Bannister, F. (1992). *Application for Applied Communication Program – 1992-1993.* Olympia, Washington: Office of the Superintendent of Public Instruction.

Shaw, M. C., and Bannister, F. (1992). *Applied Communication 30-Hour Training Session Agenda.* Olympia, Washington: Office of the Superintendent of Public Instruction.

CHAPTER 5

ALL BUSINESS IS GLOBAL

JOANNE PHILLIPS
Chattanooga Public Schools, Chattanooga, Tennessee

All Business Is Global - An Initiative To Infuse International Business into All Business Education Classes in Secondary Schools

This report is based on the All Business Is Global Project of the business education teachers in the Chattanooga, Tennessee, area in partnership with the World Trade Center Chattanooga. It was described in a presentation at the NBEA Convention in Boston, April 1992.

CHANGE

Business education courses have continuously changed to keep pace with changes in business, equipment, organization, policy, and market demands. Skills have been taught on equipment from manual typewriters to word processors, from key-driven calculators to computers, and from duplicators to copiers, laser printers, and fax machines. Business principles and concepts have changed focus from secretarial office procedures to management systems and entrepreneurship and from a local economic community to an international one.

These changes have often been gradual and unheralded. Therefore, as the emphasis of business, education, and the world news in general centered on such themes as diversity, multiculturalism, global economy, global competition, and international business, a group of business educators took advantage of an opportunity to collaborate and publicize the changing curriculum. When the Public Education Foundation of Chattanooga announced that their 1991-92 grants would be committed to partnership projects that addressed multicultural issues facing education, the All Business Is Global Project was conceived. The World Trade Center Chattanooga agreed to be the partner with the business education teachers of the area, and the proposal was developed and approved.

LITERATURE AND PRACTICES

The literature and presentations of the 1980s and early 1990s show some authors and schools are establishing international business education programs or are including the international concepts in existing programs. Many of the initiatives described are at the postsecondary level. Several secondary programs are quite comprehensive and successful. By 1990 Tennessee was developing an international business curriculum to be piloted as a semester course, which may later be approved to satisfy the academic economics credit. The direction was clear and correct, but the opportunity in Chattanooga was immediate. The business educators were ready to take the initiative to expand the curriculum to include the world. They felt that business education should be recognized for the constant upgrading that occurs as changes in the workplace require changes in the preparation for that workplace. This material is designed to help secondary business educators incorporate the global view of business and international practices for business into classes currently being taught. Incorporate the global view in small segments or as large units, but incorporate it now.

ALL BUSINESS IS GLOBAL (ABIG PROJECT)

In the spring of 1991, the Public Education Foundation in Chattanooga issued the call for grant applications for 1991-92 with guidelines detailing partnership projects dealing with multicultural issues. The guidelines sparked the thought that multicultural issues meant international business to business educators. Business educators should get a grant, get the recognition for what they would do anyway, and identify some of that topic for business education. The Public Education Foundation is a prestigious foundation established to promote and improve public education by providing opportunities for teachers and principals, opportunities that are not included in school budgets.

The idea grew, and a search for the right partner began. The World Trade Center Chattanooga was recommended, and Franz Reichert, director, agreed to the proposition. The World Trade Center Chattanooga is a nonprofit corporation that serves as a central source for resources and services that can be of assistance in international commerce. A full member of the New York-based World Trade Center Association, which has over 200 affiliates in over 54 countries, the World Trade Center Chattanooga provides businesses in the area with world market information and experts in international business fields. The fields include marketing, business development, finance, logistics, and cultural understanding. One goal of the World Trade Center is to foster the international thought process, so the partnership for education was appropriate. As the proposal was written, phase one called for several sessions to give the teachers in the area information on international business and cultural considerations for successful practice and to set their minds into a global mode. The next phase called for several work sessions for teachers to prepare instructional material. The third phase called for the teachers to reconvene, review, revise, and renew the commitment to teach that all business is global.

The All Business Is Global Project began with a kickoff meeting in May 1991 so the participants would have the idea in mind during the summer, when teachers may have opportunities to travel and read. Twenty-four teachers from the area attended the first meeting, and Franz Reichert introduced them to the possibilities and inevitability of businesses participating in a global economy. He explained the purpose of World Trade Centers, how many affiliates there are, how the membership privileges assist businesses in accomplishing international trade—either importing or exporting, either goods or services. He showed the electronic message system, the Network, that allows World Trade Centers around the world to access current market information—what someone wants to sell and what someone needs to buy.

The presentation included information about the documentation required in international transactions, the letters of credit, and how banks are involved. The banks in the area that have international departments were identified, and the clearinghouse used by other banks was explained. The role that business educators may play in training workers for employment in the international arena was stressed. The accuracy required in documents, the precision required in language usage, the awareness of differences in cultures and practices must be part of the education of future workers. Mr. Reichert gave interesting anecdotes from his experiences living and working in other countries, provided the teachers with handouts of tips for dealing with persons from different cultures, added some humorous illustrations of what not to do, and generally sparked the interest and enthusiasm of the group. The session began with international hors d'oeuvres; all agreed that the introduction of international foods would catch the attention of students, too. Mr. Reichert stressed to the group that respect and understanding are essential to successfully conducting business internationally. He wanted students to know that they may not accept another culture, but they must respect it to engage in business.

The first meeting of All Business Is Global was held in the spring as a means of involving summer activities in the process. All Business Is Global Project provided for more specific sessions to be conducted in the fall. The World Trade Center director declined to identify the markets which would be discussed in September and stressed that the world is changing and the markets are changing. This is a dynamic topic and the only way to address much of international business or the global economic community is by using current information or current events.

In the fall of 1991, All Business Is Global had three sessions. The first concentrated on the ASEAN market (Association of Southeast Asian Nations), and the teachers were introduced to Asian food, customs, and business practices. The second session concentrated on South America, and the teachers were introduced to food, customs, and business practices of some of the South American countries. This session was conducted in part by a native of Guatemala. The third session was on Europe and North America and was conducted in part by guest speakers from France and the Netherlands, and the food was pizza. The customs and practices that were identified for North America and Europe were more similar than for the other markets. Teachers were told to expect the European market to change as the European Economic Community develops. The teachers attending the sessions were all given many ideas and facts to share with students, resources to use, and contacts to maintain. Teachers were instructed in the importance and the proper use of business cards. Throughout the project, the emphasis was on respect, not only to promote business but to create understanding and concern for all people.

CURRICULUM DEVELOPMENT

From those who attended the All Business Is Global seminars, a group from Chattanooga Public Schools elected to meet and prepare some guidelines, objectives, and activities that could be used by business educators throughout the area and in classes throughout the curriculum.

When Tennessee developed curriculum frameworks and curriculum guides some years ago, the format design identified strands. Strands define the units or areas of knowledge to be included in a course. In business courses, many strands are in all courses but in varying degrees. The term *strand* is fitting since strands are used to weave a whole course. The team of teachers developed strands for this project that may be used as a separate course or may be infused into existing courses. The goals and objectives and strands are listed here.

All Business Is Global
Goals and Objectives

This course is designed to acquaint the students with the global marketplace, the role of supply and demand, cultural diversities, and the growing interdependence in the world of trade.

Strands and Descriptions

The strand headings are the units of study in which students will be engaged in this course or as these units are infused into existing courses.

ECONOMICS acquaints the student with international financial procedures involved in the importing/exporting of goods and services.

BUSINESS TECHNOLOGY familiarizes the students with the technology involved in global business transactions.

COMMUNICATION provides guidelines to the student for communicating in the international society.

PROTOCOL focuses the student on cultural differences and similarities.

LEADERSHIP creates opportunities for student involvement and leadership development.

Strands, Concepts, and Objectives

ECONOMICS - Concept: International financial transactions are involved in the importing and exporting of goods and services.

Objectives:

- To understand the role of supply and demand in the global economy
- To understand the role of the banking industry in international business transactions
- To understand documents and terminology required in international transactions
- To understand the sequential flow of trade documents
- To understand some implications of foreign investments in the United States
- To understand the extent of import/export activities in the United States.

BUSINESS TECHNOLOGY - Concept: Technology is an integral factor in the global economy.

Objectives:

- To understand the function of the World Trade Center Chattanooga
- To understand the effect of technology on markets and products
- To understand the means of transportation available in the world of trade.

COMMUNICATION - Concept: Communication is vital in successful international trade.

Objectives:

- To understand the role of business documents required in importing and exporting
- To understand the method of communication available in the international markets
- To understand the diversity of languages involved in international trade
- To understand the extent to which standard English is used in international trade.

PROTOCOL - Concept: Successful business ventures require mutual respect and understanding of cultural differences.

Objectives:

- To understand that cultures around the world vary
- To understand that respect of customs and social codes is essential in business
- To understand sources of information regarding specific cultures.

LEADERSHIP - Concept: Leadership skills are essential for competing in the global economy.

Objectives:

- To understand, identify, and develop leadership and interpersonal skills
- To understand that leadership involves mutual cooperation and respect
- To understand social and business etiquette in individual and group relationships.

CURRICULUM GUIDE EXAMPLES

INSTRUCTIONAL OBJECTIVES	CONTENT	ACTIVITIES
ECONOMICS		
The learner will identify and prepare documents involved in international transactions.	The common export documents are these: Ocean Bill-of-Lading, Export Declaration, Commercial Invoice, Certificate of Origin, and Letter of Credit.	The students will discuss documents and prepare some samples of the forms.
The learner will describe or chart the sequence of documents used in the exporting process.	The flow of documents involved in exporting is an established procedure.	The students will view the steps in exporting and arrange in order.
The learner will define Incoterms and locate the information.	Incoterms are the 3-letter abbreviations for terms of sale used throughout the world regarding shipping risks and costs per title transfer.	The students will read the terms or look at sources for such information.
BUSINESS TECHNOLOGY		
The learner will list some WTCC purposes and describe the Network.	The World Trade Center Chattanooga (WTCC) is a non-profit corporation which serves as a central source for assisting in international commerce and is a full member of The World Trade Center Association.	The students will discuss and explain WTCC goals and services.
	The WTC Network is an electronic worldwide trade and message system.	The students will read a printout from the Network and identify categories of goods for trading.
	The Network classifies goods for trading by 12 headings: non-processed animal and vegetable products; prepared foodstuffs; chemical and mineral products; plastics, rubber, wood, and building materials; textiles; base and precious metals, jewelry; electronic and mechanical appliances; vehicles, aircraft, and ships; medical, surgical, and health care products; manufactured articles; miscellaneous other; finance, real estate.	The students will use the yellow pages to find a local firm for each classification.

COMMUNICATION

The learner will detail steps in currency exchange for international activities.	All commercial banks can assist with exchanging currency; larger banks have international departments; smaller banks deal through an international clearinghouse bank.	The students hear speakers on international banking procedures.
The learner will use proper forms and reference material to prepare clear and concise documents for interpretation.	Any document which may be read and translated by a person unfamiliar with English must be clear and use words which translate the intended meaning.	The students will write a letter and verify, using a dictionary, that the first definition relays the message. The students, using a translating dictionary, will translate letters written in a foreign language.

PROTOCOL

The learner will know several cultural practices from other areas which differ from those most widely accepted in this country. The learner will understand and define customs that are common and traditional to that student.	Content will be the practices described in resource material and in the experiences of members of the class and community. Resource material such as *Culturgrams* - Brigham Young University's publications.	The students compare and discuss customs which are presented to the class. Students will do reports on culture of their family, community, or region.

LEADERSHIP

The learner will understand that social and business etiquette is important to job success.	Social and business etiquette information must be gathered from many sources. It will vary from country to country and region to region.	The students research a country to determine correct behavior, and role play situations about different customs.

INTERNATIONAL BUSINESS – A SEMESTER COURSE

The course being piloted at several sites in Tennessee was planned and promoted by Katherine Lasater, state consultant for Business and Office Education, and written by Susan Thompson, Karns High School, Knoxville. The goal is understanding the attitude, knowledge, and skills for entry level occupations in international business.

The strands identified for this course are Domestic and International Business, Cultural and Economic Features, Economic Systems of International Business, International Communications, Financial and Legal Considerations, Marketing and Promoting Products and Services, International Trade Documentation, Management for International Business, and Employment

Opportunities in International Business. Through these strands (and their concepts and objectives which follow), the course is designed to correlate with all objectives of the state curriculum for economics and may be approved at some future date to satisfy the economic credit in the social studies area.

Strands, Concepts, and Objectives

DOMESTIC AND INTERNATIONAL BUSINESS - Concept: The ability to describe the economic base of a region of a country is vital for success in international business.

Objectives:

- To understand the importance of domestic, national, and international resources to international business
- To understand the impact of American resources in international business
- To understand the components of an international/global economy
- To understand the major trade regions of the world.

CULTURAL AND ECONOMIC FEATURES - Concept: To conduct business in a host country one must understand its culture and economy.

Objectives:

- To understand the importance of a foreign language
- To understand the importance of communication for success in business
- To understand the function of art and music in a culture
- To understand the function attitudes, beliefs, and values have in business.

ECONOMIC SYSTEMS OF INTERNATIONAL BUSINESS - Concept: Economic systems with distinct factors are involved in international trade.

Objectives:

- To understand the elements of a free enterprise system
- To understand a capitalistic economic system
- To understand a socialistic economy
- To understand the communist economy
- To understand the importance of committees in a planned economy.

INTERNATIONAL COMMUNICATIONS - Concept: The ability to communicate effectively is vital for conducting business in a host country.

Objectives:

- To understand the importance of a foreign language in international business
- To understand modes of communication
- To understand the importance of the telephone in business
- To understand procedures to send telex/cable/fax messages
- To understand international business correspondence.

FINANCIAL AND LEGAL CONSIDERATIONS - Concept: The ability to understand foreign exchange rates and regulations is vital in international trade.

Objectives:
- To understand the currency unit of each of the leading industrial countries
- To understand the importance of exchange rates in international business
- To understand the importance of the balance of payments in international trade
- To understand domestic and foreign investment
- To understand the impact taxation has on international business
- To understand laws which regulate imports and exports
- To understand the concepts of expropriation and confiscation
- To understand product liability
- To understand intellectual rights protection.

MARKETING AND PROMOTING PRODUCTS AND SERVICES - Concept: Marketing principles for national and international business are the same.

Objectives:
- To understand marketing principles in the international arena
- To understand that socio-economic forces influence the marketing mix
- To understand that laws of foreign countries affect product changes
- To understand that elements of physical forces affect international markets
- To understand the elements of international advertising.

INTERNATIONAL TRADE DOCUMENTATION - Concept: Proper documentation is necessary in international business.

Objectives:
- To understand the importance of export documentation in international trade
- To understand the importance of import documentation in international trade
- To understand the flow of documentation in international trade
- To understand the importance of licensing
- To understand the importance of letters of credit
- To understand the use of specific documents in international trade.

MANAGEMENT FOR INTERNATIONAL BUSINESS - Concept: Human resources, policies, and procedures influence the effectiveness of the organization.

Objectives:
- To understand the importance of employee recruitment and selection
- To understand the importance of employee training and development
- To understand the importance of compensation and benefits
- To understand the importance of labor and employee relationships
- To understand the uses of different management styles
- To understand different international organizational structures.

EMPLOYMENT OPPORTUNITIES IN INTERNATIONAL BUSINESS - Concept: International business offers exciting and rewarding careers.

Objectives:

- To understand career clusters in international business
- To understand educational requirements of specific careers
- To understand the importance of a resume and a job application
- To understand the importance of a job interview
- To understand employee responsibilities.

RESOURCES FOR INFUSING INTERNATIONAL CONCEPTS INTO ALL COURSES

When the All Business Is Global Project began, some teachers could not envision the resources necessary for infusing the global concepts and mindset into their classes. As the project developed, the wealth of resources became evident. The teachers in the Chattanooga area are especially fortunate to have a World Trade Center in operation that is able and willing to include the secondary teachers in part of its education efforts. The World Trade Center Chattanooga is involved with the University of Tennessee at Chattanooga in developing and offering college programs in international business. These efforts both validate the goals of the secondary programs and provide a direction for students who choose a career in the field. Students can plan an educational program from high school through graduate school and know that opportunities exist. The world is not separate and isolated markets, and business will not ignore technological advances and telecommunications that promote international business.

Finding resources for the All Business Is Global Project was similar to learning a new word and then hearing it everywhere. Everything seemed related to the project. The topic was covered in all media. The international arena is in newspapers, magazines, newscasts, advertisements, and neighborhoods. There is an increase of multicultural awareness in the same sources. The information is available, timely, and vital. Students may be able to contribute more than their teacher in some phases of this infusion. Students may be the active participants and the teacher only facilitating the projects that develop from the inclusion of the global picture in business education classes.

INTEGRATING ACADEMIC AND VOCATIONAL INSTRUCTION

The Carl D. Perkins Vocational and Applied Technology Education Act of 1990 requires that vocational and academic education be integrated. Existing business education classes lend themselves to integration with language, math, and social studies in communications, finance, and economics. Including international concepts in business classes will provide more opportunities to integrate. The global concepts and the international business aspect present business classes with additional opportunities to integrate with social studies and language by including world geography and foreign language programs in integrated projects.

SERVING STUDENTS' NEEDS

Including the global picture in business education classes may provide unexpected opportunities to meet the needs of certain students. As cultural respect and awareness are incorporated into classes, students may feel included who have felt excluded because of cultural differences. Students may investigate and share their own cultural backgrounds. The classes may perform a service to the school by developing awareness of diversity and appreciation of its contribution to the community and economy.

CONCLUSION

Students in school today must live and compete in a global economy where business is international business. It is imperative that education prepares them to survive and succeed in that world, that education helps them prepare for and develop respect for life and work in a society of diverse cultures. Business education can help in this effort by making all business courses relevant to the time and place.

Adding international flavor to the business education courses will be exciting for the teachers and the students. It can open doors to the future while opening windows on the world. It is a journey not a destination. It is a challenging undertaking. It will be a rewarding experience to keep current and keep including the fact that all business is global in all business classes.

Business educators should ask themselves the question, "What in the world are we doing?"

CHAPTER 6

In Pursuit of Virtual Learning Alliances:
A Passion To Integrate Curriculum and Instruction

THOMAS HAYNES

Illinois State University, Normal, Illinois

AH! Never forget that we can only stave off that fatal degradation if we unite the Liberal Arts, which embody the sacred fire of sensibility, with the sciences and the useful arts, without which the celestial light of reason will disappear. (Bernard Lacèpéde, 1801, in Gould, 1991, pg. 366)

Over the past decade, curriculum integration has become a focal point of discussion as evidenced by conference programs, publications, grant support from state and federal governments, and educational research efforts. Over the years, leading educators have advocated learning processes that are integrative and active; where individuals make sense out of theory through practice, such as exhibited in the closing address of Monsieur Lacèpéde for the Zoology Course at the Natural History Museum in Paris.

This chapter was constructed with the aim of adding form to the sometimes elusive topic of curriculum integration. Today, a tremendous volume of professional literature is available, both theoretical and research-based, regarding curriculum integration. This chapter is the result of a concentrated effort to distill, crystallize, and clarify this literature to provide illumination to a concept that is oftentimes misconstrued. The following questions have been used to frame this endeavor:

- What is curriculum integration?
- What are the supporting theories, principles, and research for curriculum integration?
- What are commonly identified models of curriculum integration?
- What are results from curriculum integration?
- What are effective implementation strategies for successful curriculum integration?
- What are educators' roles in successfully integrating curriculum?
- What are the implications and potential directions for business educators and business education programs regarding curriculum integration?

The intent here is to shed some significant light on the broad and expanding nature of curriculum integration efforts as they relate to business education. The overriding thesis of this chapter is: If curriculum integration is of value to business educators—if information suggests that curriculum integration is a worthwhile enterprise for business education—what should we consider as we approach this in an action-oriented manner?

WHAT IS CURRICULUM INTEGRATION?

These questions [regarding how people learn and forget school-based knowledge] cannot be disposed of by saying that the subjects were not actually learned, but they were learned, at least sufficiently to enable a pupil to pass examinations in them. One trouble is that the subject in question was learned in isolation; it was put, as it were, in a water-tight compartment. (Dewey, 1938, p. 48)

The central question concerning curriculum integration, when it is first approached by curious or critically thinking educators and citizens, is: What is it? At this juncture, a variety of responses present themselves. According to Webster's (1963) *3rd New International Dictionary,* integration related to curriculum is, "the organization of teaching matter to interrelate or unify subjects usually taught in separate academic courses or departments." A common view, which is collateral to Dewey's perspective, is that curriculum integration is the process of making connections between school subjects and experiences with which learners are currently involved and may likely be engaged with in the future. These experiences add immediate relevance, as well as provide for preparation for future experiences.

In a broad sweep, an integrated curriculum is more than just interrelationships between curricular areas or subject matters. As Jardine (1990) states,

It is an ecological and spiritual matter, involving images of our place and the place of our children on "the precious earth." It raises the question of how we are to understand that we are people of this precious earth caught up in its potentialities and possibilities. . . in the end, the integrated curriculum requires a deep reflection on our desires to disintegrate children's curriculum experiences in the name of manageability, ease of instructional design, or territorial notions with separateness and uniqueness of subject matter's specializations. (pg. 111)

As this quote speaks from a wide-angled view of curriculum integration, it also focuses on bringing wholeness to subject matters via interrelationships with other disciplines to provide students with perspective, as well as skills, in being a part of the earthly community. It also forces us to think about the challenge of restructuring our schooling processes; to look at more original, and in many cases barrier-ridden, innovations that may have positive effects on student success.

However, as we pursue a formal and practical review of what curriculum integration means, many think of it as interdisciplinary in nature. Jacobs (1989) describes curriculum integration as an interdisciplinary curriculum which is integrative. It is a curriculum that has a knowledge view and an approach that consciously applies methodology and language from more than one discipline to examine a central theme, issue, problem, topic, or experience. A parallel definition of curriculum integration is offered by Bernstein (1975). He suggests a blurring of the curriculum, "Integration occurs when the boundaries between the content of various subjects are weak, weakened, or blurred; in other words, the content of each subject is subordinate to some idea that reduces the isolation from the others" (p. 135).

In addition, there are a number of prefixes to "disciplinary" knowledge and skill development that should be considered, such as:

- Cross-disciplinary: Viewing one discipline from the perspective of another; for example, the physics of music and the history of math (Meeth, 1978)

- Multidisciplinary: The juxtaposition of several disciplines focused on one problem with no direct attempt to integrate (Piaget, 1972)

- Plural disciplinary: The position of disciplines assumed to be more or less related; e.g. math and physics, French and Latin (Piaget 1972)

- Transdisciplinary: Beyond the scope of a discipline; that is, to start with a problem and bring to bear knowledge from the disciplines upon it (Meeth, 1978).

Jacobs (1989) criticizes defining curriculum integration because such efforts become too esoteric and nitpicky to be practical. She suggests that as we refine curriculum integration as a concept, we should consider several criteria:

1. It is an effort that has an organizing center which cuts across two or more disciplines.

2. It can be practically set up for a curriculum development effort, and it has a workable instructional sequence.

3. It is valid within each of the disciplines being suggested.

4. It is valid across the disciplines.

5. It has validity beyond the disciplines; there are workable parts that form a whole that resides in life experiences.

6. It contributes to broader outcomes, such as critical thinking, problem solving, group team work, and skill building.

Reviewing curriculum integration from the vantage point of business education, a number of researchers and educational leaders have developed the concept in a specific and practical light. Researchers at the National Center for Research in Vocational Education assert that integrating curriculum means revising processes of instruction such that academic programs display bountiful applications of theory (i.e., how and why the theory is used) while at the same time, business education programs and other vocational areas incorporate supportive academic skills instruction (Benson, 1991; Grubb, 1989). As will be seen later, this effort may be as simple as one teacher infusing interdisciplinary content into a course or as complicated as creating curricula that may obscure the distinction between academic and vocational to the point that disciplines almost disappear.

Pritz (1988) conceptualizes vocational/academic integration genre as a linking of academic skills instruction to vocational applications to enhance student learning. Some of the underlying components of this type of integration are the blending of curricular content and the collaboration of teachers to conduct planning and potentially to align curriculum (i.e., to dove-tail vocational and academic courses). Plihal and Johnson (1990) suggest that curriculum integration should take place in a three-dimensional arena. The first dimension focuses on teachers. For example, teachers in academic and vocational areas are assigned to work together on curriculum content and teaching methods. Their backgrounds, subject areas, and commitment may lead to a large or small degree of curriculum integration. At this initial level of curriculum integration, the curriculum, programs, and teachers are isolated; curriculum change is a solitary matter. The second dimension is the curriculum itself. Some courses include content from other subjects, while others are naturally isolated.

The final dimension is evidenced at the program level (i.e. college prep, Tech Prep, specific vocational prep) where students have a coordinated and focused program of study. In a two-dimensional environment, each of the three component parts pairs-up with one of the other component parts (e.g., teachers work on programs, or teachers work on curricula). But, in the third and most comprehensive view of curriculum integration, integration takes place with teachers working together to improve curricula and instructional practices that form the content of a coordinated and focused program of study.

In September 1990, the Carl D. Perkins Vocational and Applied Technology Education Act took effect. This new federal law mandates the integration of academic and vocational education by using the context of job skills training to enhance students' academic skills and drive students to excel in both (Wirt, 1991). An example of this legislation's initiative to address learners' needs is the High Schools That Work Program, initiated by the Southern Regional Education Board (SREB). SREB pilot-site schools pursue integration activities based on key practices and principles, such as making academic learning real and applied, integrating academic content into vocational courses, and having academic and vocational teachers work together on curriculum planning teams, staff development activities, industry visitations, interdisciplinary teaching activities, joint learning projects, school-within-a-school efforts, and committee assignments (Bottoms, Presson & Johnson, 1992).

While curriculum integration has so far been viewed from a horizontal, cross-disciplinary perspective, there is also the opportunity to integrate curriculum vertically within a given discipline. In such situations, topics, themes, and major goals or objectives for a disciplinary curriculum are delineated and aligned in such a manner as to provide for transfer of learning, develop advanced problem-solving skills, and master life-experience skills to help students pursue work and further education within a discipline. Vertically integrated curriculum is developed so that students can successfully pursue introductory and advanced study.

Dressel's (1958) perspective focuses on integrative and integrated curriculum. He explains that an integrative curriculum consists of two parts: the first provides learners with a unified view of commonly held knowledge, while the second motivates and develops the learners' power to perceive and create new relationships for themselves. He saw the first function as being an integrated curriculum, while the second function is integrative in nature. The integrative curriculum is different from interdisciplinary/correlated curriculum since it does not imply the necessity for using traditional disciplines or subjects as the central point of the curriculum. The major emphasis is on how the curricula join to form a "whole."

Although these several perspectives provide a glimpse of how researchers and theorists define curriculum integration, some questions still remain: What are meaningful supportive paradigms for such efforts? What logic, theory, and research suggest that curriculum integration has an synergistic effect upon student leaning? These are the focus points of the next two sections.

THEORIES, RESEARCH, AND PRINCIPLES
SUPPORTING CURRICULUM INTEGRATION

The solution which I am urging is to eradicate the fatal disconnection of subjects which kills the vitality of our modern curriculum. There is only one subject matter for education, and that is Life and all of its manifestations. (Alfred North Whitehead, 1929, pp. 10-11)

With the deluge of new research and data in every discipline, constructing a school curriculum for students and teachers creates a flood of challenging curricular decisions. With this unrelenting tide of new information, how does one (teacher/student) make sense of an overabundance of information? How does one make connections between these facts and figures for use in daily living? Educators are experiencing significant stress attempting to sift through the volume of new technical disciplinary information. Furthermore, they must match this technical, discipline-based information with local and state curriculum goals and objectives. But, with a logical and articulated rationale for advancing specific curricular and instructional design changes, more relevant integrated learning activities can produce positive outcomes for all students. With such a critical need to analyze curricular and instructional decisions, the following theories, principles, and research are outlined to support curriculum integration efforts.

Learning in the context of life experiences. As Dewey (1938) states, "Above all, educators should know how to utilize the surroundings, physical and social, that exist so as to extract from them all they have to contribute to building up experiences that are worthwhile" (p. 9). Turn-of-the-century academic education did not have to face the issue of relevance that Dewey describes; the school environment of desk, blackboards, and small school yard was satisfactory. Teachers did not become intimately acquainted with the conditions of the local community, physical, historical, economic, occupational, in order to utilize them as educational resources. But, a system of education that's founded upon the necessary connection of education with experience must be faithful to the principle of relevance and take the artifacts, contexts, and characteristics of life experiences into account. Therefore, students and teachers accomplish significant learning when they pursue instructional activities in true contexts and exhibit characteristics of life experiences.

Learning through a variety of styles. Another current thrust in educational improvement is identifying and using students' learning styles to their best advantage. This allows educators to match instructional design efforts with students' styles. Integrated curriculum activities usually have students pursue learning through a variety of modes. This variety facilitates the accommodation of individual learning styles.

Applied learning activities. A principle component of an integrated curriculum involves students' acquiring knowledge and skill through applied learning activities. This includes students' practicing life experiences as they take place in real world settings. As Glasser (1992) states:

Clearly, demonstrating the use of what is learned in a real life situation is one of the best ways to teach and for students to learn. If we emphasize the ability to use knowledge in every academic subject, there would be no rebellion on the part of students. (pp. 692-693)

Developing problem-solving skills. Within an integrated curriculum, it is common for students and teachers to engage in case studies, thematic projects, or schoolwide projects which allow students to work in teams to solve issues, concerns, and problems. Rosenstock (1991) crystallizes this view:

New ways of thinking about teaching and learning are already being practiced in vocational programs. Students engage in experiential and applied learning. They learn how to pose and solve problems, using tools at hand or inventing new ones. They work cooperatively, using multiple intelligences (artistic, kinesthetic, and social, as well as linguistic and logical). The proof of what they have learned is what they produce. (p. 435)

Retention and transfer of learning. Over the past 20 years, transfer of learning has become a major topic for educational researchers. Curriculum integration offers an effective means to support students' transfer of learning from the classroom to nonschool settings and other learning endeavors. Through real life contexts, students maintain the ability to use acquired principles and skills for future situations.

Raise expectations to acquire academic skills. One of the main concerns of business and industry representatives in keeping our country economically competitive in the global market place is the academic strengths of our technical workers. Curriculum integration is central to students' development of academic skills because of the applied and relevant nature of these skills. In addition, emphasizing the importance of academic skills encourages further pursuit of understanding by a student population that has, for the most part, lacked opportunities to advance these skills in postsecondary and higher education.

Collaboration among students to accomplish learning activities. Due to the industrial-age cosmology toward the structure of schools, teachers and students work in isolation, utilizing a kind of assembly-line model. As we look at the demands for the workforce for the 21st century, we know that collaboration among colleagues is and will be an increasingly important process. Through curriculum integration efforts, students work more collaboratively in cooperative-learning workgroups to complete application exercises in life contexts. As Grubb et al., (1991) state:

In particular, most learning (including learning in the workplace) takes place in quite different form than in schools. Most learning takes place in groups and requires cooperation, while most school-based learning is an individual activity; it relies on using both simple and complex tools, whereas school-based learning emphasizes thinking that is relatively independent of tools. (p. 9)

Striving for connectiveness—developing holistic perspectives. With new disciplines being developed at an unthinkable pace while overwhelming volumes of new information are being disseminated daily, there is a distinct need to have curricula and instructional practices that link disciplines. Furthermore, curricular and instructional decisions should help learners create an integrated wholeness; a holistic perspective of their surroundings. In this day and age, solving multi-faceted problems that include advanced human and technological knowledge is a common occurrence. Individuals who can sift through information and draw on colleagues' insights to make connections in solving problems have highly sought after skills. Integrated learning activities that involve collaborative student work groups, which focus on real-life contexts, support the development of students' abilities to make connections and acquire holistic perspectives on issues, problems, and topics. Jacobs (1989) supports curriculum integration because:

> *The experiences provide an opportunity for a more relevant, less fragmented, and stimulating experience for students. When properly designed and when criteria for excellence are met, then students break with the traditional view of knowledge and begin to actively foster a range of perspectives that will serve them in the larger world. (p. 10)*

Improve teaching methods via collaboration among teachers. As reported above, the structural model for schools in America developed from an industrial format. Teachers for the most part were isolated in this environment, coming in contact only during staff development activities, lunch breaks, faculty meetings, and a few irregular committee activities. When curriculum integration becomes a priority within a school, teachers and administrators need adequate time to collaborate about ideas, analyze situations, develop plans, organize curriculum integration endeavors, implement activities, and collect follow-up data to make curricular and instructional decisions. The collaboration that takes place between teachers and administrators allows for a synergy that has been basically nonexistent.

Bottoms (1992b) reports a number of benefits that result from collaboration between vocational and academic teachers:

1. Improved attitudes and ease in working together

2. Common purposes in helping students become life-long learners and workers

3. Understanding of the total school curriculum and linking of the pieces

4. Belief that every student is important

5. Realization that the current high school curriculum is inadequate to prepare career-bound students for employment and further study.

Student motivation. One of the truly exciting aspects of curriculum integration is that student motivation improves because of the relevance and action brought into the curriculum. This improvement allows teachers and students to use classroom time more effectively, pursue higher expectations within a more rigorous curriculum, and to build pride and respect for educational endeavors.

Criticism of vocational and academic skills of high school graduates. Since the mid 1970s, considerable criticism has mounted toward school curricula in vocational and academic areas. Vocational education has received criticism because of its overemphasis on specific job skills that are rapidly changing. This criticism claims that students leave vocational programs with outdated skills before they even enter the job market. In the academic arena, skills of high school graduates are so paltry that business and industry representatives and published reports suggest that the American worker cannot adequately read, write, compute, understand basic scientific principles, read a map, or understand economic theories. Because of this, academic and vocational teachers have resolved to improve basic academic skills and strengthen generic long-term workplace skills, enabling high school students to pursue future career and educational opportunities in an ever changing economy.

Stern, Dayton, Park, and Weisberg (1989) suggest that educators pursue the integration of vocational and academic education rather than training for specific entry level jobs:

> Through practical application, theoretical ideas can come alive for students. Vocational education should no longer be seen as another set of subjects competing for students' time. It should be a set of activities that help students use, understand, and appreciate what they are learning in other courses. This kind of vocational education will increase students' long-term productivity as workers by encouraging them to understand the theory underlying the work they do. (p. 50)

MODELS OF CURRICULUM INTEGRATION

As educators consider opportunities for curriculum integration to address local, state, and national needs, they will need to review models applicable to their settings. This is an important step to successfully integrating the curriculum. The professional literature regarding models of curriculum integration is quite extensive; much of it is delineated through case studies, observations, ethnographies of teacher-teams, and reports of "what works" in trade publications. A review of this descriptive literature illustrates two major collections of models: The first provides a broad look at curriculum integration. This collection includes models that bring concepts, knowledge, and skills together within an existing course, within and among disciplines, between courses, and between levels of instructions. Reports suggest that curriculum can not only be integrated, but it can be integrative; that the combination of curriculum, teacher, and learner in integrated learning activities can provide students with the ability to pull together a variety of information and apply it in an integrative manner to a new situation. This perspective puts a priority on synergistic cognitive processes that take place within students versus focusing on innovative changes in the curriculum or instructional delivery.

The other collection of curriculum integration models is discussed from the viewpoint of the Carl Perkins Vocational and Applied Technology Education Act of 1990. This collection addresses the integration of academic and vocational education. In this arena, integration is seen as a means to assist students in developing core-basic skills. (Basic skills can be described in a number of ways. Refer to Department of Labor's 1992 SCANS report, *Learning a Living;* American Society for Training and Development [ASTD] 1988, *Workplace Basics;* The Commission on Education and the Economy 1991 *High Skills or Low Wages;* and *Integrating Basic Skills into Vocational Teacher Education Curricula: Review of Literature* by Gloeckner, Cobb, Love & Grant, 1992.) The purpose here is to build the basic skills of vocational education students so they may acquire advanced technical skills at the postsecondary level. Furthermore, this application of curriculum integration has the additional purpose of building problem-solving and team-work abilities, as well as advanced systems-oriented skills. These models address these goals through the use of contextual learning and the blending of theoretical/academic content with occupationally-related activities in more rigorous vocational and academic courses.

As these collections of models reveal, several models overlap and cannot be easily separated or "partialled out" as one might like. Figure 1 is provided as a means to relate broad models to specific academic/vocational models of curriculum integration.

Figure 1
APPLICATION MODELS OF INTEGRATING VOCATIONAL
AND ACADEMIC EDUCATION

	Fragmented	Connected	Fused/Nested	Sequenced	Shared
Incorporating more academic content in vocational courses	X	X	X		
Combining academic and vocational teachers to enhance academic content in vocational programs		X	X	X	X
Making academic courses more vocationally relevant courses (e.g., applied academics adopted)		X	X		X
Curricular alignment; horizontal and vertical				X	X
Projects	X	X			
The Academy model		X	X	X	X
Occupational high schools and magnet schools		X	X	X	X
Occupational clusters, "career paths," and majors				X	X
Tech Prep		X	X	X	X
Block time/Core			X	X	X
Pulling In	X	X	X		X
Teaming		X	X	X	X

Figure 1
(continued)

	Webbed	Threaded	Integrated	Immersed	Networked
Incorporating more academic content in vocational courses	X	X	X		
Combining academic and vocational teachers to enhance academic content in vocational programs	X	X	X		X
Making academic courses more vocationally relevant courses (e.g., applied academics adopted)	X	X	X		X
Curricular alignment; horizontal and vertical	X	X			
Senior projects	X	X	X	X	
The Academy model		X	X	X	X
Occupational high schools and magnet schools		X	X	X	X
Occupational clusters, "career paths," and majors	X	X	X	X	X
Tech Prep	X		X	X	X
Block time/Core	X	X			X
Pulling In					X
Teaming	X	X	X		X

ROLES THAT EDUCATORS PLAY IN SUCCESSFUL INTEGRATION EFFORTS

In contemplating the successes and challenges facing educators who embrace curriculum integration efforts there are a number of roles that educators can play in these initiatives. Administrators', guidance counselors', and teachers' roles will be presented here. Each group of educators' roles will be discussed in terms of activities with which they can be engaged to make curriculum integration successful.

Results of studies conducted by Grubb et al., (1991), Jacobs (1989), McEwen et al, (1992), and Schmidt et al., (1992) illustrate a number of roles teachers, administrators, and guidance counselors can and should adopt for successful curriculum integration. Following are the major roles they can play:

Teachers' Roles:

- *Cooperate with Other Faculty:* Learn about other faculty; offer help/ask for assistance; instruct one another; plan together; share information about instruction; share information about students; assist with others' instruction; dove-tail instruction; schedule coordinated instruction; and support guidance counselors in efforts to promote better student choices in relation to course and program selection.

- *Develop Curriculum:* Coordinate assignments, projects, and instruction; plan meetings; align curriculum; enhance curriculum through involvement with business/industry; and develop/design student projects.

- *Develop Instructional Strategies:* Teach in teams; approach instruction through application; teach cooperatively; use community people/resources; accept student-initiated instruction; and use common teaching strategies.

Administrators' Roles:

- *Facilitate/Support Integration Processes:* Live within administrative constraints; address teacher concerns; change policy and procedures; learn from experience; give teachers authority and flexibility to solve problems; deal with teacher resentment; involve teachers; provide targeted staff-development activities; provide adequate planning time for collaborative teacher work; provide incentives for teachers to work collaboratively; provide ample support, i.e. time and resources, for guidance personnel to meet the needs of all students.

- *Develop Organizational Processes:* Utilize joint academic and vocational committees at the system and school level; unlock teachers from existing systems so they can pursue innovations; reorganize school curriculum and schedule; ensure guidance counselors are involved with curriculum integration; adjust and develop facilities to enhance curriculum integration; create networks of people, resources, and facilities; monitor planning and evaluation of instruction; update teacher evaluation procedures as curriculum and instruction change; clarify team members' roles; and provide mechanisms for teacher/student feedback concerning planning and implementation of curriculum integration efforts.

- *Develop Organizational Climate:* Assist with the development of a clear vision and mission for the school's curriculum and instruction; establish a positive climate for change; develop teachers' ownership in change; and publicize to stakeholders the outcomes of curriculum integration.

- *Building a Team Climate:* Communicate with stakeholders the importance of curriculum integration; recognize successful curriculum integration efforts; provide expertise in developing effective evaluation strategies; cultivate and maintain relationships with business and industry representatives as they relate to high school curriculum; and organize faculty to promote cooperation.

Guidance Counselors' Roles:

- *Guide Students:* Assist students in planning a rigorous academic and technical program of study; provide for career guidance experiences that will focus students' interests and aptitudes; assist students in completing aptitude and interest inventories that will assist them in making wise course/program selections; work with junior high school staff and students to help examine education and career options; work with teachers to help non-college-bound students understand the possibilities of further studies beyond high school; and provide materials and computer resources for students to review aptitudes and career opportunities in various job fields.

- *Develop Curriculum:* Assist with scheduling to make sure students with similar interests are in the same courses: collaborate with faculty as they work to integrate curriculum; and assist teachers and administrators in their work with students and parents regarding programs of study.

- *Communicate with Stakeholders:* Support information campaigns to help students and parents understand the need for a challenging program of study; assist with school handbook development; prepare information to show students the connection between school and life outside of school; provide the means for parents to be involved in the guidance process; and involve teachers in career guidance activities as co-collaborators.

- *Assist Students:* Work with teams of teachers to identify support services needed for students who need extra help; assist students in preparing four-year educational plans; and provide means for parents to be involved in the guidance process.

PURSUING QUALITY STRATEGICALLY THROUGH VIRTUAL RELATIONSHIPS

This section discusses implementation strategies for curriculum integration. The literature analyzing the theory and practice of change in the field of business relates directly to implementing change in school settings. Because of these connections, a sound understanding of the principles of total quality management and strategic planning needs to be considered as they relate to curriculum integration. Although these two concepts are popular themes in the field of business (and many times misconstrued), there are specific components of each concept that can make a distinct and positive impact on developing and maintaining quality educational programs.

First, as one pursues a new initiative, such as curriculum integration, one has hopes of successfully reaching particular outcomes. In looking for "quality" outcomes from these endeavors, educators need to engage in leadership techniques that will ensure quality through continuous efforts rather than through final inspections and adjustments. As educators pursue curriculum integration efforts, it is wise to review Edward W. Deming's quality bench marks. In addition, authors such as Joseph M. Juran and Philip B. Crosby offer useful insight in making the conscientious effort to produce quality products and services (Aguayo, 1990; Crosby, 1985; Gabor, 1990; Juran, 1989). Consistently, these theorists focus on the role of developing meaningful and focussed purposes and philosophies. From these, guiding principles are formulated that set standards for production and service. These drive training and,leadership to constantly improve the system.

These types of points are delineated in Deming's 14 points (Kirby, 1993, p. 2):

- Create consistency of purpose for improvement of product and/or service
- Adopt a new philosophy
- Cease dependence on mass inspection
- End practice of awarding business on the price tag alone
- Improve constantly and forever the service
- Institute training
- Institute true leadership

- Drive out fear
- Break down barriers between staff areas
- Eliminate hollow slogans without improving methods to reach new productivity heights
- Eliminate numerical quotas
- Remove barriers to pride and workmanship
- Institute a vigorous program of education and retraining
- Put everyone to work to accomplish the transformation.

A total quality management operation puts forth a constant effort to build in participative management, rigorous quality standards, employee participation, and recognition of efforts and achievement. It also considers customers, both internal and external, to the operation.

There are effective implementation tools available to support these principles and provide educators with the foundation to ensure their curriculum integration efforts are successful. Seymour & Collett (1991) propose three implementation models for TQM efforts: 1) The cascade model, which emphasizes the importance of educating and training senior officers of an organization. Developing a common vision and planning processes that are consistent for the whole organization is key to successful improvement. 2) The "infection" or "bubble up" model, which uses voluntary pilot programs to demonstrate successes and then promote the TQM philosophy throughout an organization by reference to these programs. 3) The "loose-tight" model, where administrative leaders function as facilitators. They demonstrate commitment and encourage staff to be responsible participants while they engage in detailed and comprehensive planning. These efforts involve employees at all levels who are typically organized into teams to execute the improvements. This model is a combination of the cascading and the infectious models.

The application of TQM to curriculum integration should utilize strategic planning processes to set in place the parameters and guidelines to reach quality outcomes. Although there are numerous published adaptations to the strategic planning process, the following steps, when focused upon quality initiatives and supported with training and resources for the participants, can lead to tremendous curriculum integration successes. The suggested strategic planning process detailed here does not preclude adaptations by practitioners, nor is it suggested that this is the ultimate synthesis of strategic processes discussed in the literature, but it does represent a review of some of the more prominent models being applied to educational situations.

Step One - Have administrative support and leadership synthesize a concentrated vision/mission statement that focuses on what skills and know-how students need upon completion from school, what is important for the future, and how, in general, teachers should carry out this vision.

Step Two - Identify broad goal areas upon which to focus.

Step Three - Set goal priorities; connect goals to all levels of the organization; review performance toward goals through existing systems; identify areas that need change; establish priorities; identify potential barriers for change; review other comparable institutions focusing on similar problems.

Step Four - Develop an action plan related to goals that delineates activities, resources needed, completion dates, personnel involved, and evaluation criteria.

Step Five - Enlist support from constituents; including staff, students, and external stakeholders.

Step Six - Utilize teams to develop and implement processes to positively impact on goals.

Step Seven - Administrators should provide staff development opportunities and resources to accomplish action plans.

Step Eight - Establish and review performance measures at onset of implementation activities and review performance throughout change process.

Step Nine - Utilize problem-solving strategies throughout process to correct performance; rethink existing policies and procedures; and build networks.

Step Ten - Develop reward systems for those risk-takers involved with the change process.

Step Eleven - Rethink and renew all processes upon completion of first cycle.

As educators initiate curriculum integration, strategic planning and total quality management principles provide excellent tools to put into place initiatives they truly believe are important for students' successes in and out of school. While maintaining a focus on total quality initiatives through strategic planning, educators must realize that they are looking to create an educational delivery system that will provide students with an education that will be valuable, now and in the future.

One of the more recent concepts being shaped in the corporate arena reflecting TQM and strategic planning attitudes is the "virtual corporation" paradigm (Byrne, 1993). As educators create integrated curricula through strategic planning and total quality perspectives, they will need to acquire the assistance of a number of stakeholders to reach their goals. In business, this is equivalent to pursuing joint ventures through strategic alliances, i.e., "virtual relationships." The virtual corporation is a temporary (maybe long term, but not permanent) network of companies that come together quickly to exploit opportunities in the key areas of an organization's goals. In a virtual organization, companies share costs, skills, and access to global markets, with each partner contributing its strengths. According to Byrne (1993), the key attributes of such organizations are:

- Excellence - Each partner brings core competence to an effort.

- Trust - These are relationships that make partners rely and trust each other more than ever before.

- No borders - "Virtually" redefines the traditional boundaries of an organization; there is more cooperation among competitors, suppliers, and customers.

- Opportunism - Partnerships will be less permanent, less formal, and more opportunistic. Organizations will band together to meet specific opportunities.

- Technology - Informational networks will help far-flung participants link up and work together from start to finish.

If we transplant this concept to educational settings, we can deduce its connection with curriculum integration. For example, in the pursuit of an integrated curriculum we will need to look for partners that can bring specific competence or skill to the effort to make the curriculum integration program successful. In addition, when developing these relationships, educators must either have or develop the ability and personality for trusting their colleagues without being too concerned about "turf" issues. Involvement with innovative educational endeavors requires trust; creating a sense of co-destiny—the fate of each partner is dependent upon the other. Furthermore, as this model is infused into educational settings, traditional boundaries, such as vocational and academic education, should become less meaningful and troublesome.

More cooperation among teachers becomes prevalent as each brings resources to bear on the problems/opportunities being confronted. These collaborative partnerships may only last a short period of time, such as until the completion of an integrated curriculum.

They may also be long-term in nature. Whatever the duration, the relationships here are opportunistic because they are based on students' needs.

Finally, as educators proceed with integration that is quality oriented, and strategically planned through virtual alliances, they will need leaders who will provide support and direction. They will also realize that they are not the sole source of knowledge and skill in delivering instruction; that they will need "virtual" relationships with other educators to reach their goals. Likewise, other educators will become more interested, trusting, and dependent upon their skills and abilities. It is a vision, goals, strategy, and working networks that will allow curriculum integration efforts to be ultimately successful in helping students prepare for learning and earning, now and in the future.

IMPLICATIONS FOR BUSINESS EDUCATORS: TEACHERS, ADMINISTRATORS, AND TEACHER EDUCATORS

In the effort to clarify the various models and strategies for integrating curriculum, the concept is still considerably fuzzy (Stasz & Grubb, 1991). As business educators develop integrative activities, they run across a multitude of questions, concerns, and challenges that can lead to frustration and failure. In gleaning the previous treatise on the subject, the following implications are relevant to business educators as they proceed with curriculum integration efforts.

Secondary teachers. Secondary teachers who are or have the potential to be involved with curriculum integration efforts need to consider the following implications:

- Involvement with curriculum integration efforts demands team building skills.

- Change takes place without consideration for personal views, but focused change is difficult to accomplish without commitment, time, and resources.

- Opportunities for business educators to integrate curricula within their own discipline and with other fields appear to be endless; they are limited only by their knowledge, creativity, and initiative.

- Teachers have strong feelings toward their individual disciplines, such as who should teach which subjects, what should be taught, when, where, and by what methods.

- Although teachers have no perceived negative connotations toward integrated curricula, once involved in these efforts, conflict and negotiating through conflict is inevitable.

- The focus of curriculum integration should be on students' needs; not nice ideas, packaged projects, or buzz-words.

- Focused, planned change may bring tremendous conflict, which can scare off some of the most ardent supporters of curriculum integration.

- Curriculum integration efforts, when planned and brought to bear systemically, can bring tremendous positive benefits to students, faculty, and other stakeholders.

- Curriculum integration endeavors demand financial, time, and material resources beyond the traditional scope of curriculum and instruction.

- As an elective area of the curriculum, business education should utilize curriculum integration efforts to build support and rapport with educators across the curriculum.

- As knowledgeable business people, business educators should take leadership roles in strategically planning and utilizing total quality management principles that will lead to integrated curriculum.

- As curriculum integration efforts are embraced, the specific domain of business education should become internally and externally stronger—not eroded; it should gain coherence and support from new groups, which can build interest and demand for business subjects.

- Guidance staff are a critical component of curriculum integration development teams. They have expertise in personal curriculum planning, evaluation, and communications.

- Staff development will be necessary to accomplish curriculum integration efforts. It should be regular, focused, and long term to meet the needs of the integration program.

- Successful curriculum integration efforts depend upon meeting measurable goals; hence assessment and evaluation must be infused in advance of implementation so that these processes are an ongoing effort, not an after-the-fact event.

- Results from curriculum integration programs need to be disseminated to all stakeholders so input can be acquired and refined.

- Since curriculum integration efforts have the potential to build new courses, issues regarding graduation requirements and admission to universities need to be investigated and resolved proactively so that students are not at risk of losing credit.

- As business educators continue to expand their involvement with integrated curricula, networks of schools and instructors should be developed locally, regionally, statewide, and nationally to provide a resource base for future efforts.

Business education administrators. This section discusses how administrators who have connections with business education should support efforts to integrate curricula. These individuals may operate as department chairpersons, district-wide facilitators or coordinators, building principals, or district superintendents. Listed below are several of the implications for administrators:

- Put aside old habits and blinders so that new innovations can be seen without inhibitions.
- Look more broadly at purposes, and develop a school mission statement for all students; communicate this to all stakeholders.
- Make the effort to build teams of teachers to act as innovators.
- Keep yourself and staff focused; keep quality innovations at the top of the agenda in planning out specific activities.
- Keep assessment/evaluation at the forefront to assure success.
- Develop explicit, yet adaptable, maps/strategies for change; curriculum integration is a journey that is shaped and re-shaped as the process unfolds.
- Make the extra effort to solve complex problems that surface when implementing innovations.
- Collaborative integration efforts demand focus and substance versus symbols and rhetoric.
- Change efforts require patience and persistence.
- Innovative changes consume resources more quickly than staying with the status quo; hence, more money, time, and materials will be needed.
- There will be a need to have staff at the school-building level lead the change process utilizing cross-disciplinary teams.
- Long-term change is systemic; it involves changes in teaching, curriculum, guidance, and is founded upon the culture and vision of those involved.
- In the midst of these endeavors, everyone involved must be considered a problem solver, not just administrators.

Teacher educators. As integrated programs involving business educators expand, especially Tech Prep initiatives, a different style of teacher will be needed. The following list of implications addresses the need to reconsider and redevelop teacher education programs.

The new style of teacher needed for curriculum integration will require the following traditional components of a teacher education program:

- Academic/humanities courses
- Business content, computer technology, research and evaluation, educational psychology, child development, adolescent behavior, and general and specialized teaching methodology courses
- Math, science, and communication courses
- Special needs courses
- Clinical and practice teaching experiences.

Teachers who will be able to contribute to curriculum integration efforts will need different experiences and backgrounds. These experiences include—

- Involvement with curriculum integration activities during practice teaching
- Experience with various school structures, (e.g., block scheduling, academies, open concept schools, cluster concept schools, and Tech Prep programs)
- Learning and exhibiting learning skills
- Building expertise in additional disciplines
- Understanding the importance of current social and family trends and issues

- Being competent in using varied teaching and learning methods
- Participating in first-year-of-teaching mentorships and/or support group activities
- Pursuing regular sabbaticals in business and industry settings
- Learning how to be an effective team player and leader
- Understanding the precepts and applications of TQM, strategic planning, and virtual alliances
- Being versed in the use of negotiations, conflict resolution, and decision making
- Appreciating diversity
- Being competent in the use of multiple computer applications, including multimedia technology
- Understanding and using curriculum development skills to build applied curriculum for business education and academic areas
- Developing skills in building articulation agreements
- Understanding and being able to plan and carry out assessment and evaluation activities
- Having the ability to plan and develop technology facilities
- Being versed in and gaining first-hand experience with Tech Prep program development and implementation.

Regarding broader issues in teacher education, business teacher educators should assist state departments and local Tech Prep efforts. These efforts include—

- Rethinking current curriculum content and delivery methodology
- Developing links to articulate with local Tech Prep programs in business to foster 2+2+2 programs that lead to business teacher education, administrative systems, or functional area business programs
- Developing supportive linkages to state boards of education and Tech Prep sites to assist with staff development, including—
  - Providing facilities
  - Planning and organizing staff development activities
  - Delivering training
  - Assessing programs
  - Developing curriculum.

CONCLUSION

In reflecting upon these curriculum innovations, the idea of curriculum integration can overwhelm even the most competent educator. We must realize that we have the ability to rethink our curriculum and instructional strategies, to build bridges between disciplines, to make our programs coherent, and to help our students better understand and operate in an interconnected world. This is especially true when we consider the real, "virtually" innovative business environment. In such an environment, we will only achieve a Pyrrhic victory if we are satisfied with just understanding the dynamics of learning through integrated curriculum and instruction. We must go beyond this sophomoric awareness and apply our knowledge. To ensure a bright future for our students obliges us to put forth our full measure of knowledge, skill, and creativity to make curriculum integration a reality.

REFERENCES

Aguayo, R. (1990). *Dr. Deming.* New York: Carol.

American Society for Training and Development (ASTD) (1988). *Workplace basics: the skills employers want.* Washington, DC.

Association for Supervision and Curricular Development (ASCD) (1992). *Resolutions 1992.* Alexandria, VA.

Benson, C. S., (1991). *Current state of occupational and technical training; The need for integration and high quality programs.* National Center for Research in Vocational Education: University of California at Berkeley.

Bernstein, B. (1975). *Class, codes and control (vol. 3).* London: Routledge and Kegan Paid.

Bottoms, G. (Ed). (1992 b). High schools that work through integration of academic and vocational education. *Outstanding practices for improving the academic achievement of general and vocational students.*

Bottoms, G., & Presson, A., & Johnson, M. (1992). *Making high schools work through integration of academic and vocational education.* Atlanta, Georgia: Southern Regional Education Board.

Byrne, J. A. (1993) February 8. The virtual corporation. *Business Week,* (3304), 98-104.

Crosby, P. B. (1985). *Quality is free.*

Dewey, J. (1938). *Experience & education.* New York: Collier.

Dressel, P. (1958). The meaning and significance of integration. In H. Nelson (Ed.) *The integration of educational experiences, the fifty-seventh yearbook of the national society for the study of education.* Chicago: University of Chicago Press.

Gabor, A. (1990). *The man who discovered quality.* New York: Random House.

Glasser, W. (1992). The quality school curriculum. *Phi Delta Kappan, 73* (9), 690-694.

Gloeckner, G. W., Cobb, R. B., Love, C. T. & Grant, B. A. (1992). *Review of literature.* Fort Collins, CO: Colorado State University.

Gould, S. J. (1991). *Bully for Brontosaurus: Reflections in natural history.* NY: Norton & Co.

Grubb, W. N. (1989). Preparing youth for work: The dilemmas of education and training programs. In D. Stern & D. Eichorn (Eds.), *Adolescence and work: Influences of social structure, labor markets and culture.* (pp. 13-45). Hillsdale, N.J.: Lawrence Edbaum Associates.

Grubb, W. N., Davis, G., Lum, J., Plihal, J., & Morgaine, C. (1991). *The cunning hand, the cultured mind: Models for integrating vocational and academic education.* National Center for Research in Vocational Education: University of CA, Berkeley.

Jacobs, H. H. (Ed.). (1989). *Interdisciplinary curriculum: Design and implementation.* Alexandria, VA: Association for Supervision and Curriculum Development.

Jardine, D. W. (1990). To dwell with a boundless heart: On the integrated curriculum and recovery of the earth. *Journal of Curriculum and Supervision, 5* (2), 107-119.

Juran, J. M. (1989). *Juran on leadership for quality.* New York: Free Press.

Kirby, C. L. (1993). Tech Prep: Planning a quality initiative. *Update on Research and Leadership, 4* (1), 1-11.

McEwen, B. C., McEwen, T., & Anderson-Yates, M. A. (1992). Business educators' perceptions regarding the integration of business education and academic courses. *Proceedings of the 1990 Delta Pi Epsilon Research Conference,* (pp 13-23). Little Rock, AR: Delta Pi Epsilon.

Meeth, L. R. (1978). Interdisciplinary studies: Integration of knowledge and experience. *Change* (10), 6-9.

Piaget, J. (1972). *The epistemology of interdisciplinary relationships.* Paris: Organization for Economic Cooperation and Development.

Plihal, J. and Johnson, M. (1990, November). Theoretical approaches to achieving integration by reorganizing subject matter of the American Vocational Association, Cincinnati, OH.

Pritz, S. G. (1988). Basic skills: the new imperative. *Vocational Education Journal, 63* (2), 24-26.

Rosenstock, L. (1991). The walls come down: The overdue reunification of vocational and academic education. *Phi Delta Kappan, 72* (16), 434-436.

Schmidt, B. J., Finch, C. R., & Faulkner, S. L. (1992, December). *Integrating academic and vocational education: An examination of vocational teachers' roles.* Paper presented at the meeting of the American Vocational Education Research Association, St. Louis, MO.

Secretary's Commissions of Achieving Necessary Skills (SCANS) (1992). *Learning a living: A blue print for high performance.* Washington, D.C.: U.S. Department of Labor.

Seymore, D., & Collett, C. (1991). *Total quality management in higher education: A critical assessment.* Methuen, MA: GOAL/QPC.

Stasz, C. & Grubb, W. N. (1991). *Integrating academic and vocational education: Guidelines for assessing a fuzzy reform* (A Working Paper). [The University of California, Berkeley:] National Center for Research in Vocational Education.

Stern, D., Dayton, C., Park, I., & Weisberg, A. (1989). Benefits and costs of dropout prevention in a high school program combining academic and vocational education: Third year results from replications of the California Peninsula academies. *Educational Evaluation and Policy Analysis. 11* (4), 405-416.

Wirt, J. G. (1991). Implications of the new Perkins Act. *Trends and Issues Alerts.* (Reprinted from Phi Delta Kappan), *72* (6), 424-433.

Whitehead, Alfred North. (1929). *The aims of education and other essays.* (pp. 10-11). New York: Macmillan.

CHAPTER 7

PREPARING STUDENTS FOR A CHANGING WORK WORLD

JAMES E. MILES

Pittsford Sutherland High School, Pittsford, New York

Americans can be proud of the many accomplishments of their public schools. As teachers, we have helped to build a cohesive and stable nation by preparing millions of students to effectively participate in family, civic, and economic life. As we near the end of this century, however, the world that most of us knew when we were growing up, and even in our adult years, is quickly vanishing. Everything about us and our environment is changing: the makeup of our population, family groups and patterns of family living, the nature of our economy, the demands of the workplace, the dramatic realignment of nations and cultures on the world scene, our increasingly threatened economic pre-eminence, and the capability of technology to transform our lives. Today's youth will live in an era very different from our own.

A CHANGING ENVIRONMENT

Two significant changes in society are challenging and placing demands upon our education system. The first is the increasing dependency of American business on sophisticated technology that demands workers with higher level skills in reading, writing, and mathematics. The mix of these required skills and how they are used in the workplace has also changed dramatically and will continue to change with the evolution of technology.

Technological changes. Emerging technology has impacted the way employees work as well as the skills they need to complete their job tasks. Technological impacts that our students will encounter in the workplace can be found in all job sectors. Robotics has changed our methods of manufacturing. In 1980, fewer than 5,000 robots were used in American factories. By 1992, 1.3 million robots were being used, and this number is projected to grow to 20 million robots by the year 2000. Today, manufacturing workers must be proficient in inputting, retrieving, monitoring, and manipulating data for these robots.

The apparel industry has developed technology that will manufacture custom-made clothing while you wait for the same cost as off-the-rack clothes. After selecting the fabric and pattern, scanners are used to record a person's measurements, which are relayed to robots that cut the fabric, weld the seams without stitching, and press the garment.

Technology is very evident in the automotive industry. The American automobile today has more electronic circuitry than Lunar I had when it landed on the moon and our cars are repaired by auto technicians who diagnose problems using sophisticated computerized equipment. The 1992 GM car manual consists of 462,000 pages and is only available in disk format. The transformation of the automotive workplace requires new and different job skills as workers interact with technology in constantly changing ways.

Societal changes. The second significant societal change placing demands on education is the new demographic makeup of our student body. The number of students who live in poverty, who return after school to empty homes, who speak limited English, or who are exposed daily to drugs and other dangers is on the rise, and each of these conditions hinders a student's chance of success in school. As educators, one of our greatest challenges will be to raise the expectations of all students—including those whose environment places them "at risk" of failure.

While many of us believe that our educational programs underwent major changes and at a rapid pace during the 1980s, the changes made in business and industry, and indeed the changes shaping society, have outpaced our educational reform five fold. The employment trend in all job sectors including administrative, service, marketing, production, and information systems has changed from an unskilled work force to a technologically-based work force. By the year 2000, it is projected that less than 15 percent of the available jobs will be unskilled. Our education system is not providing youth with the knowledge and skills needed to master the more demanding technologically-based jobs in today's market. It can no longer be business as usual. Emerging trends and changing demographics are impacting both the schools and workplace and will continue to do so for the foreseeable future.

SCHOOLS MUST PREPARE ALL STUDENTS FOR ADULT LIFE

If our schools are to meet the need of students and the business community, then they can no longer ignore the fact that too many of our students leave school without adequate preparation for adult life. Almost all of the secondary school dropouts, who account for approximately 25 percent of our population, and almost one-third of all students who do graduate with a high school diploma lack the knowledge, skills, and attitudes needed to obtain and maintain skilled employment or to successfully engage in a postsecondary degree program. June Atkinson (1990) writes that "noncollege bound students, who often take less demanding academic courses and frequently unrelated general courses are unprepared for employment or postsecondary education, and these students represent the majority of our student population." In most states, requirements for obtaining a high school diploma do not guarantee that our graduates are adequately prepared for either immediate employment or postsecondary education. Schools cannot continue to fail the majority of our youth by allowing them to leave school unprepared for their adult lives.

Employers complain that too many high school graduates lack the skills needed to qualify for entry-level jobs. Postsecondary institutions repeat a similar message, borne out by the high college dropout rates and the number of students who need remediation to handle college course work. Approximately 75 percent of the students pursuing a college degree do not complete their program in the prescribed time frame, and almost 25 percent never complete their collegiate program of study.

School reform. Before schools can provide all students with the competencies needed for success in pursuing both a career and postsecondary education, the school system itself must be changed. Schools must clearly define the knowledge, skills, and attitudes graduates must possess, determine the level of proficiency that is needed, develop curriculum to provide students with these competencies, and change their method of assessment to ensure that all students have attained these competencies at the necessary level of proficiency.

Identify what students need for success. One of the first reforms needed is to upgrade and clearly identify what knowledge, skills, and attitudes will be needed by students. Although most schools raised graduation requirements and academic standards during the 1980s, few schools made the changes needed to prepare students for the changing world of work. Willard Daggett (1993) writes, "Rarely did we identify the competencies demanded of today's citizens and workers; we simply assumed that raising standards in the traditional basics would rectify the problem. So, despite 10 years of school reform, we have the greatest gap in our nation's history between the skills young people possess when they leave high school and the skills they need to function successfully as citizens, lifelong learners, and workers."

A technological-based work force requires workers to have a new set of knowledge, skills, and attitudes that are not formally taught in the present educational system. Current literature often refers to this new set of knowledge, skills, and attitudes as the expanded basics. As its name implies, the basics, which until the 1980s included only the traditional three Rs, have been expanded to include skills such as decision-making and problem-solving, using information systems, oral communication, logic, creative thinking, listening, teamwork, and leadership skills. Today's worker does not require more or less of the traditional skills and knowledge that schools are teaching, but rather new and different skills are needed for success in the work world (Berryman, 1990).

Assessing student achievement. Another necessary school reform will be changing the method used for assessing student achievement. Student learning outcomes must be stated in measurable performance standards that can assess a student's ability to apply the knowledge, skills, and attitudes learned to his or her role as a worker, a citizen, and a lifelong learner. The assessment standard must accurately measure a student's mastery of the learning outcome rather than measuring his or her ability to attain a minimum competency level. Studies clearly indicate that expectations for all students in high school are too low, and that for the sake of our young people and our economy, schools must raise their educational sights. Schools can no longer aim only for minimum competency, which was the thrust of the 1980s, but rather, they must strive for mastery, which implies excellence, by all students across the educational spectrum. Our curriculum needs to change from its traditional focus on units, courses, and curricula to giving more attention to student learning/performance outcomes that are clearly expressed and assessed in terms of what students actually must know and be able to do.

CAREER PREPARATION VALIDATION STUDY

In April of 1989, the New York State Board of Regents, the state's educational governing body, adopted a policy requiring that "all high school graduates should be prepared for immediate employment and/or postsecondary education." Employment preparation was defined as a combination of basic skills, transferable skills, and marketable skills needed to obtain and maintain employment. Being prepared for postsecondary education was defined as being able to complete a postsecondary course of instruction without the need for remediation. A blue-ribbon steering committee was appointed to identify the skills that students must have to be prepared for immediate employment and/or postsecondary education.

Skills identified. The committee's report identified a group of skills they believed should be incorporated into the educational experiences of all students. They classified the skills needed for employment as either basic skills or expanded basic skills. The basic skills included language arts skills in reading, writing, listening, and speaking, and mathematics skills in basic operations, logic, probability, statistics, measurement, and algebra/geometry. The expanded basic skills included manual dexterity, reasoning, interpersonal skills, working as a member of a team, using information systems, setting priorities, personal work skills and behaviors, and personal and civic responsibility.

Validation procedures. Upon accepting the committee's report in 1990, the Regents directed the State Education Department to conduct a validation study to verify the competency level for each of the identified skills that would be required to perform a variety of different entry-level jobs. Using the advice of national experts, scales were developed describing a continuum of competence from simple (Level 1) to complex (Level 6) for many of the skills the committee identified as necessary for entry-level positions. These scales correspond to the six levels of Bloom's Taxonomy and reflect adult standards of performance from the lowest observable demonstration of an outcome to outstanding performance of that outcome. The most commonly used reference point in the study is Bloom's Application Level (Level 3), which means students can use information learned in a new situation.

The research method selected was to observe and interview successful workers to gain the desired data. The workers' major tasks were identified and analyzed, then matched to the kind and level of skill needed to complete the tasks using a survey instrument. If a skill was not relevant to a job, it was rated "not applicable" by the observer.

Size of the validation study. Approximately 1400 successful employees, working for 300 small and large businesses, were both observed and interviewed by 40 trained observers/interviewers to gain the desired data. The same trainer was used to train all observers for continuity and validity. From these observations/interviews, a sample of 1,000 were selected to represent the diversity of the labor market and the 35 occupational job clusters in New York State. The sample included a variety of entry-level jobs such as clerk/typist, salad chef, licensed practical nurse, inventory clerk, and receptionist . . . jobs that do not require a four-year baccalaureate degree although they may require further education or training after high school. The New York State

Department of Labor assisted the State Education Department in summarizing the data collected from what is considered to be the most comprehensive research conducted on the specific skills needed by entry-level workers.

Summary of results. The data and charts that follow identify the percent of entry-level workers whose job requires them to perform at various skill levels on the scales for language arts, mathematics, and the expanded basics. The correlation between the skill levels used in the validation study and Bloom's Taxonomy is:

Validation Study Scale	Bloom's Taxonomy
Level 1	Knowledge Level
Level 2	Comprehension Level
Level 3	Application Level
Level 4	Analysis Level
Level 5	Synthesis Level
Level 6	Evaluation Level

LANGUAGE ARTS

Observations suggest that reading, writing, listening, and speaking skill levels needed by entry-level workers are more sophisticated today than in the past. The application of these language arts skills to complete job tasks is also changing, often becoming more technical and requiring a higher degree of reasoning and decision-making capabilities.

Reading. When matched with Bloom's Taxonomy, the competency level needed to complete work tasks for more than 80 percent of the entry-level employees observed and interviewed requires the skill of READING FOR INFORMATION at the application level or higher. READING FOR INFORMATION is the ability to collect data, facts, or ideas, discover relationships, concepts, or generalizations, and use knowledge generated from text. Sixty-five percent of the entry-level workers use the skill of READING FOR CRITICAL ANALYSIS AND EVALUATION at the application level or higher to complete their job tasks. This is the ability to use personal and/or objective criteria to form opinions or make judgments about ideas and information in written texts. Although READING FOR PERSONAL RESPONSE is a valuable social skill, it is not a needed skill in the workplace.

READING
**Percent of Entry Level Workers Whose Job Requires Them
To Perform at Various Skill Levels
Levels Correspond to Bloom's Taxonomy**

SKILL	LEVEL	N/A	1	2	3	4	5	6
READING FOR INFORMATION		3%	4%	12%	28%	30%	18%	5%
READING FOR CRITICAL ANALYSIS & EVALUATION		20%	5%	10%	24%	27%	12%	2%
READING FOR PERSONAL RESPONSE		71%	8%	9%	7%	4%	1%	0%

Writing. The study found that WRITING FOR INFORMATION and WRITING FOR CRITICAL ANALYSIS AND EVALUATION are important skills for completing job tasks. Approximately half of the workers observed used the skill of WRITING FOR INFORMATION, the ability to interpret, apply, and transmit information in writing, at the Application Level or higher. Over 60 percent of the workers needed the skill of WRITING FOR CRITICAL ANALYSIS AND EVALUATION at the Application Level or higher. This is the ability to use personal or objective criteria to express opinions and make judgments in writing about issues, ideas, and experiences. WRITING FOR PERSONAL EXPRESSION, defined as the ability to use all forms of writing to investigate and express personal feelings, attitudes, and ideas, and WRITING FOR SOCIAL INTERACTION, the ability to communicate in everyday interpersonal situations, were seldom used on the job.

WRITING

**Percent of Entry Level Workers Whose Job Requires Them
To Perform at Various Skill Levels
Levels Correspond to Bloom's Taxonomy**

SKILL	LEVEL	N/A	1	2	3	4	5	6
WRITING FOR INFORMATION		8%	11%	28%	26%	17%	8%	2%
WRITING FOR CRITICAL ANALYSIS & EVALUATION		26%	11%	21%	21%	11%	8%	2%
WRITING FOR PERSONAL EXPRESSION		68%	11%	9%	9%	2%	1%	0%
WRITING FOR SOCIAL INTERACTION		47%	17%	16%	10%	7%	2%	1%

Listening/speaking. The study suggests that over 80 percent of the entry-level employees observed and interviewed need the skill of LISTENING/SPEAKING FOR INFORMATION AND UNDERSTANDING at the application level or higher. This skill is the ability to acquire, interpret, apply, and transmit information through oral language. Approximately 65 percent of the workers studied use the skill of LISTENING/SPEAKING FOR CRITICAL ANALYSIS AND EVALUATION at the application level or higher. Workers use this skill to evaluate and generate information and ideas according to personal and/or objective criteria. More than half of the workers require a skill level at the application level or higher for LISTENING/SPEAKING FOR SOCIAL INTERACTION, which is the ability to communicate through spoken language in everyday interpersonal situations. LISTENING/SPEAKING FOR PERSONAL RESPONSE, although a useful social skill, is not a high priority job skill.

LISTENING/SPEAKING

Percent of Entry Level Workers Whose Job Requires Them
To Perform at Various Skill Levels
Levels Correspond to Bloom's Taxonomy

SKILL	LEVEL	N/A	1	2	3	4	5	6
LISTENING/SPEAKING FOR INFORMATION & UNDERSTANDING		1%	3%	13%	26%	33%	17%	7%
LISTENING/SPEAKING FOR CRITICAL ANALYIS AND EVALUATION		8%	8%	18%	23%	29%	11%	3%
LISTENING/SPEAKING FOR PERSONAL EXPRESSION		45%	8%	19%	18%	9%	8%	3%
LISTENING/SPEAKING FOR SOCIAL INTERACTION		11%	6%	25%	28%	18%	8%	4%

Students in school most often receive language arts instruction at, and are assessed at, the comprehension level of Bloom's Taxonomy. There is an urgent need to correct this discrepancy between the level of proficiency needed by entry-level workers and the level of proficiency achieved by students in schools.

MATHEMATICS

Basic operations and logic. The study showed that math skills using BASIC OPERATIONS, LOGIC, PROBABILITY, and MEASUREMENT were the most essential math skills used by entry-level workers. The competency level in BASIC OPERATIONS for almost 75 percent of the workers interviewed is at the application level or higher. Approximately two-thirds of the workers interviewed use the skill of LOGIC at or above the application level. LOGIC is the ability to use reasoning to determine relationships among propositions in terms of implication, contradiction, contrariety, and conversion.

BASIC OPERATIONS AND LOGIC

Percent of Entry Level Workers Whose Job Requires Them
To Perform at Various Skill Levels
Levels Correspond to Bloom's Taxonomy

SKILL	LEVEL	N/A	1	2	3	4	5	6
BASIC OPERATIONS		3%	10%	12%	25%	27%	11%	12%
EVALUATION		8%	10%	14%	28%	24%	10%	6%

Probability and Measurement. Almost 50 percent of the workers need the skill of PROBABILITY at or above the application level to perform job tasks. PROBABILITY is defined as the ability to predict the number of times something will probably occur over the range of possible occurrences. The skill level in MEASUREMENT for almost two-thirds of the entry-level workers is at the application level or higher. This is the ability to determine size, extent, and quantity using standard and metric systems.

PROBABILITY AND MEASUREMENT

**Percent of Entry Level Workers Whose Job Requires Them
To Perform at Various Skill Levels
Levels Correspond to Bloom's Taxonomy**

SKILL	LEVEL	N/A	1	2	3	4	5	6
PROBABILITY		21%	19%	12%	22%	18%	6%	2%
MEASUREMENT		21%	7%	10%	18%	22%	13%	9%

Statistics and algebra/geometry. Math skills in STATISTICS, the ability to assemble, classify, tabulate, and analyze numerical facts or data as well as ALGEBRA, the ability to use and solve formulas and equations and GEOMETRY, the ability to describe, compare, and classify geometric figures, appear to be of minimal significance as job skills for entry-level workers.

STATISTICS AND ALGEBRA/GEOMETRY

**Percent of Entry Level Workers Whose Job Requires Them
To Perform at Various Skill Levels
Levels Correspond to Bloom's Taxonomy**

SKILL	LEVEL	N/A	1	2	3	4	5	6
STATISTICS		47%	17%	12%	11%	6%	5%	2%
ALGEBRA/GEOMETRY		21%	7%	10%	18%	22%	13%	9%

Students generally receive classroom instruction in basic math operations and measurement at the appropriate levels for developing job competency. Instruction and student assessment, however, are often below acceptable levels for developing competency in logic and probability. Instruction and evaluation in these areas must be raised at least to the application level to ensure that our students are properly prepared to assume their role as working citizens.

EXPANDED BASIC SKILLS

Major research studies conducted in recent years have concluded that the basic skills of language arts and mathematics, although an essential foundation, are not sufficient in themselves to prepare students for the rigors of today's workplace, much less for the workplace of the 21st Century (Carnevale, Gainer, and Meltzer, 1991). The Career Preparation Validation Study uses the term EXPANDED BASICS to identify the other cognitive and affective skills a student needs to bridge high school with college or the work world. The results of the study underscore the almost universal importance of a high level of competence in the EXPANDED BASIC skills for entry-level workers.

Interpersonal skills and personal work skills and behaviors. A worker who possesses good INTERPERSONAL SKILLS has the ability to interact effectively, professionally and socially, by using skills such as courtesy, tact, empathy, objectivity, tolerance of and respect for others. Over 80 percent of the entry-level workers interviewed use these skills to complete their job tasks at the application level or higher. PERSONAL WORK SKILLS AND BEHAVIORS require a skill level for approximately 85 percent of the workers observed and interviewed at or above the application level. An employee with PERSONAL WORK SKILLS AND BEHAVIORS has the ability to apply his or her efforts systematically and conscientiously to required tasks. This worker would be viewed as a self-starter with good time-management skills for organizing and completing job responsibilities.

INTERPERSONAL SKILLS AND PERSONAL WORK SKILLS AND BEHAVIORS

**Percent of Entry Level Workers Whose Job Requires Them
To Perform at Various Skill Levels
Levels Correspond to Bloom's Taxonomy**

SKILL	LEVEL	N/A	1	2	3	4	5	6
INTERPERSONAL SKILLS		1%	3%	11%	21%	28%	20%	16%
INTERPERSONAL WORK SKILLS & BEHAVIORS		1%	8%	9%	18%	27%	24%	13%

Working as a member of a team and reasoning. The study suggests that approximately 80 percent of the workers observed and interviewed require the competency of WORKING AS A MEMBER OF A TEAM at or above the application level. This skill is defined as the ability to conduct oneself according to the expressed or unexpressed norms of a group and to participate according to one's talents. REASONING, which is the ability to draw conclusions through the use of rational processes, is needed by over 80 percent of the entry-level workers at or above the application level in order to perform their work tasks.

WORKING AS A MEMBER OF A TEAM AND REASONING

**Percent of Entry Level Workers Whose Job Requires Them
To Perform at Various Skill Levels
Levels Correspond to Bloom's Taxonomy**

SKILL	LEVEL	N/A	1	2	3	4	5	6
WORKING AS A MEMBER OF A TEAM		1%	9%	11%	21%	22%	23%	13%
REASONING		1%	4%	11%	19%	32%	28%	5%

Using information systems and manual dexterity. USING INFORMATION SYSTEMS requires a skill level for approximately one-half of the workers interviewed at or above the application level. A worker uses this skill to gather, manipulate, retrieve, analyze, and synthesize data. MANUAL DEXTERITY is defined as the ability to apply psychomotor, cognitive, and affective skills in the execution of manipulative activities. The study suggests that approximately 80 percent of the workers observed and interviewed require a skill level at or above the application level to complete their job tasks.

USING INFORMATION SYSTEMS AND MANUAL DEXTERITY

**Percent of Entry Level Workers Whose Job Requires Them
To Perform at Various Skill Levels
Levels Correspond to Bloom's Taxonomy**

SKILL	LEVEL	N/A	1	2	3	4	5	6
USING INFORMATION SYSTEMS		21%	10%	17%	18%	15%	15%	4%
MANUAL DEXTERITY		1%	2%	17%	30%	24%	21%	4%

Setting priorities and personal and civic responsibility. Over 70 percent of the workers observed and interviewed use the skill of SETTING PRIORITIES at or above the application level. Workers use this skill on the job to make judgments regarding relative criticality of tasks in order to accomplish objectives and/or meet deadlines. PERSONAL AND CIVIC RESPONSIBILITY requires a competency level for almost 40 percent of the workers at or above the application level. This expanded basic skill is described as being accountable for one's actions and fulfilling one's duties as a citizen.

SETTING PRIORITIES AND PERSONAL AND CIVIC RESPONSIBILITY

**Percent of Entry Level Workers Whose Job Requires Them
To Perform at Various Skill Levels
Levels Correspond to Bloom's Taxonomy**

SKILL	LEVEL	N/A	1	2	3	4	5	6
SETTING PRIORITIES		3%	6%	15%	20%	27%	20%	9%
PERSONAL AND CIVIC RESPONSIBILITY		20%	24%	7%	7%	19%	17%	6%

The level of competency expected of entry-level workers for most EXPANDED BASIC SKILLS appears to be substantially higher than the level provided through school curriculum. Instruction and evaluation in these areas must be raised at least to the application level to ensure that our students are properly prepared to make the transition from school to the world of work.

Unfinished research. Although the Career Preparation Validation Study was submitted to the Board of Regents in March of 1991, much of the research remains unfinished due to a lack of funding. The level at which each skill is currently taught in our curriculum and the degree of student mastery of them must still be measured.

The list of validated Expanded Basic Skills is not an all-inclusive list. Additional skills identified during the observations/interviews as necessary for entry-level workers to perform their job tasks, including resource management and keyboarding, must still be assessed and validated. The validation of these skills, as well as job-specific skills and skills necessary to complete a postsecondary program of study without the need for remediation, will be left for future research studies.

CURRICULUM IMPLICATIONS

The validation process has provided us with an excellent foundation for analyzing the results of this study and for determining how the skills that have been identified and validated as essential for entry-level workers can be taught in our curricula at the application level or higher. We must begin writing performance-based student learning outcomes and developing instructional strategies for these skills so that all students will be adequately prepared to assume their adult roles of worker, citizen, and life-long learner.

Validation of the study results. The findings of another significant study, which was conducted by the U.S. Department of Labor in 1990, identified the seven skill groups that employers consider basic for employment. These seven skill groups validate the skills identified in New York's survey.

U.S. DEPARTMENT OF LABOR: 1990 Report
"Workplace Basics: The Skills Employers Want"

Adaptability: creative thinking and problem solving. Employers need workers who can use creative thinking to solve problems, overcome barriers, and make decisions in an ever-changing, multi-task environment. Schools must create learning environments that foster development of the thinking, problem-solving, and decision-making skills young people need to become successful workers in a world economy.

Personal management: self-esteem, goal setting, motivation, and personal career development. Taking pride in work accomplished, setting goals and meeting them, and enhancing job skills to meet new challenges are necessary characteristics for all employees as well as being essential skills for success in life. Schools must adopt standards and implement strategies at all grade levels to help each student believe in his or her own self-worth and maintain a positive view of self. Students must learn how to assess themselves accurately, to set personal goals, monitor their progress, and display self-control.

Group effectiveness: interpersonal skills, negotiation, and teamwork. The ability to work cooperatively in teams and contribute to the group's efforts are increasingly important for workplace success. The top-down management style of the manufacturing age has been replaced in the information age with an increasing reliance on front-line workers functioning as a team. Cooperative Learning should become part of every classroom in America. Classrooms can no longer be used to encourage students to become isolates, but rather must help students to demonstrate understanding, friendliness, adaptability, empathy, and politeness in group settings.

Organizational effectiveness and leadership. Employers want employees to have a sense of where the organization is headed and what they must do to make a contribution. Workers need a greater understanding of the production process, the products and services of the company, and their company's market. In 1980 for example, bank personnel needed to know only six services. Today, however, they must be able to explain more than 120 different bank services. Business needs employees who can and will assume responsibility and motivate and teach co-workers. They need workers who will take initiative and are able to "fill-in the blanks."

Competence in reading, writing, and computation. Employers need a workforce that has sound basic academic skills in reading, writing, and computational skills. Employees will need to be able to use these skills on the job with proficiency in summarizing information, monitoring their own work, and using analytical and critical thinking skills. All students need a rigorous foundation in academics in addition to the new workplace skills.

Listening and oral communication. Fifty-five percent of the time spent in communication is spent listening. Schools' curricula, however, focus almost exclusively on reading and writing skills, and offer minimal training in oral communications and listening. Employers want workers who can receive, attend to, interpret, and respond to verbal messages and other cues. Workers in the information age must be able to effectively organize ideas and communicate them orally.

Learning to learn. Employers are frequently shifting employees between jobs and responsibilities. They need employees who can absorb, process, and apply new information quickly and effectively. Today's worker must be able to manage more frequent and complex interactions with others, perform a greater number of more frequently changed tasks, and operate in a more uncertain and less well-defined environment.

The impact of technical change, innovation, and global competition has brought about an upskilling of work in America. Broader job responsibilities with more complex and demanding work tasks will require workers to learn and adapt to new and unique situations for which they must discover the solutions. This rapid transformation of the workplace from unskilled to skilled positions will require workers to continually upgrade their knowledge and skills through formal education and informal training. Knowing how to learn will become the foundation for building other skills and acquiring new knowledge. Promotions and job upgrades will depend on our graduates having the basic literacy skills needed to complete this training and education.

The skills employers identified as essential in the U.S. Department of Labor's study are the same skills that New York's Career Preparation Validation Study suggest as critical for satisfactory job performance by entry-level workers. Journal articles reporting similar research projects conducted in other states list like sets of knowledge, skills, and attitudes as vital for a competitive workforce. These articles also support the findings of New York's study that expectations for students are too low and that the present delivery system used in schools is functionally unable to provide all students with the preparation needed for success in their adult roles as workers, citizens, and lifelong learners.

RECOMMENDATIONS

As educators, we must move forward with integrating the knowledge, skills, and attitudes identified and validated by these research studies into our curriculum. We must identify where these basic and expanded basic skills can be taught in our business courses, write curriculum and instructional strategies for teaching them at the application level or higher, and develop performance-based learning outcomes that hold all students accountable for attaining the level of proficiency needed for success in the workplace. Simple knowledge or comprehension, the levels we typically teach to and test for in secondary schools, will no longer prepare workers for today's competitive, global job market. Research shows that when an individual uses any skill, it is at least at the application level.

Integrating language arts skills in business courses. In each business course, we can provide students with instruction and activities that will raise their level of performance in reading, writing, speaking, and listening for information and for critical analysis and evaluation. In content courses like The Dynamics of Work or Principles of Marketing, students can select and read an article related to the work world, write a descriptive summary analyzing the information in the article, and give an oral summary that includes their personal evaluation of the article to either the entire class or a small group.

In skill courses such as Information Processing or Business Analysis with Computer Applications, have students select an unfamiliar piece of software and, using the software program and the manufacturer's manual, become proficient with its applications. The students can then use a word processing program to write a summary in their own words giving an overview of the program, how to load and use the software, special features, and their recommendation with supporting reasons as to whether the software should be purchased by the school. Each student can also present a class demonstration on using the software program.

These activities increase the level of student proficiency with basic language arts skills needed for employment. The skills are developed using activities within the curriculum content area that are relevant to the learning outcomes for the course. Both activities will challenge and stretch students at all six levels of Bloom's Taxonomy.

Integrating mathematics skills in business courses. Business education courses can help students raise their level of performance with the math skills used most by entry-level workers. Activities can be designed for students to practice applying basic operations, probability, logic, and measurement to simulated job tasks. Students can use basic math operations to determine the inventory value of selected stock items, verify the sums on an invoice, mark up merchandise as a percentage of the cost, or determine the sales tax for a series of purchases in a content course such as The Dynamics of Work or in a skill course such as Recordkeeping.

In a computer applications course students can conduct an experiment in probability by playing a computer game 10 times to determine how often the computer wins against an opponent. The student can then use this simple probability to predict the number of times the computer will win in a given number of trials. The spreadsheet is also an excellent tool for teaching the concepts of logic and probability while reinforcing basic math skills and statistics. After inputting an income statement using a spreadsheet program, "what-if" applications can be performed by the accounting student to project changes in net income if one expense increases by 20 percent.

Logic can be used in many business courses to determine relationships. Accounting students can identify and explain relationships between a balance sheet and an income statement; students in business math can sort a set of numbers to subsets of odds and evens; and in business law, students can examine the conclusions to case studies to be sure they reflect the given relationships. Students in business courses often identify or measure items by size, quantity, weight, length, or capacity. Their proficiency using measurements can be increased by encouraging them, when appropriate, to convert standard measurements to metric measurements.

The application of math skills with realistic job task situations will help students in our business courses see the relationships between concepts and skills learned in school and how they are used in the work world. These activities will raise their level of math proficiency and better prepare them for entering a technologically-based work environment.

Integrating expanded basic skills in business courses. Each expanded basic skill identified and assessed through New York's validation process, and supported by the U.S. Department of Labor's survey, is important not only as a work skill for entry-level employees but also as a life skill for all adults. Business education can provide instruction and activities that will raise a student's level of performance in each of the expanded basic skills.

Keyboarding is an excellent manipulative activity for developing eye-hand coordination and strengthening manual dexterity. Students can develop their competency in using information systems through the inclusion of curriculum-related activities in all business courses that require them to interact with a computer terminal for the purpose of gathering, manipulating, retrieving, analyzing, and synthesizing data. It is projected that by the year 2001, 95 percent of all jobs will require workers to interact with computers in some manner. Reasoning skills will be sharpened in a computer programming course when a student is asked to debug a complex program and explain the steps that were followed to locate and correct errors.

Getting along with co-workers and supervisors is one of the most critical skills for workplace success. Using work-related role-play situations and case studies will help students understand the need for and how to use effective, interpersonal skills to avoid conflict and promote harmony. Students in a cooperative work experience program can provide realistic situations they have observed on the job. Local employers are another excellent source for providing teachers with realistic data for writing case studies.

The classroom is an excellent place for students to practice and be held accountable for the personal work skills and behaviors of regular attendance, meeting assignment due dates, and organizing tasks and time effectively. A short unit on time management skills will provide students with a valuable, lifelong skill. Using a community project for a class activity is an excellent way to promote personal and civic responsibility. Students in an Information Processing class can work with members of a local senior citizens organization to produce and distribute a newsletter using a desktop publishing program.

One of the most important job skills we can help our students develop is the ability to work cooperatively with others as a member of a team. In an accounting class students can work together in class on completing a major problem or practice set. An Information Processing class can produce a class newsletter with each student assuming responsibility for writing and formatting one article using a desktop publishing program. A stock market project that divides students into teams and gives each team $10,000 to invest provides an excellent opportunity for students in a finance or economics class to develop their interpersonal and leadership skills.

Businesses of the future will require better-educated employees and managers who know how to organize their work places to make the most of their human resources. Our curriculum is best able to provide future workers with the knowledge, skills, and attitudes needed in an ever-changing, sophisticated business environment. As Janet Treichel (1991) wrote, "Students need business education programs to prepare for productive roles in a global economy. Our programs are essential to the well-being of our nation's businesses, and we must promote this idea all across the country."

Changing our education system to produce graduates who are better prepared for their adult and work life will not be an easy task. It will require fundamental changes in the current structure and organization of schools—and in their approaches to such issues as curriculum, resource allocation, and teacher training. All parties in the educational process must understand the urgent need to raise expectations of students, to meet the needs of a growing number of students placed at risk, and to target resources to accomplish these objectives. A comprehensive awareness program must be initiated to create an environment supportive of these changes.

RESOURCES

Atkinson, J. S. (1990, November). Helping students plan their education for tomorrow. *Business Education Forum 45*, 40.

Berryman, S. E. (1990, July). Skills, schools, and signals. Occasional Paper No. 2. Institute on Education and the Economy, Teachers College, Columbia University. New York.

Carnevale, Gainer, and Meltzer (1991). Workplace basics: the skills employers want. United States Department of Labor, The Secretary's Commission on Achieving Necessary Skills, "What Work Requires of School: A SCANS Report for America 2000." New York State Education Department (1990). Career preparation validation study and, Northern Illinois University. (1991). Building public-private partnerships to improve vocational education in Illinois.

Daggett, W. R. (1993, Winter). Answering the call for school reform. *The Balance Sheet 74*, 2-3.

Treichel, J. M. (1991, February). Moving toward the 21st century. *Business Education Forum 45*, 52.

CHAPTER 8

PREPARING STUDENTS FOR A CULTURALLY DIVERSE WORKPLACE

JEANETTE J. PURDY

Mercer County Community College, Trenton, New Jersey

Cultural diversity and intercultural communications are rapidly becoming the watchwords of the nineties and are beginning to have profound ramifications for the American workplace. Transcontinental and intercontinental travel is a major pastime as people travel from one continent to another and from one country to another. Trade with the Orient—Japan, Hong Kong, Taiwan and Korea—continues to bind us together economically, not to mention the political ramifications for our own national security. Today's labor market is starting to "look different" and will continue to do so as we move toward the 21st century. According to the U.S. Bureau of Labor statistics, by the year 2000 women will make up 64 percent of the work population; minorities and immigrants will constitute 26 percent (an increase over 22 percent in 1990); and 32 percent will be white. The number of blacks and Hispanics in the workforce is expected to increase nearly twice as fast as the number of whites (Livingston, 1991).

For decades, the traditional American image of the melting pot was an attempt to assimilate the variety of cultures typifying a "common bond." What was a philosophical approach to bring together all nationalities, colors, creeds in pursuit of the American dream of life, liberty, and the pursuit of happiness is now being challenged by a concept that embraces a diversity of cultures—a mixture of traditions, beliefs, values, and lifestyles.

The impact of global competition has made America's loss of its competitive edge critical. Businesses are experiencing a dramatic shift in their ability to compete in the international marketplace. Production in the United States has risen more slowly (1.9 percent per year from 1950-1991) than in all other industrialized countries (National Alliance on Business, 1992). The most serious failure is the inability of the United States to sustain and nurture a highly skilled workforce. With minorities and immigrants continuing to make up a larger portion of the labor resource, business is not quite prepared to handle this new breed of workers. Those who are flexible, who have developed goals and strategies of inclusion for cultural diversity, and who view the concept as a strength rather than a weakness will be ahead of the competition.

Significant changes have made today's workforce far different from that which existed 20 years ago. The generation gap continues to widen between older and younger workers. Increasing numbers of women continue to enter the labor market each year. Ethnic groups representing a diversity of cultures have infiltrated the workplace in record numbers since Congress passed a new law in 1990 boosting annual legal immigration levels to 100,000, allowing 150,000 skilled workers to enter and stiffening penalties against employers who fear hiring foreign-looking workers. Organizations are revamping their physical environment to accommodate those with physical and medical disabilities (1993, *Business Week*).

Throughout this decade, the competition will be extremely keen for all types of workers—entry level, skilled, and seasoned. Employers must begin to look to the nonmale, the nonwhite, and the nonyoung as a labor resource. There will be a push for noncitizens as well. Over the next 10 years, only about 15 percent of those entering the workforce will be native-born white males. Building a new, more diverse workforce and making it a viable one will be among the most important endeavors for business in the coming years.

INTEGRATING DIVERSITY IN THE WORKPLACE

It is becoming increasingly clear that for organizations to become competitive, they must prepare to meet the challenges of diversity. Several organizations have already taken the initiative to put training programs in place aimed at valuing diversity. Others are becoming more sensitive to family issues, offering childcare plans and flexible work schedules.

As early as 1979, Merck began an aggressive management training program and employee awareness seminars for 17,000 employees, designed to change attitudes, policies, and systems to reflect a greater sensitivity to minorities and women.

Proctor and Gamble is committed to increasing diversity awareness for all its employees. Initiatives are designed to value diversity, including advisory teams, minority women's networking conferences, and an "on board" mentoring program to retain African-American and female managers. At Folger Coffee Company (a subsidiary of Proctor and Gamble), through a variety of roleplaying workshops, employees are helped to understand and appreciate individual differences.

Ortho-Pharmaceutical Corporation, in response to a concern for high turnover and the scarcity of women and minorities in upper management, holds three-day "managing diversity" workshops. The managers gain insight into their attitudes about race/gender and examine the impact of these attitudes on decision making and other behaviors. Action plans are then developed to help all managers integrate newly acquired principles and skills into their daily activities. For employees, quarterly symposia during which outside experts speak on issues of diversity related to the workplace are an added feature.

Hallmark's "Valuing Diversity" program addresses culture and gender on three levels—personal, interpersonal, and organizational. Both minority and nonminority managers meet periodically in small groups to discover their own personal biases about race and gender and to learn how their behavior affects their employees and the organization. Hallmark offers informal after-work gatherings called Minority Forums designed to help minority employees grow professionally and personally. Employees from all divisions of the company are encouraged to network, exchange ideas, and share experiences.

Northeastern Products Company, a division of Campbell Soup Company, has an on-site ESL program to meet the needs of Hispanic and Asian employees, who represent 36 percent of its workforce. The class meets twice a week for two hours and involves employees in activities such as applying for credit cards, reading road maps and food labels, and communicating in the work environment.

Digital Equipment Corporation, the second largest computer company in the world, has established a full-time office devoted to AIDS education for its 125,000 employees. Digital's educational format was designed by the AIDS Program office manager and engages the expertise of a health professional from the Digital staff or an outside health agency. Subjects covered include prejudice, homophobia, sexuality, grief, death, dying, and the politics of AIDS. The use of group exercises and interactive dialogues with persons living with AIDS is an important part of the program (Jamison and O'Mara, 1991).

Apple Computer has established a manager of multicultural and affirmative-action programs. Diversity-management workshops offer training for managers that explores what it means to be a minority in a majority society. A multicultural board oversees the company's diversity efforts. And a mentor program introduces new minority employees to the company's culture. Avon encourages employees to organize cultural networks. The networks help new employees adjust, arrange cultural events, and provide feedback to a top level council that includes the CEO. At Corning, new employees are rotated through different jobs during their first five years so they can get the experiences they need for future promotions.

Corporate attitudes have changed dramatically since the days of William White's Organization Man, when everyone was expected to look and act the same. Today, corporate leaders recognize the need to have a working environment in which all kinds of people can thrive (Livingston, 1991).

BARRIERS TO CULTURAL DIVERSITY

One of the goals of education is to provide a learning environment where students will be able to interact effectively and to appreciate the contributions of individuals from a variety of cultural backgrounds. Training students to appreciate cultural diversity requires a teacher who does not feel uncomfortable or threatened by the kind of dialogue and free expression that may be encouraged by this topic. An important aspect of this concept is to recognize that in order for this kind of environment to exist there are certain barriers to healthy multicultural relationships that need to be recognized. In the study of a subject that connects people so closely as culture does and yet divides people so distinctly because of differences, it is important to understand the myths that are partly responsible for intensifying those differences:

The Myth of Universality. *Under the surface all human beings are alike, members of the human race.* This belief causes people to expect others to be like them; that is, everyone acts out of the same motivation; but often they do not.

The Myth of Deficiency. *Those who are different from us are deficient in some way.* They are referred to as being the "underdeveloped" nations, the "backward" nations, or the "culturally disadvantaged." However, none of these terms is correct.

The Myth of Contact. *If people are brought together more often, they will get along with each other better. They will grow to understand each other.* Contact produces only opportunity—not necessarily friendship or understanding.

The Myth of Authenticity. *If we are sincerely ourselves, then everyone else will become like us.* The problem with this is that sincerity is culturally defined; what may be authentic sentiment in the United States may be regarded as artifice or deception in another culture.

The Myth of Knowledge. *Expertise in our field of work or professions will bring us success abroad.* However, native intelligence is not the equivalent of technical intelligence. This difference could cause serious problems in the distribution of resources, etc.

The Myth of Linguistic. *Knowledge of the foreign language will be sufficient to ensure success.* But knowledge of the language is no guarantee that a speaker will exercise good judgment, or that he/she will be aware of deep cultural differences that may be nonverbal.

The Myth of Unpredictability. *Culture is so complex, and intercultural business is so involved, that it is impossible for us ever to make a success of working or communicating across cultures.* This last myth evaporates when we realize that effective communication can turn complex concepts into understandable and simple ideas (Sigband and Bell, 1986).

Each year businesses invest millions of dollars trying to improve communication among coworkers, managers, customers, and clients. Misunderstandings occur frequently because people are not willing to rid themselves of preconceived biases and attitudes that are a detriment to effective communication and understanding of others. Among the more frequent restrictions to positive communication among diverse groups are the following:

Making incorrect assumptions. Passing judgments without having all of the facts is detrimental to harmonious working relationships. Assuming that a person is poor or illiterate because he/she speaks broken English is damaging to diverse students. Likewise, all Americans are not alike; neither are all Asians, Italians, or Mexican-Americans. Generally, a preoccupation with external characteristics about individuals who are "different" is the reason for arriving at inaccurate judgments. Premature judgments often made without all of the facts can be particularly harmful. Special care must be taken to see that assumptions about people from other cultures do not prevent meaningful interaction.

Using the "allness" theory. This is a tendency to judge the whole basis of experience with a part of the whole. Rarely do we see "all" of something, yet on the basis of limited knowledge and information, we conclude the whole. The pattern of misevaluation results from the "allness" theory. Allness statements are especially harmful. The use of words such as "always," "never," "ever" (Example: "You always interrupt me." "You never want to hear my side". . . and "You're always late . . .") invites defensiveness and can have an overall negative effect on communication in a culturally diverse environment.

Rejecting particular lifestyles. Students need to develop sensitivity to other people's values, dress, eating habits, and leisure-time activities that may reflect a particular culture. Criticism of another's right to be different is a barrier to understanding and acceptance of diversity. Recognition of individual differences allows for growth, personal fulfillment, and creativity, traits especially needed by diverse students who have low self-esteem.

Ignoring territorial rights. These are usually unwritten rules that evolve by virtue of a person's status, seniority, special merit, or some other "right" or "claim" that an individual has made. To preempt another's chair, cabinet, piece of equipment, or "personal territory" can be hazardous to effective human relations. Employees who are asked to share their "territorial rights" often feel upset by the intrusion. Territorial rights, particularly those established by older workers, may cause conflict among individuals. Territorial rights, like personal space, can be marked by cultural differences. Students need to be taught the importance of developing a healthy respect for those "rights," even though they are difficult to understand.

Being intolerant of others. Failure to understand and accept personal traits, mannerisms, or other people is harmful to effective multicultural relationships. The degree to which a person is able to accept the idiosyncrasies of another person determines one's tolerance level. A high tolerance level provides a cushion/safety net to allow people to get along with others under circumstances that normally would upset or annoy them. When a person's tolerance level is low, the slightest things will annoy him or her. The key to building effective relationships between cultures is tolerance. The more tolerant, the more opportunities for understanding and accepting individual differences. The importance of tolerance in building good working relationships cannot be underestimated as a valuable learning outcome for entry-level job training.

COMMUNICATING IN A MULTICULTURAL ENVIRONMENT

As the population of the United States becomes more varied culturally, it is extremely important that as teachers we make students aware of the need to communicate with other cultures in ways that are mutually satisfying. By connecting culturally with people who are "different" means that we must be willing to speak each other's language. Speaking the language of another culture does not mean, necessarily, that we must become multilingual; however, it does mean that we must become responsive to the communication needs of other cultures. Learning how to use our own language correctly will ease the burden of foreigners who are often confronted with the task of becoming interpreters of the English we use. The ultimate goal of communication is that participants in the process will understand each other through shared meanings. As people interact on a daily basis and participate in routine work activities, meanings are discovered that form a bond for common understanding.

Too long have Americans conveyed the message that we are smarter, faster, bigger, and better. The last several years have proved that the reverse is true. Yet, we continue to convey in subtle ways that "our way is best" and look to others to adapt. One mistake reflecting this philosophy that has made communication difficult among and between culturally diverse groups is the assumption that "we all speak the same language—the English language." Nothing could be further from the truth. As teachers, we need to impress upon our students that they never take for granted that the words they use will convey the message they intend.

Understanding the communication messages and styles reflected by other cultures is tantamount to building effective business and personal relationships. As we move toward the 21st century, the need for the United States to be a viable competitor in the global marketplace will require that we become adept at reading and interpreting correctly cross-cultural communications. Teachers must take the lead in helping students to become language sensitive. As communicators in search of successful interaction with people of various cultures, we must be extremely careful to select and use words that have the same, or nearly the same, connotations as those of other cultures. It is going to be increasingly important to observe national language differences among cultures if communication is going to be successful. Americans often fail to realize that language that is "Americanese" is frequently confusing to non English-speaking people or an "outsider." Colloquial expressions, idioms, cliches, slang, buzzwords, trendy phrases, puns, and show biz metaphors have no place in multicultural communication and only serve to heighten the ambiguity that often accompanies language differences among cultures. Expressions such as "name of the game," "good as gold," "tip of the iceberg," "go with the flow," "read my lips," "condo," "yuppie," "high tech," "feedback," etc., have been woven into the language patterns of our society as part of the local color and have become acceptable on all socio-economic levels. Add to that list the confusion of acronyms and symbols—F.Y.I., A.S.A.P., F.I.C.A., C.E.O.—and communication for an outsider will lead quickly to disaster. While preparing students for a multicultural workplace, it is important for teachers to be aware of communication problems that can arise through the use of discriminatory words. Discriminatory words are generally regarded as words that do not treat all people equally and with respect. Words in this category usually convey negative connotations associated with nationality, race, sex, age, and disability. Young people are particularly vulnerable to the volatile repercussions often reflected in discriminatory words. Frequently, these kinds of words are used without much thought about the effect they have on others, particularly when used stereotypically with regard to race or nationality. Students should be made aware that it is unfair to suggest that "all Jews are stingy;" that "Italians are hot-blooded;" that "Hispanics are breeders;" that "blacks are lazy." On the contrary, words that suggest that members of diverse groups are exceptions to stereotypes also carry discriminatory messages that are subtle although well-meaning. For example, to refer to an "articulate black businessman," "a Hispanic female lawyer," or "an Asian supervisor" are, in fact, discriminatory. Words that discriminate against the old and young are just as capable of arousing negative responses as those related to race or national origin. Particularly sensitive to older persons are terms such as, "senior citizens," "golden agers," and "mature citizens."

Equally damaging to the young are, "adolescent," "immature," "juvenile," and "yuppies." Special care should be taken in addressing disabled persons. Words such as, "handicapped," "disability," and "learning disabled" are extremely sensitive. This kind of labeling can do much to create insensitivity to those who already feel less than a "whole" person.

Another area of concern that affects the appropriate use of language with negative ramifications for diversity is the word *man,* and the masculine pronouns *he/his* used generically for men and women (i.e. Every man must pull his own weight) are clear examples of sexist language. Terms that are gender-neutral, such as *persons, individuals, people,* and *their, your, they,* do not reflect negatively on communication.

As the workforce moves more and more toward a diverse population, the need for language-sensitive personnel is going to be the biggest challenge facing the work population. Equally challenging is the tremendous opportunity for teachers to provide classroom forums for students to converse and discover ways that lead to mutual respect and understanding of other cultures.

DEVELOPING A STRUCTURE FOR CULTURAL DIVERSITY TRAINING

Today our high school students are exhibiting negative attitudes that lead to violence, racism, drugs, and hate crimes. They are responding vehemently to a society that has failed to teach them how to live effectively in a world where individual differences are the norm. Teachers at all levels are going to have to take a proactive or more aggressive role in helping young people cope with cultural differences. As business educators, we must face the reality that the labor market is beginning to look, sound, and act "differently." The challenge is to help students learn how to manage or cope with this phenomenon.

To determine a basis for cultural diversity training, a developmental approach devoted to awareness, knowledge, and skill seems to provide manageable and meaningful guidelines. The objectives of a viable program would be to—

1. Ascertain the level of awareness students have or do not have about a particular culture.

2. Determine the extent of knowledge or accurate information students may or may not have about the culture.

3. Provide opportunities for developing a level of skill for appropriate responses after the learning objectives have been identified.

Awareness: The first phase provides the students with an orientation to cultural diversity. This phase gives the students an opportunity to become introspective. Awareness brings students in touch with their own belief system about the culture and encourages them to examine the system in terms of the following questions:

a. What is the level of students' awareness about a particular culture?

b. What perceptions, attitudes, opinions, or assumptions do the students hold about the culture? What are the frames of references from which these attitudes have evolved?

   c. To what extent are the students aware of the myths and stereotypes of the culture?

   d. Are students aware of the resources available to secure accurate information about various cultures?

   e. Are students aware of the communication and language systems, verbal/non-verbal, that distinguish one group from another?

   f. How effective are students in understanding and dealing with individuals from other parts of the world?

   g. How much are students aware of their own culture and to what extent are they able to articulate elements of their culture in relationship to other cultures?

Knowledge: The second phase is an attempt to discover how much students actually know about the culture. Is the information they have accurate? Do they have all of the facts? Often there are serious gaps in the information students have and they are not able to substantiate where, when, or how they received it. This level will provide students with an accurate base from which to change incorrect attitudes and false assumptions.

   a. What specific knowledge, if any, do the students have about cultural diversity?

   b. What knowledge do students have that focuses on cultural background relative to history, education, economy, social status, lifestyle, customs, etc?

   c. What information is readily available concerning the educational advantages to other cultures and/or where to locate such information?

   d. What do students know about the social services to other cultures?

Skill: The third level of the triad requires techniques and procedures to bring about positive change. Developing skills provides the teacher with opportunities to help students establish rapport with culturally diverse students.

   a. What skills do students have to interact with persons from other cultures?

   b. Are students equipped with communication and correct language usage?

   c. Have students developed a level of tolerance for another's habits, mannerisms, lifestyle, values, speech or dress?

   d. Do students demonstrate concern and interest in the welfare of others? Do they show support, acceptance, friendliness, or appreciation in their interactions with others? (Peterson, 1988).

INSTRUCTIONAL STRATEGIES TO ENCOURAGE CULTURAL DIVERSITY

Business education teachers can do much to heighten students' awareness of and appreciation for cultural diversity. Perhaps the most meaningful, significant role for the business teacher is to accept the role of catalyst in fostering a supportive, interpersonal environment. The teacher should set the tone for "accepting" students who are diverse. The need for students to feel accepted and to develop a sense of community in the classroom is critical to the students' mental, emotional, and intellectual well-being. Part of their sense of belonging is related to the attitude and behavior of the classroom teacher toward students who are culturally diverse. When teachers express sensitivity through a caring attitude toward students who are different, this attitude becomes infectious among the rest of the students. When diverse students feel supported, encouraged, and respected, they are more likely to be successful.

PERSONAL STRATEGIES

Increase Sensitivity to Diversity. Business teachers have a unique responsibility in creating a classroom climate that encourages and facilitates quality interaction among diverse students. Preparing students for a successful transition from school to work begins with successful human relationships in the classroom.

Examine personal biases. Take a good look at your own prejudices, racial attitudes, fears, and generalizations about people who are "different." Unpleasant memories often contribute to feelings of anger and fear. Avoid the tendency to "lump together" all persons of one race because of a bad experience with one. Attitudes and beliefs you bring to class often hinder the potential for a positive learning environment.

Increase awareness of exclusion and inclusion of diversity. Become a student of the social attitudes concerning diversity. Observe TV shows, advertising commercials, radio discussions, speeches, and documentaries, etc. Look for examples of whether various ethnic or cultural groups are portrayed and, if so, how are they portrayed. Are they included or excluded? Look for the overt as well as the hidden messages of inclusion and/or exclusion.

Find an interpreter. It is not always easy for teachers to admit they are unfamiliar or uncomfortable with those who are "different." One of the best ways to overcome this feeling is to find someone from a diverse group who can speak openly to provide information and understanding about the needs, desires, attitudes, problems, and cultural differences of non-white students. Teachers with this kind of background information can make a significant impact on the climate established within the classroom and the school.

Be a risk taker. Take a stand for those issues that promote multicultural causes, programs, and practices. Read credible newspapers and magazines; challenge the status quo. Become aware of the kinds of issues that foment misunderstanding, that propagate misinformation, and that seek to divide rather than unite people.

Maintain high, but realistic expectations. Some teachers have a tendency to set either excessively high or low expectations for diverse students. Other teachers sometimes perceive culturally diverse students as having learning disabilities because of their English language difficulties and as a result, an inability to grasp learning material quickly. A great disservice is done by overacting to a disability or lowering expectations for achievement. Students with learning disabilities may only require more time or the use of different strategies to meet expectations.

Reach out to diverse students. Try to remember unique information about a student. This is one of the best ways to establish rapport. Contact between student and teacher motivates students and encourages them to excel. Don't be afraid to form supportive, interpersonal relationships with students whose cultural orientation is different from your own. Communicate to diverse students that the advantages of being bicultural can be an asset. Students who represent other cultures need to understand that they do not need to renounce their heritage to be accepted. Very often a student's perception and understanding of cultural diversity is grasped more poignantly during verbal interchange with the instructor and others in the class.

CLASSROOM STRATEGIES

Help diverse students experience success. Provide a learning environment that will help students gain the confidence needed to take responsibility for their own learning. Emphasize their strong points; help them overcome weak ones. Be alert to how diverse students interact with other students in the classroom. Note differences and similarities among the groups' perceptions. If all groups report similar views, explore the reasons why. What specific learning experiences accrued from the discussion/project? How can this be applicable on an individual level?

Let diverse students know you *expect* them to succeed. Diverse students need to know that you believe in their ability to meet course requirements. They will perform well when they know they are expected to perform well. Use a variety of test data to evaluate their performance. Communicate expectations clearly and frequently. Try stating them in a variety of ways. Explain and illustrate what is acceptable and what is not acceptable performance. Give test results as soon as possible and follow up with reinforcement work when necessary. Provide verbal and written feedback that is not only negative, but positive as well.

Use mistakes as learning tools. Often teachers spend more time focusing on mistakes and not enough time on using the mistakes as a means to help diverse students learn. Provide increased repetition or a variety of learning strategies in confronting areas of weakness. Diverse students need to understand that making errors is a natural part of learning. Individualize instruction for students with special needs. A one-size-fits-all learning approach does not allow for individual differences, since students do not all learn and process information at the same rate.

Establish a "buddy system" among students. Develop a buddy system or support group so that students can communicate freely with each other. The system should permit students to exchange telephone numbers (with permission) based on geographic location, academic major, similar interest, etc. The buddy system will be a resource for students to get special help from peers; i.e. work missed because of absences, assignments, events or activities the student may not otherwise know about.

Provide opportunities for small group work. One of the most valuable experiences in developing a sensitivity to diverse students is to arrange small groups for study, discussion, project work, or peer tutoring purposes whenever such groups are conducive to the learning environment. The use of experiential exercises in the form of games, role playing, case studies, oral and written presentations is an excellent way to clarify concepts, perceptions, and attitudes. Those students who are less articulate seem to gravitate to a smaller, nonthreatening group where they feel more comfortable participating. Culturally diverse students are often "late bloomers." Initially they do not do as well as other students. Therefore, a program of study that facilitates their academic adjustment and helps them to set goals that are reachable can contribute immeasurably to their success.

Initiate a diversity table. This technique involves the individual's awareness of his/her own feelings and the feelings of others. In a classroom setting, it allows people to release and express their innermost thoughts and share feelings and attitudes, with the teacher deciding upon the rules, goals, and how to achieve those goals. For example, the group might take turns sharing about traditions, customs, attitudes, beliefs, or other native observances. Group members learn to communicate more openly and honestly, improve social relationships, and achieve a better perception of themselves.

IMPLICATIONS FOR BUSINESS EDUCATION

The decade of the nineties will bring the greatest challenge for cultural diversity ever witnessed in the workplace. The necessity for education and training at the secondary level becomes more apparent as technology continues to become more sophisticated.

In spite of management's efforts to enrich the quality of work life by relieving the office worker of boredom and mental fatigue, research studies continue to purport that over 70 percent of employees are terminated each year because of the inability to interact effectively with co-workers and superiors. Maintaining a multicultural perspective in a highly technological office setting will be one of the salient challenges facing the workforce throughout the decade. The electronic office will not only affect patterns of change in organizational structure and in employee tasks and responsibilities, but the potential for creating unhealthy interpersonal environments needs to be recognized as people become more involved in teamwork relationships.

While many high school students may underestimate the need to become sensitive to cultural diversity in the work community, training in human relations should be addressed by business teachers as a key element in understanding and coping with the ramifications of a changing work environment. It is not unrealistic to suggest that with imminent changes in new technology, job procedures, and job patterns, social and psychological adjustments in multicultural relationships may be more difficult to achieve and sustain. As today's office becomes more high-tech, office workers will become more interdependent through flow-of-work activities and will interact to discuss work-related issues, solve problems, and make decisions on all work levels.

The necessity for business education to provide training in cultural diversity at the secondary level is quite apparent. Students preparing for entry-level positions must be ready to meet the challenging demands of a multicultural workplace. The success students achieve on the job in being able to respond positively to cultural differences will be directly proportional to the preparation, training, and motivation they experience in the classroom.

REFERENCES

Human capital: the decline of America's workforce. (1993, September 19). *Business Week.* pp. 112-113.

Jamison, D., and O'Mara, J. (1991). *Managing workforce 2,000.* (pp. 86-87, 95). New York: First edition. Jossey-Bass.

Livingston, A. (1991, January). Cultural diversity: 12 companies that do the right thing. *Working Woman.* p. 45.

National Alliance on Business. (1992). *Helping America work.* (p. 2). Washington, D.C.

Petersen, Paul (1988). *A handbook for developing multicultural awareness.* (pp. 9-11). Virginia: American Association for Counseling Development.

Sigband, N. and Bell, A. (1986). *Communication for Management and Business.* (p. 70). Scotts Foresman and Company, IL.

CHAPTER 9

SUCCESSFUL PROMOTION OF BUSINESS EDUCATION

CARLA GRIES
Omaha Burke High School, Omaha, Nebraska

JOSEPH NEBEL
Omaha Bryan High School, Omaha, Nebraska

"Stand still and silently watch the world go by—and it will." Does this anonymous quotation describe what has happened in business education? Yes, in various degrees many business educators may have done just that. While the merits of business education have been discussed by those in the field, and while many have bemoaned and complained about the fate of business education, much of the world has passed by.

It is now obvious to most business educators that this is not business as usual and they can no longer wait for students to enroll. Business education has traditionally been the most popular elective; however, the following are some factors that have contributed to the decline of enrollments in recent years:

1. The back-to-the-basics movement
2. Universities' increasing admission standards
3. An increase in high school graduation requirements
4. The lack of adequate funds and administrative support to acquire and maintain up-to-date curriculum, hardware, software and training
5. Fewer students from which to recruit.

As a result, effective, on-going marketing strategies need to be implemented.

No business that has a product or service to offer would even think of eliminating or minimizing its marketing activities. Why then do some business educators overlook their responsibility to market the program and sit silently waiting for someone else to do it? Business teachers must use ingenuity to market their programs successfully. Quality marketing of business education is no longer a luxury; it is mandatory.

Despite all the challenges, there are many successful programs. A review of recent literature reveals that such programs have many of the following characteristics in common:

1. Relevant curriculum that meets the needs of students and the business community
2. Effective rapport with counselors and administrators
3. Strong commitment and teamwork on the part of all business educators

4. Outstanding recommendations and testimonials from students

5. Active student organizations

6. Effective, on-going marketing strategies.

See Exhibit 1, a portion of a sample timeline, which was taken from Nebraska's *Promotion of Business Education Handbook.*

DESIGNING THE PROGRAM

Prior to designing a marketing program, it is suggested that an analysis be conducted of the program to determine:

1. What is the most important aspect of the program?

2. Who needs to know about the program and why?

3. What are the special needs of the constituents?

For the plan to be effective, the following target audiences should be included:

1. Current students

2. Prospective students

3. Community

4. Alumni

5. Parents

6. Faculty

7. Local media

8. Administration

9. School board

10. Counselors

11. Elementary students

12. Legislators/governors

13. Business/industry

14. Community organizations

15. Other educators

16. Non-business-oriented students

17. Advisory committees.

Upon reflecting on this list, it becomes quite obvious why business educators may have fallen short of achieving the goal of full classrooms, for they have a tendency to market to current and prospective students and because of time constraints, frequently overlook other audiences.

Communication in any marketing program must be well planned and consistent. The focal points, of course, are the value and benefits of the program.

MAIN STREET AMERICA

Main Street America—friend or foe? Businesses succeed on Main Street America, and so can business education! Members of state legislatures and

Exhibit 1

NOVEMBER
1. Parent-teacher conferences
   a. Distribute flyers or brochures on business program
   b. Show video: "Business for All Seasons"
   c. Recommend to parents that their child continue with additional business classes
2. Begin initial recruiting for next year's classes
   a. Distribute handouts promoting new business classes
   b. Distribute handouts on classes which need special promotion
   c. Talk to students one-on-one
3. Promote American Education Week
   a. Host a coffee for faculty, counselors, administrators, school board, and advisory council
      (1) Show video: "Business for All Seasons"
      (2) Demonstrate equipment
      (3) Review curriculum
   b. Wear promotional buttons
   c. Prepare a bulletin board
4. Promote American Enterprise Day – November 15
   a. Air a radio spot on a local radio station
   b. Publish a news article
      (1) Local newspaper
      (2) School newspaper
   c. Purchase ads in local and/or school newspaper
   d. Distribute flyers
      (1) Place flyers in sacks from local businesses
      (2) Place flyers on windshields of cars in parking lots
      (3) Place flyers on students' lockers
   e. Prepare a bulletin board
   f. Prepare a display to be placed in a local business
   g. Prepare announcements for school bulletin

ADDITIONAL IDEAS

FEBRUARY
1. Enter a business competition day
2. Promote Vocational Education Week and Future Business Leaders of America Week
   a. Air a radio spot
   b. Run promotional spot in school announcements
   c. Prepare buttons advertising the week
      (1) Give to students
      (2) Give to administration/counselors
      (3) Give to business people
   d. Recognize outstanding vocational students
   e. Show video: "Business for All Seasons"
   f. Host coffee for business people in community
   g. Place tent cards in school cafeteria and/or businesses
   h. Put placemats in school cafeteria and/or community restaurants
   i. Place posters in school cafeteria and/or businesses
   j. Purchase an ad on business education to be published in the local newspaper
   k. Hold a Vocational Education Week proclamation signing with the local mayor
3. Distribute information on business curriculum to community
   a. Place tent cards in businesses
   b. Put placemats in restaurants
   c. Distribute flyers in grocery sacks

ADDITIONAL IDEAS

the United States Congress are listening to their constituents. Because educators are often perceived as a special interest group, it would be advantageous for them to enlist help from all possible sources. D. Ross Thompson, community relations specialist for the New York State Department of Education, recommends the HUGS formula: Hold events; Use media; Give recognition; Seek help from specialists.

Student ambassadors. Our products, the students, are our pride, so why not showcase them as our ambassadors? For example, invite the local media when students use their business skills helping local charities. Utilize student organizations—FBLA, Business Professionals of America, DECA, Phi Beta Lambda, and Pi Omega Pi—for public service activities. These organizations could assist the United Way and the March of Dimes, for example, by processing mass mailings, keying newsletters, and answering phones during a telethon.

Students in the business internship programs are also involved in an ongoing, highly effective public relations program as they showcase their skills in the business community.

People without school connections. Excellent opportunities exist to garner the support of people who no longer have or who have never had children in school. Numerous creative teachers have worked with these people in conducting short, after-school workshops on the topics of computer education, consumer education, and credit. Some nontraditional students attend classes with their younger counterparts. When working with older people, student assistants can be of great help as they usually relate to this age group in a very positive and special way. One should not overlook the expertise that has been developed by many senior citizens, who would be perfectly willing to share their expertise with a class or student organization. What an incredible resource!

Community organizations. Lion's Club, Kiwanis, Rotary and similar groups are always looking for new members and programs. The successful business educator should take advantage of the opportunities to speak at their functions in order to expose them to the business education programs. Business persons who belong to such organizations not only hire people, but they also have children, grandchildren, and neighbors in school, thus giving them a special interest in school. In addition to the teacher, have the students speak. Select student speakers who are enthusiastic, intelligent, well-versed, and poised. They would enhance such presentations and would project the pride and merits of the program.

Advisory committees. Nearly every successful business program has an advisory committee, which may consist of internship training sponsors, adopt-a-school partners, parents who are business persons, and other leaders of the business community. Since it is important to take the business person's time into consideration, advisory committees meet anywhere from once a month to once a year. Student accomplishments and curriculum content should be discussed during meetings. The meeting is also an opportunity for business persons to inform the school of new developments in the workplace. Members of an advisory committee frequently serve as speakers and interviewers and offer advice on such things as equipment purchases. *Remember to include* *advisory committee members when letters of support for a program are needed.* If a legislative network is in place, advisory committee members should be included.

School-business partnership programs. School districts across the nation have established elaborate, well-organized school-business partnership programs. An example is the Omaha Public Schools Adopt-A-School Program, which involves over 175 business/community partners. They range from banks, insurance companies, restaurants, hotels, and hospitals to Fortune 500 companies. The exchange of human resources and services between the schools and partners is endless. Partners are matched with the entire school while others are matched with a specific program.

A very successful program at Omaha Burke High School is the annual Business Talk Show, where business partners, or their professional colleagues, conduct a question and answer forum with students from various disciplines. As a result, students are made aware of opportunities in business.

Offering scholarships to deserving students helps to enhance the visibility of the business program. Advisory committee members and school business partners are often in a position to establish funds for scholarships.

Parents. Too often it is assumed that parents know everything that goes on in school. One only needs to be a parent to know the fallacy in that assumption. An excellent way to bring visibility to a student organization is to invite a parent to be a chaperon when taking students to state, regional, and national conferences. Most business teachers are impressed when they attend their first student organization conference. Why not share that feeling with parents? If it is shared with one or two parents, it will be shared with many, for word travels fast! Always seize the opportunity to distribute brochures and other materials at open houses and parent-teacher conferences. Better yet, have students distribute the information at such special events. If a promotional video is available, set it up either in the area where parents stand in line to pick up report cards or next to the coffee service.

School boards. Business educators need to recognize politics as a part in the decision-making process. Perceptions of business education are important in bodies where decisions are made. Nearly every decision that affects business education is political. It is advantageous to maintain communication with these political bodies. School boards, for instance, provide facilities, approve budgets, and appropriate funds. It is essential that business education be highly visible to the local school board. Frequently, board members are business leaders and understand the importance of the business curriculum in meeting needs of students and the business community. When making presentations to the school board, students and alumni should be involved. An invitation should be extended to the members of the board to tour the business education facilities.

Many schools recognize cooperative internship employers each year at an employer-employee banquet. This provides an excellent opportunity to showcase an important part of the business/marketing education program. Seize the opportunity to include central office administration and school board members and acknowledge them during the program.

Legislators. Legislators play a key role in business education. Concerned business educators from across the country have united into "One Big Voice," a legislative network that speaks on behalf of business education. NBEA has recently published *Hot Tips: Legislative Strategies for Business Education*. This publication includes samples of communication appropriate for local, state, and national legislators. Every business educator should correspond with his/her legislator about the relevancy of business education in meeting the needs of business and industry.

WITHIN THE EDUCATION CIRCLE

Other faculty members. Within the circle of educators, business education has many target audiences, some of which have been virtually untapped. *All* faculty must be kept informed of special events in the business department and they, along with their students, should be invited to participate in special events. Involving other teachers can go a long way in showing how their curriculum interrelates with the business curriculum. More and more business educators are coordinating curriculum and activities with other disciplines. International business, fashion marketing, applied business communications, and applied math are among the cross-curricular subjects being taught. Interdisciplinary projects range from well-developed courses, to units, to daily lessons.

Counselors and administrators. Who is in a better position to promote business programs than counselors? They, along with the administrators, need to be kept informed of current trends and activities in the business program through memos and internal news releases, such as the school newspaper and daily bulletin. Plan informal visits and joint meetings with them to explain curriculum, prerequisites, and course content. Encourage them to participate in field trips, student organization conferences, and visits to internship-training sites.

Elementary students and staff. Since students are exposed to careers from their early days in elementary school, business educators have the responsibility to see that business is represented in the information that is shared with them. Most elementary teachers would welcome a well-prepared and age-appropriate pamphlet to use with a career unit. Some business educators have a rather unique opportunity to gain a great deal of visibility. Have a business educator teach keyboarding at the elementary level to enhance the articulation between the elementary school and the secondary business program. See Exhibit 2, a sample letter to a fourth grader, which was taken from Nebraska's *Promotion of Business Education Handbook.*

Junior high/middle school students and staff. Across the country, junior high/middle school business programs have emerged in recent years. These programs present the perfect opportunity to orient junior high students to the high school program. A teacher exchange for a day is fun for both the teacher and students. Some schools sponsor a business competition day for high school and junior high students at the high school facility, thus exposing the junior high students to the senior high setting.

Current students. The nucleus of any business education program lies with the students who are currently in the program. Computer keyboarding is generally a student's first exposure to the business education curriculum and offers the largest number of students from which to recruit. This recruitment should be ongoing, with greater emphasis just prior to registration. Recruitment activities could be conducted by both staff and advanced business students.

TOOLS OF THE TRADE

Letters. Students are an excellent resource for recruitment and can be utilized to make recommendations. Ken Kaser, business management instructor at Lincoln Northeast High School in Lincoln, Nebraska, uses the following technique. He distributes a business management fact sheet to each student in his business management classes and offers them an opportunity to recommend one or more students for the class. Students who recommend other students have their names submitted for a prize drawing. Their names are submitted once for each person recommended. Recommended students are then contacted by a letter.

Exhibit 2

DATE

Fourth Grade Students
District _____
City, State, ZIP

Dear Fourth Grade Student:

Your assignment is to write a story. Wouldn't it be exciting to be able to type your story on a computer!

We at _____ school are happy to offer to you the chance to learn keyboarding. Beginning this _____ , we are offering any time, you will learn the alphabet, number, and punctuation keys. Using a computer, your story will probably take less time to write and will be neat and easy to read.

You are the workers and leaders of tomorrow. We as business teachers want you to be ready to learn about how computers can help you.

Join us—bring a friend if you like—for an exciting adventure in KEYBOARDING.

Sincerely,

Name
Business Education Instructor

Letters can also be sent to students whose responses to a survey have shown they have a career interest in business. At Lincoln Northeast, students sit at a table in the hallway and survey students. (Of course, to entice students, it helps to set treats out on the table.) At Burke High School in Omaha, Nebraska, letters are sent to all freshmen, sophomores, and juniors who make first-semester honor roll. To recruit for the office internship program, the teacher checks the records for the past three years of those students who have completed first-year keyboarding successfully. Personalized letters are then sent to them.

Brochures. Student brochures should be designed with students in mind. Bright colors with large photos and graphics work well. Information in the brochure should be brief so that it will be read. It should be scaled down to a two-color publication on the best quality paper available within the budget.

For the corporate community, a brochure, produced by the Omaha Public Schools was sent by the superintendent to over 300 businesses, and is an effective means of communication.

The NBEA "9 Facts" brochure is also an excellent resource that can be used just prior to spotlighting individual courses.

Other written communications. Inserting business cards and flyers in the program for football games is an effective means of communication. Such printed information should include names of business courses, student organizations, and other business activities and programs. Sending business education newsletters to target audiences periodically informs them of student successes and special projects and events.

Technology to the rescue! Yes, there are several ways business teachers can put technology to good use. One would be to produce a video tape. This project can be very expensive, but it is essential in any good recruitment program. A brightly colored, funky, and upbeat video with little or no narrative is an "attention getter." Show the video in the school cafeteria, hall, student lounge, and at open-house presentations. Allow students and parents to check out the recruitment video, and/or air it on cable TV for a nominal price.

Cindy McWhirter, of Omaha Northwest High School, conducts workshops to recruit junior high students. She has created a template which includes all of the school course offerings. While the template is on the computer screen, Cindy discusses the various courses offered, with special emphasis on the business courses. Students enjoy working on the computer and are exposed to the curriculum, including the computer labs.

It has also been suggested that a Hypercard or Linkway tour of the business department be created. Card stacks could be built to describe the courses and programs available. Such programs are also available for students and parents for home use.

ARTICULATION

Articulation programs between high schools and community colleges have taken on a new sense of importance with the passage of current federal legislation. Such programs allow graduating seniors who complete a sequential program in business to seek advanced standing at the community college. These programs motivate students to take business courses at both levels. The following elements are paramount when developing a quality articulation agreement:

1. Develop a partnership between a secondary and a post-secondary institution.
2. Identify courses with similar curricula that are taught at both the high school and the community college.
3. Standardize offerings, competencies, curriculum, texts and materials.
4. Develop measurements to be used at both levels.
5. Involve the business community.
6. Recruit students.
7. Secure administrative support.
8. Conduct in-service training for counselors and business education teachers.

Other key elements include board of education approval, involvement of faculty, equipment, responsibility, funding, advanced college courses, and public relations (Briggaman, 1991). Exhibit 3 is an example of a Competency Certificate, which is a component of the articulation agreement between the Omaha Public Schools and Metro Community College.

Exhibit 3

Similar competency profiles (Exhibit 4) are given to students for each high school vocational course that meets the requirements of the articulation agreement. The student then completes an Advanced Standing Application Form and is interviewed by the respective college chairperson to determine advanced placement standing.

Exhibit 4

OMAHA PUBLIC SCHOOLS
Business Education
Omaha, Nebraska

Competency Profile for Accounting

Semesters completed _____

Student _____ School _____

I hereby certify that this student is competent to the extent indicated in the tasks listed on this profile.

Instructor _____ Date _____
Signature

1	2	3	4	
				Accounting Careers
				Debit/Credit Principles
				Accounting Terminology
				General Journal
				Special Journals
				Worksheet/Spreadsheet Preparation
				Financial Statement Preparation
				Adjusting & Closing Process
				Accounts Receivable
				Accounts Payable
				Accounting Cycle
				Payroll
				Checking Account and Bank Statement Reconciliation
				Voucher System
				Petty Cash System

1	2	3	4	
				Accounting for Plant Assets
				Accounting for Uncollectible Accounts
				Accounting for Accrual Items
				Accounting for Prepaid Expenses & Unearned Revenue
				Financial Statement Analysis
				Automated Accounting
				Management/Financial Accounting
				Cost Accounting
				Inventory Control
				Departmentalized Accounting
				Corporate Accounting
				Tax Accounting
				Other: _____

RATING SCALE

1 = Skilled - Can perform task independently with no supervision

2 = Moderately Skilled - Can perform task with limited supervision

3 = Limited Skills - Requires additional instruction and supervision

4 = No Exposure - Does not have experience or knowledge in this area

EXCELLENT	GOOD	FAIR	POOR	Interpersonal Skills:
				Attendance
				Punctuality
				Task Completion
				Confidence
				Perseverance
				Comprehension
				Initiative
				Reliability
				Loyalty
				Enthusiasm
				Cooperation
				Adaptability
				Housekeeping
				Personal Appearance
				Human Relations
				Attitude
				Other: _____

Restructured business programs. Because of restructured business programs, business students spend less time in the classroom than they did a decade ago. Schools are accommodating students by streamlining many full-year courses to one semester. Conflicts with required courses can be reduced by offering one-semester courses or by offering classes before school, after school, or in the evening.

Alternative credits. In spite of valiant recruitment efforts on the part of business educators, enrollment continues to decrease. To minimize this decline, many business programs have experienced excellent results by offering business courses for alternative credits—business economics to meet a social studies requirement, accounting and/or applied math to meet a math requirement, business communication to meet an English requirement.

BACK TO THE BASICS

All gimmicks aside, the most powerful form of recruitment is word of mouth—student to student, student to counselor, student to parent, parent to parent. Diligent efforts on the part of the teacher to make a class interesting and informative pay dividends. What the teacher does in a caring, nurturing classroom environment is the most basic of yearlong recruitment plans. Effective body language and a positive attitude are vitally important as a part of subtle public relations.

SUMMARY

To meet the challenges confronting business education, it is essential for each business department to implement on-going, effective marketing strategies. All business educators must work together enthusiastically and willingly to ensure a bright future. By all means, the business education curriculum is relevant for today's global and technological world and must be effectively marketed to all targeted audiences in order to prepare students for the 21st century.

REFERENCES

Briggaman, J. S. (1991, Spring). Recruitment program builds win-win relationships. *The Balance Sheet 72*, 3.

Hays, D. G. (1992, January-February). Getting the word out—selling the business education story. *The Balance Sheet 73*, 3.

NBEA (1991). *Hot tips: legislative strategies for business education.*

Moore, D. L. *Effective strategies for marketing and promoting business education.* M-PBEA Service Bulletin 32.

Nebraska Department of Education—Vocational Division. (1986). *Promotion of business education.* Lincoln: pp. 6 and 10.

CHAPTER 10

TEACHING BUSINESS EDUCATION TO SPECIAL GROUPS

RENAE HUMBURG
Laramie County School District Number One, Cheyenne, Wyoming

A high percentage of America's youth and adults will have great difficulty rising above the poverty level. A major barrier in their transition from school to work is lack of marketable skills. Many members of special groups are unemployed. If they are employed, they are engaged in jobs that pay poverty level wages with little or no benefits. A number of government and privately funded programs have been established to eliminate barriers for special groups in their transition from school to work. Business educators need to be actively involved in these special programs as grant writers, service providers, and project directors.

SEEKING FUNDING FOR SPECIAL GROUPS IN BUSINESS EDUCATION

Almost all public and private education grants provide support to schools or agencies to improve or expand services to target groups. Projects need to be of the size, scope, and quality to be effective in meeting each target group's special needs. Special groups include youth and adults with disabilities, youth and adults who are educationally and economically disadvantaged, individuals with limited English proficiency, and individuals in correctional institutions. Other special groups include teen parents, single parents, and displaced homemakers. A displaced homemaker is one who has worked as an adult primarily without remuneration caring for the home and family and, for that reason, lacks marketable skills. Many displaced homemakers have been dependent on public assistance or on the income of a relative but are no longer supported by such income. A high proportion of special groups would benefit by enrolling in business education programs. Business educators should respond to the challenge: to initiate, improve, and expand services to special groups needing employability skills.

Business education involvement needed. Historically, business educators have customized their programs to meet the needs of special groups. Business education is indeed the untapped resource. Too often, grant writers and proposal development committees do not know about the unique and special services provided by business educators. In order to generate more funding, business educators should actively offer their services, materials, and advice to grant writers. Moreover, they should write proposals for competitive grants, seek new funding sources, and be the leaders in helping target populations overcome the barriers to employment.

Generally, employability projects serving special groups involve hands-on learning in alternative programs; career assessment; vocational-academic integration; basic skills reinforcement; job training; school-work linkages; flexible scheduling and extended day program; and special support services such as counseling, day care, community service, transportation, and job placement.

Too many classrooms are characterized by passive learning. Students do not see the connection between academic skills and the world of work. Business education has experience in providing applied academics courses as well as opportunities to apply skills in cooperative work experience, simulations, and internship projects.

At-risk youth need meaningful relationships with adult mentors to help them in the transition from school to work. Business education might propose to systematically connect students to adult volunteer mentors in the workplace. Students might connect with adults through vocational student organization community service projects. Business education programs might provide job coaches for students on the job. For the less-abled, a community transition case manager would assist in connecting services such as vocational rehabilitation, YMCA, adult learning, and other community-based organizations involved in dropout prevention.

Disadvantaged youth and adults need flexible schedules and day care services that respond to the demands of their family life and work schedules. Business educators might propose to team with home economics teachers to help teen parents access parent-skills classes, day care, and transportation services so that they will stay in school and complete their business program.

Students need a learning plan that provides for a smooth transition to postsecondary education. Business educators should be leaders in developing articulation agreements with community colleges to help students master skills needed to succeed in their Tech Prep associate-degree program.

Youth and adults need to overcome barriers that prevent them from succeeding in school: illness, poor nutrition, violence, abuse, and lack of adequate housing, for example. Special groups need to learn in a place that provides meaning and coherence to their work life. Academics, work life, and family life need to be connected in a safe, convenient, and well-equipped learning environment. Business educators should systematically meet with a variety of school departments to help students overcome economic and social obstacles. For example, the home economics department might provide day care services for single parents enrolled in business education classes. The business educator and counselor might volunteer to serve on community coordinating councils to network public assistance and health services in a variety of locations. One-stop referral agencies would be organized to help save time and resources. Skills training would be provided in convenient locations that offer comprehensive family, education, and human services day and night. The school would be open from early in the morning to late at night to accommodate family and work schedules.

Students need a support system that helps them overcome obstacles to their citizenship and leadership training. They need to show pride in their community. At-risk youth need adult role models and business mentors. Business educators might propose to develop projects to revitalize the community—projects that will provide hands-on learning and relationships with adults who would model nonviolent resolutions to conflict. Youth and adults might promote service through volunteer community projects that promote drug free schools and work environments. Vocational student organizations (such as FBLA) might improve the appearance of neighborhoods and volunteer clean up services for the elderly. Business educators should work with community groups such as the Chamber of Commerce to help to integrate the at-risk youth into the community. A number of business communications and leadership skills would be strengthened in these projects to emphasize good citizenship and employability skills for the youth.

Special groups are especially affected by changes in the global economy. Automation, changes in consumer demand, and substitution of imports for domestic goods will continue to cause employment to stagnate in jobs held by members of special groups. All workers will need computer literacy skills. Business educators are well-equipped to provide computer training and re-training to dislocated workers.

Most members of special groups will be employed in the service-producing industry. Business educators need to help students to learn how businesses are organized and managed. They might propose to provide small-business development courses or entrepreneurial training for at-risk groups in economically depressed areas.

In summary, business educators should offer their invaluable services to grant writing teams as team leaders, writers, planners, learning facilitators, advocates for special groups, promoters of hands-on learning, designers of innovative programs, and as community agency linkers.

Networking with community groups. Funding will not be available to maintain the status quo. Most of the grant requests for proposals mandate linkages among community service providers. Grants require that the education program will change to meet the needs of special groups.

Community teams should develop strategic plans for special groups to help them overcome barriers such as: educational deprivation; ignorance; poverty; drug and alcohol abuse; teen pregnancy; violence; and inadequate housing, health, and transportation services. Proposed interventions will need to address the problems that impair the student's ability to make the successful transition from school to work. All programs will emphasize linkages between education, business, and public agencies. Special groups will need alternative learning settings and financial assistance to help reduce welfare dependence.

Support services might include extended day schools, night schools, adult basic-skills remediation, transportation services, training in correctional institutions, additional equipment and instructional supplies, counseling support services, mentorships, and training on the job. All of the direct instructional services in the program will need to be linked with health, transportation, day care, and rehabilitation services.

GETTING STARTED

Call state or local granting agencies. Volunteer to be on grant proposal reading teams. Obtain copies of funded and unfunded proposals. Analyze the common mistakes of grants that are not funded. In most cases, grants are not funded unless they meet the needs of the special target group. If the grant proposal looks like a "give me" application, readers will not fund it.

Link up with other interested parties. Discuss ideas with colleagues. Visit winning projects. Consult the city directory. Call education and training or economic development agencies or the Chamber of Commerce in the community or region. Contact local grant management officials, the state department of education, welfare agencies, or the department of employment. Attend grant writing workshops.

Initiate project plans that identify student special needs in business education programs. Deliver these reports to a variety of groups. Convene or join coalitions of community service providers to write for a diverse spectrum of grants in education and training.

A grant writing team for special groups should include representatives of city government, corrections, business, health services, job service and employment agencies, vocational rehabilitation, teen parent support services, family services, worker associations, adult learning centers, community-based organizations, public assistance or welfare offices, safe houses for victims of domestic violence, secondary and postsecondary public and private agencies, or any agency that helps special groups in the transition from school to work. Barriers to employment may require systemic changes in schools or proposals to provide alternative programs. Members of the committee will provide letters of support at a later date.

Any funding source will require the writer to demonstrate that the needs of a specific group will be met through improved or expanded services. The primary goal of the planning team should be: to identify the needs of the special groups and design strategies to help special groups overcome barriers to employment. After the needs and interventions are outlined, the grant writer will seek funding that matches up with the needs of the special at-risk groups.

The group will design a plan or a set of interventions. The committee will develop a variety of grant proposals based on the needs assessment information.

Order the proposal application packet. Contact the grant program office to see if separate guidelines are available. Order copies of kinds of projects supported in specific grant areas from the federal or state agency.

Begin proposal applications well in advance of the deadline. Some agencies ask for a pre-application. Call grant program officers and ask questions. Study copies of previously funded grant requests. Privately owned telephone and research services are also provided.

SOURCES

Many instructional grants are available from a variety of funding agencies. Every year, many requests for public and private proposals are not answered.

Hundreds of worthy projects go unfunded. Why? Applying for grants is not a simple process.

Volumes of grant writing information and funding sources are available. Many federal grants are awarded to improve schools or provide training for work. The key is to match up student or special client needs with specific program needs. In order to help special groups, other agencies need to be tapped. Much of this information will be learned through involvement on planning teams. Not all of the grants are awarded by the Education or Labor departments. Grants are also awarded by lesser known agencies, foundations, or businesses.

A number of government publications list new grant opportunities. The *Federal Register* is published every weekday, except holidays, and is the official publication listing new grant opportunities. Using the *Federal Register*'s notices section, seek announcements of grant programs organized by agency. It describes the eligibility requirements, where to obtain application forms, deadlines, and criteria for review and evaluation. All federal government publications may be ordered through the Superintendent of Documents, U.S. Government Printing Office, Washington, DC 20404.

Save time by subscribing to newsletters that summarize grant and contracts announcements. Contact state education and labor agencies to obtain information on available newsletters related to education for the disadvantaged, vocational education, job training, and adult education and literacy. Obtain requests for proposals from state or regional education and labor agencies.

Not all grants are listed in the *Federal Register*. The federal government sends information to state agencies to notify them of the availability of funds. State agencies notify local public and private school agencies of the availability of subgrants. Most of the education and training grants are awarded by formula to states. Contact state agencies to obtain technical assistance and requests for proposals. The greatest opportunities for funding will come from education and training grants awarded by formula to states. Contact state agencies for proposal guidelines for vocational education, job training, and adult education/literacy grants. State agencies will grant funds to local applicants. The following outlines the grant categories most often used by business educators to improve services to special groups:

Vocational education. The Carl D. Perkins Vocational and Applied Technology Education Act of 1990 emphasizes services to special populations. The Act revitalizes vocational education by integrating basic academic and vocational skills and focusing more resources for special populations. A limited number of vocational programs—those with the highest concentration of special groups—must be identified for local program improvement. If business education programs are identified, funds may be used for upgrading curriculum, purchasing equipment, in-service training, counseling, remedial courses, and support services for special groups, such as child care and transportation. Other programs include guidance and counseling, support for community-based organizations, programs to eliminate gender bias, and services for pregnant teens, single parents, and displaced homemakers.

Get involved in Tech Prep. Tech Prep is also funded by the Perkins Act.

Tech Prep supports a new model of vocational education: a combination of secondary and postsecondary education that leads to an associate degree or 2-year certificate, provides preparation in vocational areas including business, builds student competencies in the basic academic skills, and leads to employment.

Job training. The Job Training Partnership Act 1992 Job Training Reform Amendments also emphasize services for disadvantaged youth and adults. State and local governments have the primary responsibility for the management of the programs. The Act creates separate youth and adult training programs that stress basic education and literacy and promotes linkages between education and job training programs. The Act targets services to economically disadvantaged adults and youth, dislocated workers, and others who face significant employment barriers. Adult retraining services include classroom training, career assessment, occupational skills training, on-the-job training, basic and remedial education, entrepreneurial training, and other activities.

Get involved with JTPA programs. Many adult students will be eligible for services. Other programs include Job Training for the Homeless, Community Service Employment for Older Americans, and the Job Opportunities and Basic Skills Program (JOBS). JOBS provides welfare recipients with job training and educational programs. Many welfare recipients must participate in JOBS in order to receive a welfare check that reflects their needs. Business education programs will no doubt serve many welfare clients who need extra assistance.

Adult education and literacy. Many out-of-school adults lack the basic skills needed for them to benefit from job training. Business educators are in a unique position to help adults to master both basic and job skills. Major amendments were enacted as part of the National Literacy Act of 1991. Funds help adults to get their high school equivalency degree. Funds are also set aside for services to adults in correctional facilities. Subgrants may be used for literacy projects in public housing authorities. Literacy projects are linked with job training projects through cooperative agency agreements.

Business educators should gain knowledge about the National Workplace Literacy Program, which emphasizes business-education partnerships offering literacy training in the workplace. The Stewart B. McKinney Homeless Assistance Act authorizes literacy programs for homeless adults.

Education and training, adult education, and services for disadvantaged are interconnected. The workplace demands basic literacy skills. Every federal job training program includes a literacy component. Adult basic education is an important component of vocational education. Coordination and dialogue are required among job training, vocational education, and adult education agencies at the state and local levels.

Education for the disadvantaged. Education for the Disadvantaged programs include Chapter One. Chapter One is the largest program of aid to elementary and secondary education. Chapter One programs are funded in areas with the highest concentrations of low-income students. Most Chapter One programs provide extra help to students and parents in elementary schools located in low income areas. The Even Start program provides basic skills and literacy for parents of disadvantaged children.

A number of programs help disadvantaged students: Talent Search, Upward Bound, Student Support Services, Educational Opportunity Centers. Contact school counselors to help students enrolled in business education programs.

School Improvement Programs include Chapter Two block grants to school districts. Contact Chapter Two program coordinators at the local level. The National Diffusion Network disseminates nationwide any instruction method deemed exemplary by a federal review board. Contact the state education department for information on innovative education approaches. In many cases, National Diffusion Network teacher training workshops on best instructional practices are provided at no expense to the local school. Many of the NDN projects provide unique approaches to how to improve services to special groups.

Other public funding information. Become acquainted with *Commerce Business Daily*. Federal agencies use the publication to purchase products under specific terms. They solicit bids on work they want done. Procurement announcements summarize the work, service, or supplies needed by the agency. Some announcements invite organizations to do the job. A section also lists auctions of property ranging from motor vehicles to office equipment.

Contact state and local agencies to determine other education funding sources for compensatory education for special groups. Legislatures, county commissions, and city governments in some states authorize grants to help educators initiate innovative projects to serve special groups.

Foundation grants. Funds are also available from public and privately funded foundations. Find the right foundation by using the Foundation Center services. The Foundation Center Grants Index (1992) is housed in libraries across the country. The Foundation Center is a national service organized to help grantseekers. The Foundation Center is a network of offices established to collect and report information. The Center reviews types of grants and lists thousands of foundations.

Find out when a regional Foundation Center will do periodic grant writing seminars. Public librarians will help to provide foundation directory information.

Company sponsored, operating, or community foundations are identified in the directory. Company sponsored foundations receive annual gifts and contributions and endowments. Grants are usually related to corporate activities in the community where the company operates.

Operating foundations usually use funds to conduct research. Some of the research, however, might be directed toward improving basic skills and business literacy within the workplace.

Community foundations are publicly sponsored by charitable organizations. They may provide grants for special purposes within a region. Many of the foundations direct funding for special target groups. For example foundations help programs to provide supportive services to out-of-school youth needing basic literacy and employability skills.

Community-based organizations (CBOs) often work with school districts or colleges to help severely economically and educationally disadvantaged youth in their transition from school to work. Link up with a CBO to write a proposal for foundation or public funds. CBOs may offer alternative education sites and case management services.

Develop a plan that meets the intent of the foundation request for proposals. Prepare a cover letter and a complete detailed proposal. Sell the foundation on how the grant might be a publicity advantage. Use simple, direct sentences. Appeal to the specialty or unique services of the business. Do not waste space. Use clear and concise statements.

Business partnerships. Business partnerships offer important sources of funds and volunteer services. Volunteers serve as mentors for at-risk youth. They provide tutoring services, help students in career explorations, provide speakers, sponsor field trips, and are involved in the cooperative work program. Many businesses contribute equipment and instructional materials. Others sponsor scholarships for disadvantaged students.

CONCLUSIONS

A number of special grants are available to eliminate barriers for special groups in their transition from school to work. Business educators should volunteer to be on grant writing teams as team leaders, writers, and designers of alternative programs. Education and training grants are available from a variety of government agencies, foundations, or businesses. Many federal grants are awarded to improve school or provide training for work. In order to get involved, business educators should:

- Contact local grant management officials, the state department of education, welfare agencies, or the department of employment for information on funding sources.

- Join coalitions of community services agencies to write for a diverse spectrum of grants in education and training.

- Subscribe to newsletters that summarize grants and contracts announcements. Contact state education and labor agencies to obtain information on available newsletters related to education for the disadvantaged, vocational education, job training, and adult education and literacy.

- Obtain application packets from state or regional education and labor agencies and private foundations.

- Attend grant writing workshops.

- Volunteer to be on grant proposal reading teams.

- Obtain copies of funded and unfunded proposals. Analyze the common mistakes of grants that are not funded.

The following grant categories are most often used by business educators to improve services to special groups. Both granting agencies require networking and coordination among community service providers:

- The Carl D. Perkins Vocational and Applied Technology Education Act of 1990, Department of Education.

- The Job Training Partnership Act 1992 Job Training Reform Amendments, Department of Labor.

Funds are also available from public and private foundations. Contact public libraries for foundation information. Find the right foundation by using the

Foundation Center Directory. Business partnerships also offer important sources of funds and volunteer services.

Business educators cannot serve the needs of special groups in isolation. Begin now to meet with other groups that can help improve services to special groups enrolled in business education classès: representatives of city government; Chamber of Commerce; corrections agencies; health services; job service and employment agencies; vocational rehabilitation; teen parent support services; family services; worker associations; adult learning centers; community-based organizations; public assistance or welfare offices; safe houses for victims of domestic violence; secondary and post secondary public and private agencies; or any agency that helps special groups in their transition from school to work.

REFERENCES

AVA Guide to the Carl D. Perkins Vocational and Applied Technology Act of 1990. Alexandria, Virginia: American Vocational Association, 1990.

Crockett, Lib, and Smink, Jay. *The Mentoring Guidebook: A Practical Manual for Designing and Managing a Mentoring Program.* Clemson, SC 29634-5111: The National Dropout Prevention Center, 1991.

The Foundation Grants Index 1992. New York, New York: The Foundation Center, 1992. The Foundation Grants Index covers 57,443 grants. The grants have a total value of $4.47 billion. The Foundation Center is an independent national service organization established to provide a source of information on private philanthropic giving. A complete set of U.S. foundation returns are in the New York and Washington, D.C., offices of the Foundation Center. Participants in the Cooperating Collections Network are libraries or nonprofit information centers throughout the country.

Guide to Federal Funding for Education (Volumes I and II). Arlington, VA: Educational Funding Research Council, 1992.

Ohman, Diana. *A Healthy Wyoming: Start with Youth Today.* Cheyenne, Wyoming: Department of Education, 1991.

Whole Nonprofit Catalog: A Compendium of Resources for Nonprofit Organizations, Los Angeles, CA; The Grantsmanship Center, Fall 1992.

Wyoming's Education Progress Report. Cheyenne, Wyoming: Department of Education, 1992.

Youth Apprenticeship in America: Guidelines for Building an Effective System. Washington, DC: William T. Grant Foundation Commission on Youth and America's Future, 1992.

Zahn, Donald K., and Poole, Vicki A. "Education and Work Partnerships, *The Hidden Curriculum: National Business Education Yearbook 30.* Reston, Virginia: National Business Education Association, 1992.

Part III

EXPANDING HORIZONS IN BUSINESS EDUCATION: POSTSECONDARY EDUCATION

CHAPTER 11

BUSINESS/INDUSTRY TRAINING SEMINARS

DEBORAH RILEY

Manatee Area Adult Vocational Center, Bradenton, Florida

Current business literature stresses the need for retraining and reiterates in document after document that society's members must be lifelong learners. Reports reveal the necessity for retraining for basic skills, technological change, and constant quality improvement. President Clinton's administration is championing the need for retraining. Disney Corporation's success is built on its strong commitment to training. Now is the time for local business educators to assist in the retraining process.

Where does a training program start and how does it develop? The training program begins with a specific strategy for development, an analysis of what is to be accomplished, a design to accomplish the goal, expert trainers, appropriate media, and methods for continuous evaluation.

PROGRAM DEVELOPMENT

Is the school system ready to commit the resources, time, and marketing expertise to create a quality program?

A quality program doesn't just happen by chance. It must be designed with precision and care by an expert trainer. Organizational development training is an easy item to eliminate in tight corporate budgets. To survive the 1990s' cost-cutting, any training program must bring about measurable results. An individual in the school organization must be assigned the development responsibility. This initial step requires resources of time and money unless a trainer is presently on the staff with a background in corporate training. Otherwise an educator must develop corporate training skills including a knowledge of what is happening in corporate training programs today and what is appropriate to the training level expected in the local community. To develop corporate training skills for the trainer, many short seminars are available in most geographic areas of the United States. The training coordinator should attend one or several of these commercially available programs to study current trends in corporate training.

Customer Service or *Telephone Techniques* are ideal course offerings to start business/industry liaison programs. In today's business climate any computer training has a guaranteed market. If resources are available to continually update equipment and the trainer's expertise, an entire business liaison could be established in this area. If effective computer software training programs are developed, they are guaranteed immediate participants. Short seminars are feasible for most businesses and are affordable in time and dollar resources. Once the programs have won support from several local companies, they provide a springboard to further develop longer and higher level training programs, such as *English Grammar* and *Punctuation Skills for Business, Proofreading for Business Professionals, Supervisory Training, Teambuilding,* and *Mid-Level Management Skills.*

To start small and perform well cannot be too strongly recommended to ensure the development of an effective liaison program with the business community.

CLIENT/TRAINER RELATIONSHIP

Establishing an effective liaison program requires expert communication skills. The client must have accurately assessed the needs of participants, set realistic expectations, and be committed to the goals of the seminar. Responsibilities must be negotiated so that both client and trainer share equally in the seminar outcome. Successful trainers deal with the "wants" of the client in relation to their capacity to meet the client's expectations. Have the trainer and the client identified the "real" client? Sometimes what the liaison client perceives as the organizational needs for training is not perceived as a need by the participants who will be the "real" clients.

Danger signals for training include:

1. Feeling a need to get the project off the ground but being unrealistic about current resources
2. Feeling obligated to deliver a program that is out of the area of expertise
3. Allocating time to a client organization that does not have the commitment to expend dollars for quality training
4. Inadequate training environment.

Communication is the key to program success. Listen with empathy to the concerns of the client and set a realistic training timeline; assess the power line of the client for genuine follow-through; plan for the unexpected. Ensure that there is genuine agreement for program objectives. Does the client have realistic expectations for a behavior change or technical knowledge application? Have materials been approved for purchase? Is there a feedback mechanism? The trainer MUST be accessible and give timely support and feedback. This type of working relationship takes time and trust to develop.

ADULT LEARNERS

In recent years much has been written about adult learners. Adult learners, according to current literature, must find relevance and perhaps even application in order for them to become active participants in any training endeavor. Research indicates that adults are more motivated by single-concept courses that can be readily applied to a relevant problem. Adults also tend to integrate new ideas into their present data. Totally new concepts must be integrated more slowly. Adults like to have time to achieve mastery of the new skill and are often bothered by trial and error.

Adults need to adjust to the different "value sets" of persons in different life stages. All of these factors must be considered when the training program is developed.

PROGRAM CONTENT

The most difficult task of any trainer is to narrow the focus to the specific content to be included in the seminar from the wide body of knowledge available. Before developing seminar content, it is critical to assess what employees "know," "need to know," and what they would "like" to know. In technical training, content should be developed that enhances how one can do a task faster and better.

Textbooks are perhaps the least effective model for training development. They are useful as instructor resources for most short seminars. For a true business liaison, program content must include pertinent "technical" and/or "people-development" skills. The trainer should ask, "Can this training be applied to the everyday work situation?"

In a customer service seminar, the trainer must address the specific concerns of the client. For example, a service organization has objectives and challenges different from a manufacturing environment. The geographic location also has its own particular implications. For example, in Florida, there is a large retired population that enjoys the social interaction of business transactions. Consequently, in most customer service training seminars in Florida, a training objective addresses how to be efficient and courteous in bringing closure to a telephone or face-to-face business transaction.

In seminars such as *Supervisory Training, Team Work,* and *English Grammar,* the material must be pertinent to the perceived needs and wants of the client organization and its participants. As the demands of our complex society require high level intellectual and interpersonal skills, the trainer should supplement lectures with role playing, simulations, case studies, and team-work sessions which simulate creative thinking.

Trainers know that involvement, problem solving, discussion, and "learning by doing" enhance the learning process; they recognize the value of a case study. The case study should be written in a conversationally interesting style that sustains interest, incorporates human interest, has clarity and simplicity, and is job-related.

There are many commercial publishing companies that market professionally prepared seminar materials that can be invaluable in augmenting training goals. Companies also develop self-assessments for communication, listening, management style, team building, as well as change inventories and surveys for quality customer service, time management techniques, and stress indicators. Participants enjoy this style of activity; it gives excellent feedback to the participant, and it can be quickly reviewed for reinforcement. Most are reasonably priced.

Effective professional video support is available for most business topics. Video tapes can be costly items and must be selected with maximum care. A maximum time frame of 30 minutes is usually ideal; longer videos are often programmed for segmented viewing.

In planning for program content, a variety of learning strategies incorporating participatory activities must be included as part of the program. The input of participants with worthwhile business experience can enhance the training; although participatory involvement is a teaching strategy with a limited range of applications. It must be expertly applied to the appropriate subject, with pertinent knowledge of participants, and in an appropriate situation. If the subject matter is technical and new to the participants, participatory involvement may not produce the desired results. It lends itself well to participants with a relational, verbal learning style; the analytic learner may prefer formal training with the instructor viewed as an information giver. The trainer must be highly skilled in guiding the group to conclusions and be prepared for the participant who tends to monopolize feedback sessions.

LEARNING ENVIRONMENT

Elements of a conducive training environment must be clearly stated to the client before the training session. This seems a simple request, but is often difficult to obtain. Learning environments can be limited by inadequate space for the number of people or by a facility too large for the group, uncomfortable chairs, no writing area, inoperable VCRs, lack of promised overhead, or an area with frequent interruptions from other employees. Each of these factors must be effectively negotiated to ensure program success.

TRAINERS

The trainer is an important catalyst in a business/industry liaison program. For example, a trainer can tap talented retired persons from industry and education who are often willing to put their skills to use at a cost less than the customary business pay scale. Persons with corporate training experience immediately flow into the program. For most educators, business/industry training seminars are a new concept which requires new skills and a period of adjustment. The tight delivery time frame, the learning styles of the adult learner, and the lack of extensive business experience often are great challenges to the trainer.

A visit to the work site before the seminar begins is important to get a feeling for the work environment and to negotiate any environmental factors. Become familiar with the jargon of the trade and use it in the seminar to make case studies or for problem-solving activities.

Arrive early and stay late to observe. Listen with empathy, and convey that somebody listens who cares. Dress comfortably and appropriately to the situation.

The corporate trainer is challenged by classrooms of people who are different in age, experience, education, and learning ability. Today's participants will be different from yesterday's, and success will often depend upon the trainer's ability to be flexible. Rapport must be established quickly through effective introductory remarks and icebreaker activities, "mix and mingle," use participants' names, experiences, and situations. Provide name tents to encourage use of names by all participants.

Stimulating relevant material must be launched immediately, while the trainer is constantly monitoring the environment to be certain that communication is ongoing. The trainer must be comfortable communicating with participants in order to determine their likes and dislikes, language style, as well as power and political structures. Maintain everyone's self-esteem while disarming the negative, relieving the anxious, and encouraging the reluctant. Three key words for the trainer are "respond," "support," and "assist."

Often participants will know more about the technical side of the job than the trainer. In many cases clients have been promoted to the position based on their technical knowledge, but they lack the people skills to be successful leaders, facilitators, team and people developers. Encourage them to lead discussions on technical facts.

Adjusting to the situation is always necessary, no matter how much care is extended in setting up the training. One can get caught in a poor learning environment or with negative participants. Challenge the student's thinking process whenever possible. Well-organized notes and handouts are necessary to establish credibility and conduct a productive session. Only a very experienced trainer can draw on an internal data base. A bad habit of a new and inexperienced trainer is to arrive with boxes upon boxes of unorganized handouts.

EVALUATION

1. Training programs must be continuously improved and changed. Legislation, economics, and our changing corporate, community, and national culture brings change into the business environment.

2. Developing a standardized form can be useful for feedback, but some client companies will want to customize it for specific information.

3. The essential criterion for evaluation is that it should be useful to both the trainer and the client. It should provide information that helps in the development and delivery of the seminar as well as document the value of the seminar.

MARKETING

What is the competitive edge the school organization has to offer, and what is currently available in the locale? From advisory committees, the local Chamber of Commerce, and professional or trade associations, the trainer can determine the content for the seminars, as well as identify the area in which businesses conduct training and use outside consultants. If there is a successful, locally owned, national seminar group, their topics may have a corner on the market. Topics should augment what is currently available. Once the seminar is developed, prepare a professional handout to introduce the program. Selling a program is an ongoing challenge.

SUMMARY

Start small with course offerings and gradually expand the base. Develop quality seminars. Expect an ever-changing focus of the subject area to meet the business needs in the area. Remember to follow through on the details. Take time for planning. Expect to have temporary setbacks due to economic conditions, funding problems, staff change, and new program development. Seek quality professionals to present seminars. Seek effective feedback and use it to be continually improving oneself as well as the product.

REFERENCES

Anderson, D. E. (1991). How to prepare for presentations. *Effective training delivery.* Minneapolis, MN: Lakewood Publications.

Broadwell, M. M. (1991). Broadwell, P. C. Reading for rapport. *Effective training delivery,* Minneapolis, MN: Lakewood Publications.

Carr, C. (1992, June). The three r's of training. *Training.*

Carter, J. H. (1991). Participatory training: Separating fantasy from reality. *Effective training delivery.* Minneapolis, MN: Lakewood Publications.

Owenby, P. H. (1992, January). Making case studies come alive. *Training.*

Szarek, E. (1991). 16 ways to save time in the classroom. *Effective training delivery.* Minneapolis, MN: Lakewood Publications.

Zemke, R. and S. (1991). 30 things we know for sure about adult learning. *Adult learning in your classroom.* Lakewood, MN: Lakewood Publications.

CHAPTER 12

OPEN ENTRY—OPEN EXIT CLASSES

CHARLOTTE MONTANUS AND MARK MONTANUS

Glendale Community College, Glendale, Arizona

For years many of us in business education have searched for alternate ways to help students learn. When teaching skill subjects, business teachers know they must provide self-paced drill and practice opportunities in order for students to be successful. In the past the hard work that went into the creation of these materials provided only minimal success both for teachers and students, because the available media was expensive, difficult to manage, and not always available. Yet, in these small successes, most of us believed that the development of alternate methods of learning would one day occur. Enter the microcomputer! This marvelous tool has become the vehicle for making great strides.

In 1983 Glendale Community College created a small 30-station microcomputer lab dedicated solely to the open laboratory process. Two individualized business courses started the open entry—open exit (OE/OE) style of learning. The motto for these classes was start when you want, finish when you can.

The early success of this lab was phenomenal. After one semester, the president of the college agreed to tear down the wall of an adjacent room and fill it with more computers. Thirty more computer stations were added, and a half-dozen new OE/OE modules saw the program swell to 2,000 students. Within three years the walls of the remaining rooms were destroyed, creating a large open laboratory with 200 microcomputers. One-half of the 14,000 students at the college were using the facility.

This prototype lab led to the building of a new 32,000-square-foot high technology center. This computer laboratory, which is two-thirds the size of a football field, contains 300 microcomputers and computer terminals. Currently there are over 35 OE/OE business modules and a great variety of open lab activities serving 27 disciplines within the college. Today the college has 18,500 students with 16,000 of them using the center. The center is open seven days a week, from 7:00 a.m. to midnight during the week and 8:00 a.m. to 5:00 p.m. on weekends. A support staff is available during all open hours. Our business education staff is elated as student completion rates soar over the 90 percent mark. Many disciplines use a variety of alternative teaching styles in the center. The OE/OE style has proven to be extremely successful and has become the heart of the center. The subject of this chapter deals with the elements that must be incorporated into a program to teach successfully in the open entry—open exit style.

PROBLEMS

Computers solve many problems in our current educational system, but users must understand the nature of the computer relative to these problems. What are the problems?

Financial requirements. Finding dollars to support technology seems almost impossible. Most departments are asking for an exclusive lab, and administrators demand computing power to run the school. It does not seem possible that public education can afford technology.

Inflexible instructional systems. Inflexibility exists in our schools. Many traditional teachers tend to believe that the status quo is acceptable and that traditional methodologies should prevail. Is it possible to break away from standard class schedules where all students dance to the same tune?

Inflexible administrative systems. Current administrative systems hamper a true OE/OE style. Is it possible for a student to enroll in a class two weeks before the end of the semester? The system requires that all students receive a grade at the end of the grade-reporting period. How can we trace the amount of time a student spends on different classes in the same lab period? How can we get funding agencies to approve non-traditional attendance systems?

Compartmental hierarchies. Instructional territories developed over many years. Is it possible that a student could study business math, geography, accounting, and writing all in the same laboratory experience? We have built compartments that will be tough to break down.

Lack of technology accessibility. Large departments can garner their share of computers while other departments go without. There is much ado about who owns what and how much sharing is going to happen. Extremely expensive computer labs are opened at the start of the school day and closed by mid-afternoon. They are often not fully used even when school is in session.

Fast learners are unchallenged. Accelerated classes are only a partial solution and still deny true opportunities for unlimited growth potential for the gifted.

Slow learners get left behind in the current system. Time is the real enemy for many of these students. There really is never enough time for slow students to truly master the necessary skills, which often results in social promotion and high drop rates.

Low retention. Shrinking dollars, larger classes, and myriads of social problems seem to push us further into this awful hole.

Lack of instructional materials. Instructional materials using computers in an open style of learning are not available. Many schools have computers, but what can be done with them?

Staff inexperienced in technology. How can teachers use something they don't fully understand? How do we network? What kind of computers do we buy? Who will fix them? Is there enough time for training and upgrading skills? How and where do staff members get training?

A lack of tutorial support. Students often cannot get help when they need it most. Sometimes the learning centers are remote and require students to jump through hoops before help is available, thus contributing to the problem.

Inflexible time periods. Suggesting that all students master the same performances within the same time is indefensible. Making time a constant does not consider individual differences nor situations such as illness, personal problems, accidents, changing personal responsibilities, and a host of other detractors.

These problems are here, and in great abundance. How can computers help solve these problems? Light appears at the end of the tunnel, based upon what business teachers know about computer use in education. Technology is the vehicle for change!

PHILOSOPHIES

The computer provides a solution for each major problem cited above, but it will require some serious mind-set changes. Of one thing we are certain at Glendale, trying to use computers using the old teaching methodology simply does not work. The small cadre of innovators who faced the difficult task of addressing this change decided to establish a philosophy to serve as a base from which to work. Once established, the philosophy became the base for our personal commitment and served as the guiding force to success.

Frequently, various political and financial forces create obstacles for technology leaders. Good ideas must withstand the traditional assault that accompanies change. It is imperative for the group that becomes the change agent to establish a defensible, clear philosophy and make an uncommon commitment to it. The technology will quickly change, but the philosophy must stay constant throughout this rapid change.

Our philosophical base, established in 1983, is still viable with only a few new additions through the ten-year growth period. Only five people were committed to the philosophy at first. Now there is overwhelming support from our faculty and administration.

Cooperative centralized computing is essential. The plain fact is—there is not enough money to satisfy decentralized equipment, software, or support. About 80 percent of all technology requests from departments are nearly identical. By combining purchasing power into a central lab and creating a technology committee of all users, common ground was found that would satisfy everyone. The central lab required changes in teaching methodology, but all users in the institution have access, and all users continue to drive the process cooperatively. The cooperative process has forced departments to think of satisfying their needs with respect to all other institutional needs, elevating planning to a very functional plane. Current financing can meet the needs of all when using a cooperative centralized computing process.

Maximum access is a major component to success. It is foolish to spend millions on technology, then lock it up. Students need continual access to these powerful tools. Our current definition of maximum access is keeping the center open 102 hours each week with a full-support staff available. The lab is now closed only 10 days out of the year. Expensive equipment is available 12 months each year, 17 hours each day, with an average utilization of 75 percent.

Nonownership of technology equipment must be a central theme. Departmental territories of the past fall short when dealing with technology.

Departments have proven to be uncooperative when sharing facilities, and this lack of cooperation leads to low utilization and even misuse of equipment. Put expensive equipment to its highest and best use. Departmental ownership does not allow efficiency.

Technology must be shared. Many schools have an administrative computing system separate from the instructional system. This eventually leads to an electronic nightmare for technicians to administer. Combining all systems into a powerful centralized computing infrastructure and sharing all equipment will reduce technical maintenance and provide more power for everyone.

The highest levels of innovation need support. The training of an inexperienced staff is the beginning point for innovation. Full support services must be available for the faculty to solve technical problems as they encounter them, allowing new instructional materials to move quickly into the computer laboratory. An innovation center, with a technically competent staff, can house the latest equipment and software where the staff can experiment, learn, and develop new materials.

Using computers for grade and report management systems is essential. Develop a database that will automatically take attendance and track log times for each student. Grade the completed work immediately, and record it into the database. The database should also provide facilities for withdrawing students, providing extensions, sending messages, and creating grade reports. Removing mundane tasks from teaching responsibilities will free teachers to create, teach, facilitate, advise, etc. Make the database available to students for monitoring their own progress and sending messages to their teacher(s).

Using interdisciplinary learning approaches is essential. An interdisciplinary approach leads to new levels of teaching and learning as computers break down the walls of the "compartmental hierarchy." What department should have control over computer graphics? If you consider every department that has an interest, you will include business, art, journalism, CAD, and others. It is logical for these departments to collaborate in creating the instructional materials, teaching the computer graphics courses, and sharing the same facilities.

Full-service instructional support must be available. The teaching team includes student assistants who respond to many routine questions, full-time instructional technicians who help manage the lab and assist with technical questions, and the faculty who develop the instructional materials, facilitate the learners, and serve as role models for all workers and students. The open lab provides a great opportunity for expanding the role of team teaching during all open hours.

Time must be the variable with performance as the constant. Traditionally, time is the constant and performance is the variable. The arbitrary time constraints created in our system have much to do with nothing, but the open lab is effective in removing these constraints. Allow students as much time as they need to reach defined performance levels for the OE/OE courses. Some do it very fast, others take more time, and some require considerable time. A time constraint placed upon students by the system is arbitrary.

Some students are in a retraining mode for a new position and need intensive work to develop new skills immediately. Others take whatever time they need to learn the skills. Students can and will take the responsibility for their own learning, and this philosophy will let learning happen.

Create maximum visibility and an open environment. The open visible setting considerably enhances the ability to manage a large computer laboratory. The teaching team can see any student who may be having difficulty, and students can see that immediate support is available. An open lab can be soundproofed and ergonomically arranged to be very attractive. Students seem to take pride in an open and attractive lab. Most important, if something does not work, it is immediately visible and demands spontaneous correction. The same kind of problem can linger for weeks in a closed class setting.

Instruction drives technology. No dollars should be spent until the need in the classroom dictates it. The purchase of equipment and software is solely the function of the instructional need. While most administrators will agree with this philosophy, most do not really understand it. The budget or someone's bias frequently affects the decision to purchase a DOS computer as opposed to a Macintosh, or vice versa. The purchase of software falls into the same trap. The needs of our business community and students determine what we will teach; therefore, demand dictates what we buy and develop.

Technology must focus on flexible learning formats. All users of the technology do not have the same needs. The learning strategies dictate the instructional materials, and all agree that a great variety of learning strategies is available. OE/OE works beautifully for teaching computer applications; but business law, general business, or speech may require other strategies. Using technology in a flexible manner seems to work best. Computer uses in learning will change dramatically as multimedia comes into broader use. The point is to remain flexible and create whatever learning formats seem to work. Plan, experiment, and develop with the technology to see how it can work for you.

The various philosophies provide a possible solution for each problem discussed in the chapter. The question now is, what are the solutions?

SOLUTIONS

Success of the program at Glendale Community College led to the building of a second high tech center, creating a technology complex. GCC has conducted more than 1,000 tours for visitors from around the world. Visitors often remark that they are unable to build high tech facilities like this. Building facilities to match what another college has is not the point. The point is to understand the nature of the problem, the philosophy, and the process. With that point in mind, anyone can start a small one-room lab dedicated to the open style and help it grow. The solutions include three areas: 1) high tech center, 2) learning materials, and 3) instructional team.

High tech center. Create as large an open area as possible, and place the required combination of computers needed by your students into the lab.

There is a walkway around the open lab and the lab itself is sunken but entirely visible from any point in the building. All walls except for storage and restrooms are glass to provide maximum visibility.

Use tables that hide the wiring, and try to avoid arranging them in rows, if possible. At Glendale we use Y-shaped tables, putting 11 stations at each Y table, with a laser printer serving the 11 stations. Positioning these tables in the lab randomly avoids the unattractive look of rows. Students need space; don't try to jam everything into the lab that you can. If you do, you will create a general feeling of discomfort. Never allow the central lab to become a scheduled room. It must be committed totally to an open lab. Keep the library concept foremost in your mind, and serve students and the faculty on a walk-in basis with no time restrictions.

High schools have a different agenda and must work with time schedules. However, several high schools in Arizona are creating open lab times before school starts and will run open labs in the late afternoon. The high level of activity in the open labs before and after school surprises many administrators.

Select a central area in the lab for grading to take place. House the grading database and the grading manuals in this area. As students bring their work for grading, evaluate it immediately. While computers can grade much of this work, we prefer human contact in helping students to evaluate what must be done to improve their work. After grading, students may be asked to return to their station to make the necessary corrections. The student makes corrections, submits the assignment again, and continues the process until the work is perfect. The grader enters the score into the database and signs the student's progress sheet. Students learn by doing, but they also learn by evaluation and reinforcement.

Create the database so it will perform automatic queries according to student progress. Students making little progress receive a letter verifying their status in the course. The letter should be positive and supportive, encouraging the student to meet with the teacher. Our database can create four different letters for students as they progress through the course. These letters include a completion letter congratulating the student and suggesting the next course of action open to him/her.

A disk-checkout area should be placed near the main entrance of the lab. You may have a computer network, but students still need floppy disks. The employees at the disk-checkout area issue software that may not reside on the network, issue data disks used in many courses, issue syllabus materials for various courses, and provide a place where students can ask questions about how the lab operates. Keep the computerized log-in system in this area. Attendance is taken by scanning the student's ID card at the start of each session. The card is kept at the checkout counter until the student returns the software and quits for the day. The ID card is scanned again for logging out. Complete attendance records are available for the teaching team and the students.

In the true OE/OE style, the checkout area serves as a place where new students start their first day in the lab. Each student receives an individual orientation. The orientation includes viewing a video tape of how the lab works, reviewing student progress sheets that track student progress, learning how to send messages electronically to the teacher, learning how to see grades in the grading database, and other first-day activities. Staff mail boxes are kept in this area because it serves as a communications center for everyone. Laboratory managers and lead faculty persons should have offices in the same area if possible.

House the centralized computing equipment such as LAN servers, production printers, tape storage, telephone devices, etc., in the immediate area if possible. In addition, this area should have glass walls. Students like to see the devices that make it all work for them and are proud of their environment. Keeping these devices close to the instructional area also keeps a wealth of talent nearby to help with technical problems that may arise in the open lab. Frequently, network managers, VAX operators, and programmers are working in the open lab with the faculty and students to solve perplexing problems. The rule is—don't let this wealth of talent retreat into isolation. They will if you let them.

Manage your laboratory similar to a library. We encourage students to help each other solve problems, but we also set a standard that shows respect for fellow students. The teaching team sets the pattern by speaking in a low tone when helping students. All members of the teaching team are out in the open lab watching for students who need help. The open, visible environment makes this an easy job. Keep the traffic flow areas between tables clear so that students and teaching-team members can move about without aggravation.

Do everything you can to soundproof the facility. The goal is to achieve a place that is very active, quiet, attractive, and functional. On the job, students will work in open environments with much activity going on about them. Let's make it real.

We were fortunate to receive a grant to decorate our high tech center. Silk plants, live plants, and simple but rich decor has added a touch that makes a difference. Make the area attractive and, above all, keep it clear of clutter. We put all CPUs on the floor to lower the profile of equipment on the table. It is surprising what differences small changes can make.

The learning materials. All business teachers are well aware of the difficulty in finding the perfect textbook for the open environment. Most of the textbooks that teach the latest applications are written for a lecture/lab combination and don't really work well in the open lab environment. It is difficult to take incomplete materials and write additional labs, syllabus materials, step-by-step instructions and combine them for use in the individualized instructional environment. Most of the time, students are confused trying to figure out which of the documents they should be using. This confusion adds to the frustration of trying to learn difficult computer applications. Publishers are moving toward self-paced materials, but still have far to go. What are the solutions?

Ideally, the instructional material should be a complete treatise for the student. Include everything in the materials that will lead the student to mastery of the performances for that course. The materials should include information on the logistics of how the lab runs, how to get assignments graded, how to log into the network, how to view grades in the database, and how to get extensions. No gaps or holes can be tolerated in the information; everything must be included in the instructional materials for the students to be successful.

Fortunately for GCC, several faculty members are writing in the style just described. Observations of the courses using this material show a very high finish rate, a strong sense of accomplishment by students, self-disciplined students, and fewer instructional problems. Survey results show that student performances are suitable to the job market. Materials written in this manner become the focal point for all members of the teaching team when helping students. It is not just a matter of a correct keystroke sequence. It is really a matter of understanding the logic of a keystroke series. That logic is made clear by focusing on the textbook with a student. Our facilitators never touch the student's keyboard; instead, they help the student in understanding the concepts, the logic, and the keystrokes using the text as a focal point. Students then use the textbook to master what they have just learned.

The creation of these instructional materials is not a simple matter, but most of us have written instructional lab materials. Developing a complete textbook is an extension of this. Weave the concepts into the fabric of specific steps to tie the learning materials into a complete package. Include reinforcement exercises, mastery self-checks, and assignments.

Here are possible ways these materials can be created:

1. Get your administrators to budget dollars to provide release time for faculty who are willing to write. The material written at GCC is published by our local authoring center and placed in the bookstore, where a small charge eventually recovers all or part of the cost for release time. These dollars stay with the authoring center and are used to create more material.

2. Write for a federal, state, or local grant to create the needed materials. Sometimes our faculty will take full release time to write, and in other cases specialized writers from our business community are hired to write.

3. The more entrepreneurial faculty members can use their own time to produce instructional materials. At least seven of our faculty members have written in this manner. Most of them use a quick turnaround publisher and take a reasonable royalty. Others have become self-publishers. Materials written in this manner are submitted to a college-standards committee that reviews and monitors the process to verify that all objectives for the course are met and the writing style is acceptable. These materials are subject to the approval of our Governing Board. Often several institutions will agree to use the materials assuring that writers receive reasonable reimbursement.

4. Publishing companies are aware of the movement toward the open lab environment and are searching for ways to write the kind of material needed. Keep in close contact with your publishers, and you may find good writing opportunities for yourself.

If you cannot create your own instructional materials, what is next? Many current textbooks produced in the self-paced style come very close to meeting the needs for a true OE/OE environment. While some staff members produce in-house instructional materials, many OE/OE teachers use published textbooks. If you find a good book that is complete and meets the standards for your course, you will still do some writing. While the textbook is the main learning tool, the syllabus is the focal point for the students. The syllabus for many of our courses may be 40 or 50 pages in length and include all orientation procedures. By way of definition, orientation is an ongoing process. The initial orientation helps students get started, but later they must be oriented to the grading procedures, using the grading database, and extension procedures.

Items needed in the syllabus include:

1. Letter of welcome to the student

2. Description and competencies for the course

3. Description of the laboratory procedures

4. Progress sheet to record finished work

5. Including the configuration process in the syllabus when using a student version of software

6. Instructions for creating data disks, backup data disk, copying data files, etc.

7. The main body of the syllabus, which includes directing the student through various learning experiences in the textbook. Being explicit, clear, and accurate is crucial; otherwise, students are confused and frustrated. You may need to include additional assignments in the syllabus if the textbook does not meet that need. Properly written, students learn that the syllabus is their central document.

8. You will need to include other orientation materials in the body of the syllabus, especially if there is something unique about a given exercise. For example, students may be directed to use a special color printer for one assignment, or they may complete another assignment in a different lab.

9. Include special reminders throughout the syllabus. For example, at an appropriate point in the syllabus, tell students they are 60 percent complete, and remind them to check their end date to see if they need a time extension.

Our experience has shown that a poorly-written syllabus accompanying a well-written textbook causes students to experience serious difficulty. Students are frustrated when they cannot understand what the teacher wants.

The syllabus materials for all courses are kept at the disk-checkouts counter for distribution and become part of the orientation process. All members of the teaching team are generally expected to know how each of the OE/OE courses work. The information in each syllabus becomes part of the training materials for our high tech center staff.

The instructional team. While much of the discussion relates to community colleges, high schools and elementary schools are beginning to experiment with different kinds of support. The point is that computing power is going to move us into a new teaching environment that matches certain kinds of personnel with specific tasks to be effective, both functionally and financially. What follows is a detailed description of what is working at GCC. The purpose is not for you to emulate the exact model, but to pull from it what you need in your own operation. The instructional team consists of three groups: 1) student assistants, 2) instructional technicians, and 3) faculty.

Lab assistants. Student assistants make-up the bulk of the personnel because of our extended hours and because so many questions and problems are of a perfunctory nature. Their job duties include putting paper in a laser printer, helping a student log in, plugging in a loose electrical connection, issuing disks, etc. In terms of frequency, most of the tasks in the lab fall into this category; therefore, it is reasonable to use someone earning four or five dollars per hour for these kinds of tasks. The faculty must be free to work on a higher plane.

Try to find employees with excellent human relations skills and a strong background in the technology. The goal is to have the broadest skills coverage possible in the lab at any given time. The assistants are classified as specialists in certain areas and are scheduled according to specialization.

Using student assistants has turned out to be far more successful than we imagined. Our center currently has 125 student assistants, each working 19 hours per week. They are part of the backbone of the lab, and the quality of their assistance is remarkably high.

Instructional technicians. Instructional technicians are full-time employees with a good technical background and strong human relations skills. Do not confuse this group with the computer technicians. Computer technicians at our college keep the main frame running, service the DOS and Macintosh networks, do backups on the main systems, etc. Instructional technicians, however, work on the lab floor managing the process to be certain all instruction is functioning smoothly. Their tasks generally are to—

1. Schedule and manage student assistants
2. Monitor the activities of orientations, grading, disk checkouts
3. Meet with faculty users to resolve lab problems
4. Respond to the more technical questions that student assistants can't answer
5. Do initial trouble shooting on nonfunctioning equipment
6. Serve as role models for all student assistants
7. Conduct training seminars for student lab assistants
8. Help the faculty in presenting seminars and workshops
9. Help with technical training of the faculty and staff.

Our lab now has 12 instructional technicians working in two centers, and their role continually expands. Salaries range from $18,000 to $30,000. The instructional technicians and student assistants are the backbone of the system.

Faculty. The faculty serves as both the heart and the brains of the system. Instructional ideas usually begin with faculty members, are usually created by faculty members, and are ultimately driven by faculty members. Some of our faculty friends who fear loss of a job because of computers must read this section.

Computers are forcing us to question the old paradigms with some fascinating results. Our observations at GCC show that faculty members who embrace technology generally work hard, are excellent planners, work smart, are very creative, and show tremendous enthusiasm for their work. The faculty responsibilities are broken into three categories: 1) authors and developers, 2) managers, and 3) facilitator.

Faculty authors and developers. These faculty members have the task of getting the necessary instructional materials into place. We cannot view this work as writing a book; instead, it is developing a system. The system requires us to consider hardware and software availability, training other staff members who will help in the lab, adding the activities and/or assignments to the database, preparing the database queries for sending letters, developing an orientation for the course, etc. Development of the system must involve the department chairperson, lead faculty in the subject area, interested faculty members, the laboratory center personnel, and the appropriate administrators.

With your lab infrastructure in place, the faculty authors get assistance from student assistants who keystroke the materials to check accuracy, instructional technicians who edit for clarity, and the faculty who edit materials to meet departmental standards. By the time the work is completed, the laboratory staff is trained and the software installed on the proper equipment. A pilot course is conducted getting the appropriate feedback from students, the faculty, and the laboratory staff. The author maintains a constant vigil on the success of the material used in the lab, with any negative feedback noted and made ready for the first revision. What you have is an authoring center built right into the centralized lab. The work is created, edited, revised, piloted, and finalized in the same space.

Faculty managers. Faculty managers are responsible for making the newly created system work in the open lab. The system must run smoothly, and the faculty managers work with the instructional team to smooth out the rough spots if any occur. Faculty managers also work with the database people to see that letters go out at the proper times, that data entry is current, extension requests properly expedited, and the integrity of the system is assured. The faculty managers are also responsible for sending grades to admissions and records regularly.

Faculty facilitator. Faculty facilitators have the main responsibility of providing quality one-on-one instruction in the laboratory. A referral system summons specific faculty to help solve unusual problems. The faculty facilitators are the bottom line in helping students find solutions to their problems. This requires the faculty to be very knowledgeable in a variety of technology courses and, in particular, to be skilled in teaching strategies and human relations. All faculty members serve as role models for the teaching team, but the facilitators are expected to be especially skilled because of their visibility in the open lab.

SUMMARY

The open computer laboratory concept is springing up all over the country and in all levels of education. We now have very powerful tools that can help make it happen. The change is going to upset budgets, job descriptions, faculty contracts, traditional teaching methodologies, traditional schedules, etc. Change is painful for many, but very exciting for others. One thing is guaranteed, if you want excitement and a renewed commitment to your profession, join the technology charge.

CHAPTER 13

EXPANDING HORIZONS BY TEACHING COURSES FOR BUSINESS

LENA M. CUNNINGHAM SMITH
Southwest Missouri State University, Springfield, Missouri

The "one career, one job" phenomenon has all but ended. Instead, as the jobless rate climbs above seven percent, the highest since 1986, the "five careers, 15 jobs, and many geographic moves" phenomenon is now upon us. The future is becoming synonymous with change. To manage such an impact, training and development are becoming critical strategies for corporations fighting for a competitive edge.

For example, U.S. business currently spends an estimated $210 billion annually on employer-based training—and expects that figure to keep growing. An investment of such size signals an emerging career field for corporate trainers, the professionals who assess needs and then design, develop, and deliver training/retraining programs for employees at all levels, offering courses that range from basic literacy to computer operations to international communication. In addition, a recent study by the American Society for Training and Development, the world's largest professional organization devoted to the use of human resources, shows 80 percent of the largest U.S. companies have maintained training and development budgets at full strength even though 54 percent have laid off workers in other areas. Even more significantly, 65 percent of the companies expect to increase training funds in the near future (Kleiman, 1992).

The needs of business. As more and more jobs require technical skills and as the job market becomes restructured in response to the emerging high tech/service economy, profound changes in the way people are used on the job are becoming apparent. Many people in the current work force are lacking in the skills needed to survive such changes. Deficiencies in basic skills of reading, writing, and math have been the first to surface, but increasingly higher-level skills are being needed but not found.

A report by the American Society for Training and Development and the U.S. Department of Labor, *Workplace Basics: The Skills Employers Want* (1988), says employers seek these skills:

- Adaptability, including creative thinking and problem solving
- Listening and good oral communication
- Group effectiveness: interpersonal skills, negotiation and teamwork
- Organizational effectiveness and leadership
- Competence in reading, writing, and computation
- The ability to learn—to absorb, process, and apply new information quickly.

When deficiencies affect the bottom line, employers have traditionally responded with training or replacement. The latter option is becoming less practical because the supply of workers in our U.S. labor force is shrinking. Increasingly, employers are forced to make rather than buy productive employees.

The training skills of educators. The field of training and development calls extensively upon a broad range of teaching skills, and the justification for training-styled teaching to become a formal part of higher education appears strong. The ASTD's *Models For Excellence* (1983) identifies the following skills for trainers: researching, analyzing, writing, teaching, leading group meetings, and platform speaking—skills which postsecondary teachers practice continually. Simply put, the study describes the main focus of training and development as "identifying, assessing—and through planned learning—helping to develop the key competencies which enable individuals to perform current or future jobs." The following ASTD list of generally accepted basic skills for trainers has great similarity to a job description an educator would draw up:

- Analyze performance problems to determine applicable training solutions
- Identify training needs
- Identify skills and knowledge requirements of jobs
- Assess performance before and after training
- Establish behavioral objectives for programs
- Design training programs
- Determine program content
- Apply adult learning theory in developing programs
- Evaluate instructional methods
- Develop training materials.

More specifically, the following model describes the knowledge and skill areas which an ASTD Competency Study has identified as important for excellent performance in the training and development field (reprinted from ASTD Handbook for Training And Development, (c) (1987), by permission of McGraw-Hill, publishers). The model contains 31 competencies:

1. **Adult learning understanding.** Knowing how adults acquire and use knowledge, skills, attitudes; understanding individual differences in learning.
2. **Audiovisual skill.** Selecting and using audiovisual hardware and software.
3. **Career development knowledge.** Understanding the personal and organizational issues and practices relevant to individual careers.
4. **Competency identification skill.** Identifying the knowledge and skill requirements of jobs, tasks, and roles.
5. **Computer competence.** Understanding and being able to use computers.
6. **Cost-benefit analysis skill.** Assessing alternatives in terms of their financial, psychological, and strategic advantages and disadvantages.
7. **Counseling skill.** Helping individuals recognize and understand personal needs, values, problems, alternatives, and goals.
8. **Data reduction skill.** Scanning, synthesizing, and drawing conclusions from data.
9. **Delegation skill.** Assigning task responsibility and authority to others.

10. **Facilities skill.** Planning and coordinating logistics in an efficient and cost-effective manner.

11. **Feedback skill.** Communicating opinions, observations, and conclusions such that they are understood.

12. **Futuring skill.** Projecting trends and visualizing possible and probable futures and their implications.

13. **Group process skill.** Influencing groups to both accomplish tasks and fulfill the needs of their members.

14. **Industry understanding.** Knowing the key concepts and variables that define an industry or sector (e.g., critical issues, economic vulnerabilities, measurements, distribution channels, inputs, outputs, and information sources).

15. **Intellectual versatility.** Recognizing, exploring, and using a broad range of ideas and practices. Thinking logically and creatively without undue influence from personal biases.

16. **Library skills.** Gathering information from printed and other recorded sources; identifying and using information specialists, reference services, and aids.

17. **Model building skill.** Developing theoretical and practical frameworks which describe complex ideas in understandable, usable ways.

18. **Negotiation skill.** Securing win-win agreements while successfully representing a special interest in a decision situation.

19. **Objectives preparation skill.** Preparing clear statements which describe desired outputs.

20. **Organization behavior understanding.** Seeing organizations as dynamic, political, economic, and social systems which have multiple goals; using this larger perspective as a framework for understanding and influencing events and change.

21. **Organization understanding.** Knowing the strategy, structure, power networks, financial position, and systems of a SPECIFIC organization.

22. **Performance observation skill.** Tracking and describing behaviors and their effects.

23. **Personnel and human resource field understanding.** Understanding issues and practices in other human resource areas (organization development, organization job design, human resource planning, selection and staffing, personnel research and information systems, compensation and benefits, employee assistance, and union labor relations).

24. **Presentation skills.** Verbally presenting information such that the intended purpose is achieved.

25. **Questioning skill.** Gathering information from and stimulating insight in individuals and groups through the use of interviews, questionnaires, and other probing methods.

26. **Records management skill.** Storing data in easily retrievable form.

27. **Relationship versatility.** Adjusting behavior in order to establish relationships across a broad range of people and groups.

28. **Research skills.** Selecting, developing, and using methodologies and statistical and data collection techniques for a formal inquiry.

29. **Training and development field understanding.** Knowing the technological, social, economic, professional, and regulatory issues in the field; understanding the role T&D plays in helping individuals learn for current and future jobs.

30. **Training and development techniques understanding.** Knowing the techniques and methods used in training; understanding their appropriate uses.

31. **Writing skills.** Preparing written material which follows generally accepted rules of style and form, is appropriate for the audience, is creative, and accomplishes its intended purposes.

A changing climate in higher education. Although the training and development field has maintained an informal association with the academic world over the years, strong ties between the two fields have not developed, according to Theodore J. Settle in the ASTD's *Handbook For Training And Development* (1987). However, not only the increasing pressure for trainers in business but also emerging trends of growth in the field of higher education make it clear that workplace trainees are becoming an important segment of the postsecondary population.

For example, Settle notes the traditional full-time student core of 18-to-22-year-olds is shrinking (or stabilizing at best) while the number of part-time students who are also full-time employees is expanding. In addition, many college students today are older adults returning to the classroom for a complete overhaul in career paths, retirees preparing for new careers, or those merely seeking personal enrichment and coping skills for a rapidly changing world.

While the reasons for the new environment in higher education are many, the results are a growing interest and willingness for the college-campus community to assist business in meeting its educational and training needs.

A changing climate for training. Increasing availability of academic resources is changing the traditional role of business trainers who, in the past, have been responsible for the complete package of training services. Yet even with this emerging source of support, trainers are hard pressed to keep up with the demand for their services, evidenced in one way by the growth in membership of the leading training organization, the American Society for Training and Development, whose membership has multiplied at least five times in the past 25 years.

A new role for trainers. With the specialized skills, teaching resources, and physical plants of a broad range of business faculty becoming more accessible, many business training departments are evolving from the "hands-on delivery" role to that of a managerial group involving multiple development and delivery options. Being able to utilize the external resources that college campuses provide now allows them to appeal to multiple learning styles, to offer greater choices in curriculum, and to greatly increase the efficiency and effectiveness of their services.

Sources of support. Higher education offers an amazing smorgasbord of academic courses, credit and noncredit continuing education workshops and seminars, internships, and cooperative education experiences—on-site or on college campuses—at relatively modest costs.

Training support may be obtained from some of the following centers on many college and university campuses: Management Development Institutes; Extension Services; and Departments of Continuing Education, Cooperative Education, and Internship. In addition, campus-wide public relations offices may maintain files on faculty members who are available for extracurricular teaching assignments.

Although many college/company agreements are in effect, several major associations of colleges and universities are also actively extending the relationship between private business training needs and college/university campus support systems. One such group, the American Council on Education, has developed three significant programs to strengthen private business/academic partnerships: first, a conference to explore college/corporation connections; second, a Business-Higher Education Forum for discussing mutual concerns; and third, a Program on Noncollegiate-Sponsored Instruction for articulating in-house academic programs and campus coursework.

Two other organizations, the American Association for Higher Education and the College Board Office of Adult Learning Services are promoting discussion on business/higher education linkups.

Another group, The Council on the Continuing Education Unit (CCEU), has made a significant contribution to the development of standards to use in self-appraisal of the quality of business training programs.

A final example of major national higher education organizations working to strengthen the relationships between higher education and business is the National University Continuing Education Association (NUCEA), whose primary purpose is to encourage the further expansion and improvement of continuing education for adults.

In addition to the previously mentioned major support groups, other educational institutions which typically enter into contracts with individual businesses for training services and which serve to strengthen education-business ties are two-year (community) colleges; vocational schools; private trade and technical schools; state educational cooperatives; and secondary school continuing education, adult education, and/or cooperative education centers.

Professional societies comprising trainers and/or educators also can be helpful in strengthening higher education-business relationships. Some of the larger groups are the American Association for Adult and Continuing Education (AAACE), American Society for Personnel Administration (ASPA), American Society for Training and Development (ASTD), Association for Educational Communications and Technology (AECT), National Society for Performance and Instruction (NSPI), and Society for Applied Learning Technology (SALT).

Although they are not education oriented, many industrial trade associations can be helpful as direct providers or sponsors of training and continuing education programs; they often include members with high, specialized educational backgrounds. Some of these trade associations are the American Arbitration Association, American Association of Industrial Management, American Bar Association, American Electronics Association, and the American Hospital Association.

Guidelines for academic/business linkups. To those exploring the possibilities of using campus resources to augment business training departments' capabilities, close observance of some time-tested guidelines is recommended. Virginia Mee, director of the Management Development Institute at Southwest Missouri State University, Springfield, who is an expert in planning training programs, offers the following practical suggestions:

1. Know the faculty members being considered for use as teachers in training programs, because excellent classroom teachers are not necessarily excellent

trainers. Learn their areas of expertise, their professional reputations in their fields, their personalities, and their values.

2. Spend time with potential faculty trainers to size up their compatibility with company representatives as well as with trainees who may have been out of the classroom for a long time. Seek to determine if the potential teacher has a sincere appreciation for knowledge and skills quite different from the academic environment. Ask: Does he/she have the type of empathy which will create comfortable communication with trainees?

3. Constantly use opportunities to network among the workplace and college campuses. Social occasions, church and civic meetings, sports activities, children's school events, and local news publications are sources of information about area postsecondary faculty who may have unique qualifications for training needs.

By getting to know each other, building personal confidence and trust, and creating mutual commitments to training goals, the teams of training professionals and higher education faculty can develop new, cost-effective ways to address both the education and training needs of today's work force.

Characteristics of effective training programs. The first step in designing successful training programs which educators might conduct is to clearly and precisely answer the question, "What is the problem?" A clearly-defined problem not only suggests the path to its solution but may even reveal that training would *not* be the right path to take. Training is not the answer to all workplace problems, but careful collection and analysis of all data relevant to the work situation in light of company goals will begin to identify those areas where training will be of benefit.

To help determine if training is a possible solution to a current problem, planners may clarify the picture by working through the following steps:

1. Write out a broad, general background of the current situation, then narrow down the description, one level at a time, to the present problem. (Sometimes this relationship can be more easily constructed by working backward from specific to general conditions.)

2. Study all conditions and changes occurring just before the problem emerged, using all available data such as job descriptions, task analyses, performance evaluations, and production records.

3. Make a "best guess" list of cause(s) of the problem.

4. Determine the type of training (if appropriate) needed to eliminate the problem.

Once the particular type of needed training has been identified, the familiar concepts of performance-based teaching methodology come into play: determining objectives and standards, developing course content, selecting instructional methods and media, pilot testing, and finally conducting the training program with trainees. Following training sessions, important follow-up tasks are initiating appropriate evaluative measures, revising, and replanning for future presentations.

Most postsecondary faculty members have backgrounds in teaching methodology and are trained to perform all of the steps just described. In addition, some university faculty, although lacking the educational pedagogy background, may nevertheless make excellent trainers because they are able to bring much rich experience into their classes and are able to relate very positively to work-oriented trainees.

The needs of adult learners. In past times, educators assumed that the same teaching/learning principles that were effective with children, known as *pedagogy*, would be equally effective with adults. However, research and experience have proven that such is not the case. Now, a unique set of teaching/learning principles for adults, known as *andragogy*, are found to be most effective in successful training programs. Some of the unique characteristics of adult learning include the following:

1. **Adults must want to learn.** They learn most effectively when they have a strong inner motivation to develop a new skill or to acquire a particular type of knowledge.

2. **Adults will learn only what they feel a need to learn.** They want to know "How is this going to help me right now?" Good trainers will explain what to do, how to do it, and why it must be done in terms of this need.

3. **Adults learn best by doing.** The importance of active participation in the learning process is greater among adults than among children. Retention of new knowledge or skills is much higher if the adult has immediate and repeated opportunities to practice what has been learned.

4. **Adults focus on realistic problems.** Research shows that adults learn much faster if they deal with real-life business experience and work out practical solutions from which broader principles may be drawn.

5. **Past experiences affect adult learning.** Such conditioning can be both an asset and a liability to present and future learning.

6. **Adults learn best in an informal environment.** Many adults may have negative memories of earlier school days. A nonthreatening, positive, supportive atmosphere increases self-confidence and motivation.

7. **Adults like variety and personalized applications.** Monotonous, time-wasting assignments are quickly rejected.

8. **Adults desire personalized feedback and positive, practical guidance rather than grades.** They react negatively and learn least in overly competitive, stressful situations.

While the individual is ultimately responsible for his/her degree of motivation and learning, a trainer can greatly encourage or discourage that process as learning needs are addressed. Postsecondary teachers are uniquely able to meet those needs.

Factors in selection of a training site. Different kinds of learning require unique environments. Experienced instructors can identify certain general characteristics, however, that are common to all good adult learning sites: easy access, quiet location, adequate space, flexible furniture, lighting and sound control, adequate wiring, and healthful ventilation. In addition, some other basic questions to be considered in selecting a meeting site are the following:

1. Are transportation services available to and from the site?

2. Are parking and handicap access adequate?

3. Are restrooms and food service conveniently close?

4. Are costs of vendor-provided services reasonable?

5. Is the facility's track record for this service a good one?

When researching facilities for training locations, generally speaking, nothing should be taken for granted; nothing takes the place of a written checklist of needs (see Exhibit 1) and a personal inspection of the site. Some critical though often overlooked needs for a good training site are the following: convenient placement of electrical outlets and light switches, room-darkening drapes or shades, heating/air conditioning thermostats or controls, storage areas, wastebaskets, and movable furniture.

Exhibit 1

Southwest Missouri State
U N I V E R S I T Y

Center for Business Research and Development
(417) 836-8907
(417) 836-5650

REQUEST FOR INFORMATION

Name _____ Phone _____

Company _____ FAX _____

Title _____ SS# _____

Address _____

Presentation Title: _____

1. Audiovisuals needed for presentation:
     Overhead projector – 35mm Slide projector _____
     VHS projector_____ Film projector _____
     Other needs (please specify) _____
2. Presentation Materials: (Please check one)
     _____ I have enclosed a copy of my presentation materials for the Management Development Institute to duplicate.
     _____ I will be sending a copy of my materials by the deadline date of_____to be duplicated by the Institute.
     _____ I will be bringing copies of my materials, collated and stapled.
     _____ I have no materials to be prepared.
3. Travel Arrangements:
     _____ No arrangements necessary.
     _____ Arrangements have been made through my company.
     _____ Please make the following arrangements for me.

Expenses are my responsibility unless arrangements have been made with Southwest Missouri State University in advance.

Please return all information to: JOYCE TRAYLOR, PROGRAM COORDINATOR
MANAGEMENT DEVELOPMENT INSTITUTE, SOUTHWEST MISSOURI STATE
UNIVERSITY, 901 SOUTH NATIONAL, SPRINGFIELD MO 65504

Used with permission of Joyce Traylor (1993).

A simple worksheet on which to itemize needs (and even sketch room layouts) can also serve as a written contract (see Exhibit 2 and 2a). Such a written agreement listing date(s), time(s), facilities and services to be provided, and costs/ payment plans agreed upon will not only lessen the possibility of foul-ups due to faulty communication but also will provide valuable records for future budgeting and planning. Another example of a convenient recordkeeping form is an income and expense statement designed by Joyce Traylor of Southwest Missouri State University's Management Development Institute (see Exhibit 3).

Exhibit 2

Title or description of training session:

Facility _____
Room Name(s) or Number(s) _____ Date confirmed _____
Facility Address _____
Contact Person _____ Phone _____
Date(s) of Meeting _____ Date confirmed _____
Estimated attendance _____
Confirmed attendance _____ Date confirmed _____

Hotel/Department to provide:

Setup by: Date _____ Time _____ a.m./p.m.
      Furniture: _____ tables, dimensions _____
          _____ chairs; number per table _____
      Furniture set-up style (back of page for diagram):
         _____ classroom style   _____ herringbone
         _____ theater style   _____ hexagon
         _____ U-shape   _____ V-shape
         _____ conference table   _____ multiple tables
         _____ closed square
      Service per table:
         _____ ice water   _____ ash trays
         _____ other *(please describe)*
      Handouts table (size, location) _____
      Easel (size, location) _____
      Speaker's table (size, location) _____
         Speaker's chair (description) _____
         Speaker's table service _____
         Speaker's table lectern _____

AV requirements:

         _____ overhead projector
         _____ TV/VCR
         _____ projection screen
         _____ flipchart frame, pad, markers
         _____ other *(please describe):*_____

Total cost (itemized list attached) _____
Payment plan _____

Signature/title of person placing order _____
Signature/title of person accepting order _____

Exhibit 2a

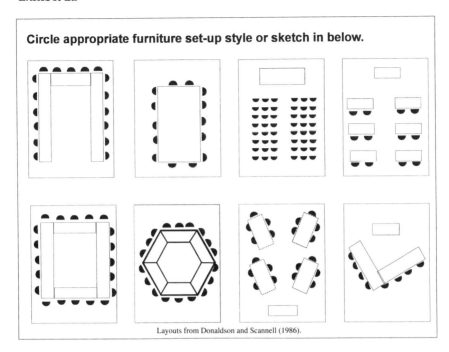

Circle appropriate furniture set-up style or sketch in below.

Layouts from Donaldson and Scannell (1986).

Generally speaking, although a place for conducting training need not be elaborate, it must be flexible—quickly adaptable to the group's changing needs as training progresses—and it must be isolated enough that trainees clearly understand that their purpose in being there is to learn. A well-chosen training site will contribute to the following results:

1. Objectives of the training session will be met, and the benefits promised to participants will be delivered.

2. Opportunities for group discussion and other interaction will be possible.

3. Physical facilities and equipment will be appropriate to the training situation, skill level, and personal needs of each participant.

4. Similarities between the training site and the work site will be close enough that measurement and evaluation of training effectiveness will be valid.

Summary. If the United States is to be competitive in the world market-place of the future, both business and education must work together to meet the needs of a new generation of workers. One such need is for continuous training or lifetime learning. Such heavy demands cannot and need not be borne solely by training staffs of individual companies, when nearby institutions of higher education have the faculty, the facilities, and the expertise to help with this new educational mission.

When planners realize the great similarity between the fields of training/ development and education, and when educators realize that training and re-training will be lifelong requirements for the future, the partnership will be sealed.

Exhibit 3

SOUTHWEST MISSOURI STATE UNIVERSITY
MANAGEMENT DEVELOPMENT INSTITUTE
INCOME AND EXPENSE STATEMENT

COURSE: _____

DATES: _____

REVENUES:
  ATTENDANCE:
  _____ @ Full Price of _____   = _____
  _____ @ Disc Price of _____   = _____
  _____ Guests
  _____ Total Attendance

  TEXT/MATERIAL FEES:
  _____ @ Price of   _____   = _____

  COORDINATION FEE   = _____

              TOTAL REVENUES   _____

INSTRUCTOR EXPENSES:
  Salary _____ Hours @ _____ per hour = _____
  Social Sec. Benefits   _____ @   7.65% = _____
  Retirement Benefits   _____ @   9.90% = _____
  Transportation/Food/Lodging   = _____
  Contract Price: _____ Attendees@ _____ = _____
  State Reimbursement:
  _____ Hours @ $25.00 = _____ @   50.00% = _____

              TOTAL INSTRUCTOR EXPENSES   _____

OTHER EXPENSES:
  Books   @   = _____
  Brochure Printing   = _____
  Brochure Labeling   = _____
  Certificates   _____ @ $0.18   = _____
  Name Tents   _____ @ $0.13   = _____
  Food Service Charges   = _____
  Refreshments   = _____
  Name Tags   _____ @ $0.25   = _____
  Notebooks   _____ @ $2.65   = _____
  Folders   _____ @ $0.85   = _____
  Postage/Confirm. Ltr _____ @ $0.50   = _____
  Postage/Brochure   = _____
  Photocopying   _____ @ $0.04   = _____
  Mailing List Rental   = _____
  Other: _____   = _____

              TOTAL OTHER EXPENSES   _____

              TOTAL OPERATING EXPENSES   _____

              NET INCOME   _____

Used with permission of Joyce Traylor (1993).

REFERENCES

Carnevale, A. P.; Gainer, L. J.; and Meltzer, A. S. (1988). *Workplace basics: The skills employers want.* The American Society for Training and Development and U.S. Department of Labor.

Donaldson, L., and Scannell, E. E. (1986). *Human resource development—The new trainer's guide,* (pp. 145-147). Second Edition. Reading, Massachusetts: Addison-Wesley Publishing Company.

Kleiman, C. (1992, January 12). Employer-based training is a growing job source. *Chicago Tribune.* Section 8.

McLagan, P. A., and McCullough, R. C. (1983). *Models for excellence: The conclusions and recommendations of the ASTD training and development competency study.* Alexandria, Virginia: The American Society for Training and Development.

Settle, T. J. (1987). Colleges and universities. *Training and development handbook.* Third Edition. (Robert L. Craig, Editor-in-Chief.) Alexandria, Virginia: The American Society for Training and Development, Chapter 46.

Traylor, J. (1993). Sample Information Forms. Springfield, Missouri: Management Development Institute, Southwest Missouri State University.

CHAPTER 14

EXPANDING HORIZONS OVERSEAS

BURT KALISKI

New Hampshire College, Manchester, New Hampshire

As you have read in many other chapters of this yearbook, change is taking place in what has been the traditional role of American business education and the American business educator. Our mission is changing, and our curriculum is changing. Our teaching materials are changing, and our methodology is changing. There is yet another change underway, one that will provide tremendous opportunity for the business educator. It is a change in the site at which we carry out our work. In Chapter 13, you read about teaching away from the traditional classroom by professing in the business environment. In this chapter, you will read about another, more distant change of locale.

The expansion of international business has brought with it many opportunities for the American business educator, especially at the collegiate level. We are in a position to expand our horizons to practice business education overseas in some very interesting and challenging ways. One of these ways is traditional teaching for a college or university in another country. Yet another is serving as a consultant for business education abroad. Another way is to open one's own business overseas.

Every new opportunity brings with it challenges in such areas as language, culture, finances, and personal concerns. What we hope to bring you in this chapter is a glimpse of how opportunities overseas occur, how they are planned and executed, and how one can deal with the challenges of such a venture. We'll travel from Bulgaria to Malaysia to Tanzania to East Africa to New Zealand in the next few pages with personal testimony from those who have traveled. Come along for a glimpse of ways to expand your horizons overseas.

BULGARIA

The American University in Bulgaria is an American-Bulgarian joint enterprise. Its organization came quickly on the heels of the collapse of the Bulgarian Communist Party's (BCP) last dictatorship under Todor Zhivkov, in November of 1989. Both American and Bulgarian faculty were recruited; some 200 first-year students were selected; and the former BCP regional headquarters in Blagoevgrad was readied to house the university. The city is located high in the Pirin Mountains in southwestern Bulgaria. Classes began in the fall of 1991.

I saw an ad in *The Chronicle of Higher Education* in August of 1991. At once I applied for a position teaching English, and one month later I found myself in Bulgaria, where my colleagues and I set about establishing the first American-style university in a formerly communist country. Readers can imagine what a breathless month I had that August: arranging for a leave of absence from New Hampshire College, where I was a professor and coordinator of the Business Communications Program, renting my house for a year and seeing that it was looked after, selecting books to take with me, packing only two suitcases with enough clothing and other personal items to last a year, making banking arrangements, and taking care of mail, etc. The pace was breathless, but the adventure and the idea of participating actively in one of history's watershed moments spurred me on.

I travelled to Harvard Square to visit book shops. I bought a four-volume English-Bulgarian/Bulgarian-English dictionary at about $70 per volume. Later in Sofia, I could have picked up all four volumes for $4. I bought some language tapes and practiced survival phrases. We had a few books about Bulgaria in our library, which I read with relish—only to find that conditions had almost no relation to what I read about. In transitional economies, one just does not know what one can find in the shops; preparation is a key task. I would look long and hard for such things as pencils, ballpoint pens, writing paper, and file folders—even simple aspirin tablets were scarce.

Medical issues also need attention. We were told not to drink, or even brush our teeth with tap water due to risk of Hepatitis A infection. The region also has endemic Hepatitis B, which required a series of spaced shots. The embassy in Sofia, a hardship posting, also told us to avoid Bulgarian dentists due to risk of HIV infection caused by improper sterilization techniques. Some observed the warnings; some did not. I did not hear of colleagues getting into trouble.

The actual teaching was a joy. Our students came from the 20 or so English-language high schools scattered around the country. The American University administered the SAT's, and our students averaged over 1100 combined. The scores are remarkable, since the tests must be culture-bound to some degree, and our students took them in a second language. Aside from an exceptionally rosy view of all things American, the students were critical of our curricula from the outset—mostly that we were not sufficiently demanding. They are eager to succeed, and most of my students were particularly eager to learn about business. As opposed to their immediate predecessors, who often sought to make lives for themselves in the West, most of my students were determined to stay in Bulgaria to make their country work. This new attitude was one that students themselves often mentioned.

The professional class in Bulgaria truly needs business know-how. For example, my landlord was a skilled surgeon employed by the Commission of Mines. At the age of 50 he was forced to leave the government job. He was often bored to death merely looking after the building that we shared with other members of his family, but he had neither the resources nor the knowledge of how to open his own private practice. The same was true for many psychologists I met. They were free for the first time to open private practices, but they did not know the first step. Two very skilled psychologists I met worked all day giving tests to prospective long-distance truck drivers—and did nothing else in spite of their training as counselors. There is a tremendous amount of talent going unused in Bulgaria for want of some expensive resources—but most importantly, for want of information.

Another problem I saw relates directly to the transitional economy. There was high inflation and tremendous unemployment during my year in Bulgaria. I should point out that *all* of our students were on scholarship because they could not afford even modest tuition. In communist days, the centrally-directed economy kept people fed and working. Now there was a lot of unrest and a marked increase in violent crime. Many authorities, like chiefs of police or mayors, were holdovers from the previous regime. The current government had won general elections by the narrowest of margins, and the increasing social and economic dislocation began to make the old regime look relatively good. Old communists had hopes of a return to power, or at least to regain some of the power they had lost. As a result, the country experienced "selective enforcement" of law and a notable rise in crime. The increase in gang violence that is marking city life in the former Soviet states is also occurring in Bulgaria. One Bulgarian friend opened a tiny restaurant on the outskirts of Blagoevgrad. He had been open for less than a month when the Bulgarian "mafia" demanded protection money. Within a week of my friend's refusal to pay, his building was destroyed by high explosives. The police basically shrugged their shoulders.

Life in Bulgaria is difficult, especially if one is living on one's own and without the support of a family. I noticed that the Bulgarian family was particularly close. This closeness really is a necessity. For a time during the depths of winter certain commodities would disappear from the shops. One might go days without dairy products in town. People could get by if Uncle Bogdan from the countryside could bring in some cheese, maybe a container of milk, and some yogurt. In turn, he might want to borrow a few litres of benzene to make the trip. As a single person, I did not have a network to help with shopping and other chores.

We also had severe shortages of electricity, often having service two hours on, two hours off, around the clock. I found this shortage to be very difficult psychologically. The darkness and the icy winds are a lot to bear when days turn into weeks. My colleagues and I often found ourselves teaching in our winter coats in the dark. The unreliable water supply also caused some "Bulgarian moments," as we came to call them. A reader might find it humorous; but as a participant, I can vouch that it is not so funny, when, having mustered the courage to attempt a cold shower in a fifty-degree flat, and when having gotten thoroughly covered with soap, I discovered that both the electricity and water were suddenly off—and would be off for the next few hours. Some colleagues did not last the year under these conditions.

I would close by noting that business education is desperately needed in Eastern Europe. Over the next generation, I foresee a tremendous need for both theoretical and practical training. My brief experience with university students suggests that the university will be only one setting for business education. Persons like my surgeon-landlord and my psychologist friends do not need professional education as much as they need information on applying their skills in private practice. My friend and his obliterated restaurant show that education in the ways of entrepreneurship is only part of the answer. The political and social climates are currently in turmoil, so it is not difficult to see why investors would think twice before taking risks in countries like Bulgaria. But my own American optimism and the ingenuity of the people I met bode well for them in the long run. The next several years will be very difficult but exciting for American business educators in Bulgaria, where they will not so much be learning the ropes as creating them.

John P. Fleming
Professor of English & Communications at
New Hampshire College, Manchester, New Hampshire

MALAYSIA

I was anxious to embark on a new personal odyssey after attending an American Collegiate Retailing Association conference where one of the panel discussion topics was international retailing, my ongoing research topic. However, I did not know at that time that an opportunity would soon come my way that would take me to the other side of the world.

For several months I had been working with one of our senior marketing majors, who intended to open a fashion business in his native Malaysia after graduation. Although he had never been a student in any of my retailing or fashion merchandising classes, a colleague had recommended that he contact me as a resource person. As educators, I believe we all try to help students outside the classroom, but we are also aware that seldom do undergraduate projects become a reality. As this young man's twice-a-month visits became twice a week, I became impressed with his persistence, tenacity, and desire to make his dream come true.

Later that spring I was invited to be a guest of his family in Malaysia as we explored the feasibility of a silk apparel and accessory business. In the mid-eighties I had thoroughly enjoyed teaching in London for a year, so I had no qualms about accepting the offer. In fact, certain of my colleagues take great pleasure in chiding me about my habit of carrying my passport with me should someone ask me to travel on short notice. My only stipulation was that I be allowed enough time to study and photograph Malaysian retail institutions.

Since the five-week trip would take place in the summer, it was not necessary to secure sabbatical or personal leave. I prepared personally by having lengthy discussions with my host and reading up on the business and cultural background of the country. In retrospect I should have done more, although there's nothing that can actually prepare you for the time-warp-culture-shock aspects of a journey to a developing country.

Having survived the 26-hour trip to northern Malaysia, I did have many opportunities to learn and grow personally and professionally. I did tour the retail stores and shopping centers as planned and also had the opportunity to meet with a public relations director of a large department store chain who was instrumental in helping me gather materials for a textbook that I was writing at the time. I took hundreds of slides which I use in virtually all of my classes and kept a journal to record my observations. As an informal visiting professor, I did have the opportunity to visit the new University of Northern Malaysia, speak to faculty there, and even locate the first edition of my text in their library. I enjoyed helping some of the friends of my host, who were recent graduates, develop their resumes and cover letters and fine-tune their interview techniques as they prepared to enter the job market. Many young Malays are educated in the United States or the United Kingdom and go back to teach in Malaysian universities. Several of the professors I met were in their twenties.

The highlight of the trip for me was to visit the east coast batik country, where fine cotton and silk fabrics are prepared using a wax relief method and then painted or block printed in glorious colors. It was these products that had originally piqued the interest of my host. We also visited the state training center called Kraftangan, which serves as a school where young people can learn traditional crafts such as batik painting and songket weaving. Often these students have completed the equivalent of British "O" level exams, but will advance no further academically. Many learn craft production because they must, not because they want to or are necessarily talented in those areas. The program lasts a year and although there is no formal placement service or follow-up with the graduates, the center director did mention that only about 25 percent of the people would stay in the field. The others would probably marry or find other work. There seemed little motivation to be entrepreneurial.

Since that first visit I have returned to Malaysia four times. Fortunately, my trips have been synchronized with the academic calendar. I recognized the business potential of the batik products and also the opportunity to use my creative talents that had been a bit dormant. Somewhere across the Pacific on the first return trip I became a partner in Sy Lyn Enterprise Senderian Berhad, a trading and manufacturing company. My Malaysian counterpart is a shareholder in Silk Accent, Inc. the U.S. sales and distribution division.

In the fall of 1992 we exhibited our line of hand-painted batik silk scarves in trade shows in four major U.S. cities. In the spring of 1993 we shipped our first orders of Malaysian-made goods to specialty-store retailers in the United States and in the Caribbean. We now have sales representatives in two U.S. regions and are continuing to develop the market as we move into our second fashion season. This summer, Silk Accent U.S.A. will open its first retail store in Alor Setar in the state of Kedah, Malaysia, carrying women's apparel, accessories and cosmetics made in Malaysia and in the United States. We hope it will be the perfect blend of East and West.

Every trip has made me more and more aware of the challenges that must be faced in the course of doing business internationally and living in a foreign country for extended periods of time.

Malaysia is shifting rapidly from an agricultural to an industrial economy. Their Vision 2020 plan sees the country fully industrialized by that year. The labor wage rate is low by Western standards, as is the cost of living—for the moment. Many government and business leaders feel that the ethnic balance of Malay, Chinese, and Indian races must be kept. They also believe that Malaysian industries should be protected and exports encouraged. Banks are advertising low interest loans for Malay-owned businesses. Yet progress is not taking place without growing pains.

Doing business in the country is a challenge and, for the expatriate, communication is sometimes difficult. Although most everyone speaks some English,

I found that even though a discussion may begin in English, it soon lapses into Malay, and often important points are lost in the transition. Even Malays joke about being on "Malaysian time"—in other words not overly concerned if appointments aren't kept exactly on time. Inefficiencies frequently confound schedules. For example, it took me almost an hour to cash travelers' checks in a local bank. It took threats from my partner that I had an appointment with the Sultan to get them to hurry. (I didn't, by the way.)

The general attitude toward environmental concerns and the role of women is much like it was in the United States in the 1950s. The conservatism and restraint of a Muslim country are very much a part of the social fiber but are being challenged by what is perceived as "Western values." Often, however, it seems to be the worst of the West that is exposed and the best overlooked. It is the young people—my partner's generation—who will begin to see changes.

Overcoming jet lag and living in 90-degree heat with near 100 percent humidity takes getting used to. I found I could not work a 10-or-12-hour work day as I often do in the states; four to five hours productive time was more realistic. Food is largely rice-based and can be very, very spicy. This also requires a period of adjustment. Accepting differences—from sometimes primitive toilet facilities to distinctly different tastes in home decor or apparel, to shopping at outdoor food markets where dinner may be brought home still alive—is the key to not only surviving, but flourishing in a foreign country.

Muslim women in Malaysia are expected to dress covered up from head to toe, although I was not held to such stringent standards. The females in the household where I stay frequently dress Western themselves, but they do expect me to follow some of the proprietaries. For example, they prefer that I not wear shorts outside the house and do cover up a bit more than I would in 90-degree summer heat in the United States. I have found some of the constraints difficult for an independent American woman to adjust to. Because I am an unrelated female in the household, I am not allowed to be alone in the house with my male partner. By Muslim law it doesn't matter if I'm 18 or 80, married or single, or in my case, a grandmother. It's sometimes difficult to be a gracious guest. With each trip I find my cultural awareness has expanded, but I find the East-West differences more rather than less apparent.

Personal reflections: There is no question in my mind that at this stage of my life I do have two demanding full-time careers—college educator and business executive. This is not for everyone.

Though the pressures of getting a new business up and running are omnipresent, the experiences I have had and the knowledge I have gained continue to enrich my teaching on a daily basis. Most of my students will probably never go to Malaysia, but all will need to interact with people in our global economy. Perhaps some will work for foreign companies or divisions of U.S. corporations abroad. It is my hope that one shred of information or personal experience that I have been able to share with them in the classroom will help to open their eyes to a whole new world.

When I stop to consider what brought me from New Hampshire to Malaysia I do wonder, why me? My new business partner says it's because I took the time to listen to him, took him seriously, and was willing to share my expertise with him, whether or not there was financial gain for me. These might be good points to consider for other educators seeking unbounded opportunities to travel, learn, and maybe become part of the international business community.

Some advice to others who would do what I have done:

1. Keep an open mind.

2. Have patience.

3. Learn the language.

4. Talk to people.

5. Listen even more.

6. Try everything new.

The real risk and reward:

I find that when the time comes to go home I'm not always sure where that is.

Lynda R. Gamans
Associate Professor of Fashion Merchandising
New Hampshire College, Manchester, New Hampshire

TANZANIA

As my sabbatical approached in 1986, I continued to assess the possibilities of doing something different. Our college allows us one-half year at full pay or one full year at half pay for approved sabbaticals. For many educators, money is a key issue, and hence, many stay at home and conduct research and write to avoid losing money on a sabbatical. I also found it much easier to find many more reasons why I shouldn't do something different, than why I should. House and pet-sitting, children's education, friends, relatives and parents, the spouse's job, and, of course, money, were all likely reasons to advocate business as usual. However, a number of other factors were impacting on change. My wife and I love to travel and were both approaching 40 years old; international experience was becoming a necessity in my field; and frankly, we needed a change. An overseas "experience" sounded like the right medicine.

I had seen a number of Fulbright brochures, and after reading one, I called the Fulbright office in Washington D.C. and talked to an area coordinator in my discipline. A complete packet was forwarded to me and, after some discussion with my wife, I decided to apply. The Fulbright process is long and inefficient. September applications for the following June through August often aren't decided on until May. Your application may make the first cut, but not the second or final cut. Hence, as in my situation, you may be held in limbo until the very end, and then told you didn't make the final cut. My first Fulbright application, a sabbatical leave, came down to two applicants. I was told in May I was not the one selected. I took my sabbatical leave in September, as I had applied on a dual project basis, and you guessed it, wrote an article. With the knowledge that my institution might grant me leave-without-pay, I reapplied immediately for the following September. We found out May 15, 1987, that we would be leaving two months later to work in Tanzania for one year. With my institution's blessing, my leave-without-pay was granted, and we booked flights, sent telexes, found house and pet-sitters, sent books and materials, talked to our children's teachers, got shots, passports, and visas, arranged for our affairs to be looked after, packed, and in general, almost had a nervous breakdown. The Fulbright selection process has little concern for the time constraints of the applicant or institution.

My position was as a senior lecturer at the Eastern and Southern Management Institute (ESAMI) in Arusha, Tanzania. ESAMI is a regional teaching institute that offers management programs for both mixed and homogeneous groups of middle and upper managers all over eastern and southern Africa. The programs are presented on campus in Arusha, and in Kenya, Uganda, Lesotho, Burundi, Zambia, Zaire, and Swaziland, as well as in other locations. The programs are intensive and run from two to six weeks. Classes meet from 9:00 to 5:00 daily. I participated in a number of teaching and consulting assignments, and almost nothing can be presented the way it normally is in the United States. Teaching adults in a foreign land is difficult enough, but most of the courses at ESAMI included representatives from as many as eight East African countries, each with its own unique business, political, and cultural climate. Consequently, part of each class was often devoted to understanding and discussing the similarities and differences existing in the respective environments. I was given no orientation at ESAMI, and like most teachers, I responded by reiterating what I had been doing successfully in the past. However, given that most management theories were developed largely in and for the Western world, there is little direct application for those theories in many developing nations. Students were not interested in Western generalizations, and everything I was accustomed to doing in the U.S. classroom was open for analysis. I was forced to reassess my pedagogical assumptions and reexamine completely the content, style, and meaning of all my material. Much of what I did became a result of trial and error. It was an excellent experience in teaching in an ad hoc environment where one is forced to truly think about the end product. Few of us do that on a regular basis in normal teaching environments. As might be expected, the differences in culture are both obvious and subtle. Attitudes and values involving family, women's rights, corruption, adultery, education, politics, and religion made teaching an entirely new experience. As a teacher, I could no longer assume anything and expect it to be correct. This made for a sometimes stressful, but wonderful learning experience. Our home and social lives were different as well. My wife, Lynn, substituted and volunteered at the local international school that our children, ages 7 and 9, attended. Spouses often have difficulty getting employment overseas due to visa restrictions. The international school turned out to be a very positive experience for our children, and making friends was not a problem. Our grocery shopping revolved around weekly open-air market ventures, and the closest medical and dental facilities were in Nairobi, four hours away by car. One of the highlights of our stay was the many good friends we made among the expatriate community. We went to more parties and danced more than we had in years at home. During our stay we were able to travel on both business and pleasure to Mauritius, Madagascar, Lesotho, and many parts of Tanzania and Kenya. We visited the Serengeti three times and other parks at Lake Manyara,

Tarangarie, and many others. We also stopped in Europe and camped on the way home.

Fulbrights in developing countries are the least competitive and can be financially workable. If one is out of the country for 330 days, any salary received may be tax exempt. This is critical, as, given the current tax laws (foreign tax credit), one may end up paying taxes in two countries at a total marginal rate of 50 percent or more. A complete understanding of the tax implications before accepting an overseas position may avoid financial hardship and general disappointment upon return.

A year away in a strange and different culture is a wonderful experience, and it forced us to reexamine the values and assumptions that shape our lives. The culture shock upon returning home was worse than when we arrived in Tanzania. We were shocked to be back in a system that seems to pay tribute to the clock, even though it inevitably squeezes our lives into smaller and less meaningful segments. Overall though, it was a wonderful experience, and I would recommend it to someone who is interested in experiencing change. As someone mentioned to us before leaving, treat it as adventure, as you will surely experience both positive and negative aspects.

EAST AFRICA

The American Participants (AMPART) speakers program is a program sponsored by the United States Agency For International Development (USAID) that serves to expose Americans to international environments, as well as provide Western views on a variety of subjects to the international community. It is generally open to educators, business men and women, and administrators who have written articles about or have worked in areas that may be of interest to the international community. During my Fulbright stay I had met a number of Americans who were touring Africa and lecturing under the AMPART program. Upon returning from my Fulbright, I contacted an AMPART representative and discussed the possibility of conducting a speaking tour in East Africa. The AMPART representative matches up the topics being requested, the countries requesting them, and the speakers' interests, and attempts to put together a speaking tour that must involve a minimum 10-working-day assignment, that, including travel, will often end up being about three weeks or more. After a long period of discussion and negotiation, I contracted to speak in Somalia and Zambia on a variety of subjects during a three-week period in the summer of 1990. I was to be paid $100 per day honorarium for the days I actually lectured, plus per diem and travel expenses. I was routed through England, Zambia, Kenya, Somalia, Kenya, Greece, and back to the United States. The most difficult part of this trip was that one had to be able to speak on a variety of prearranged topics, and even these often changed once one arrived in the host country. I had brought enough material to be able to put lectures/speeches together for different audiences. I often would change or even prepare a new lecture the night before. Also, the travel schedule was very difficult, and one had to be prepared to work almost immediately upon arrival in the host country. My experience as a Fulbrighter prepared me for everything but my experiences in Somalia, which due to curfews made the stay unpleasant and nerve-wrack-ing. Educationally, I was again able to learn more about a variety of countries and also test many of the ideas and concepts I had written about with a variety of audiences, including students, the general population, and business and government workers and managers. Overall, the experience was rewarding, as I was able to visit and learn about additional countries and learn firsthand many things about USAID.

NEW ZEALAND

As my next sabbatical approached, my wife Lynn and I investigated various possibilities and decided on New Zealand. We had started writing letters to schools in Australia and New Zealand about two years prior to my sab-batical, which was to commence in 1992. After the experience in Tanzania, we had decided to try an English-speaking country. After a large number of faxes, I accepted a nine-month position as a senior lecturer in the Depart-ment of Finance at Massey University on the North Island of New Zealand. Massey is a government-funded university with approximately 12,000 stu-dents. Since the appointment coincided with their school year, a March start, I would be alone for the first four months. We were somewhat apprehensive about three things: being separated for four months, Lynn's having to quit her job (as a middle school librarian her school would not grant a leave of absence for three months), and our teen-aged children's anxiety about mak-ing new friends and being "forced" to spend their summer in school in New Zealand.

My position, as a visiting senior lecturer, focused on supervision of stu-dent research, guest lecturing, and a graduate case-study course, Mergers and Acquisitions. For some of my students, this was their first case course, as most of the classes in New Zealand are lecture-focused. I also got the oppor-tunity to teach in a large-lecture format to 260 students. My department had a Reuters machine that provided on-line global stock market, quotations, news, and sports information, and there was a variety of U.S. television broadcast daily. Massey operates as does any large university in the United States and provides a variety of experiences both socially and academically. On any given day, there are many faculty presentations around Massey that provide an opportunity to meet faculty in other disciplines. A faculty club, with a $12 annual fee, allowed for social contacts on Thursday, Friday, and Saturday evenings, where discussions over a pint of bitter took place. Be-cause of the small size of New Zealand, one can get to know almost all of the major players in one's academic or business area of interest. Within a short period of time I knew many of the people in New Zealand in my specialty area.

One of the positive aspects of being situated in New Zealand was the possibility for travel. Our family visited Indonesia, Australia, Fiji, and the North and South Islands of New Zealand. On the negative side, there is little central heating in New Zealand, and while we were there New Zealand experienced the coldest winter on record (our summer). The children had to wear uniforms in school, which they didn't enjoy, and found five months a short time period to make friends. Hence, their experience wasn't as positive as we had hoped. Also, the transition into the New Zealand schools, and back into our U.S. system, was not as easy as we anticipated. We felt there didn't seem to be consistent and comprehensive school policies at either end for situations such as ours. Flexibility doesn't seem to be in the vocabulary of some teachers and school systems.

Overall, the adjustment we experienced in coming to New Zealand was easier than we expected. As an academic, I experienced a new educational system and gained many new ideas and a broader perspective on Asia, Australia, and New Zealand. We also enjoyed spending time where stress is not nearly as prevalent as we know it in the United States.

R. Larry Johnson
Professor of Finance
New Hampshire College, Graduate School of Business
Manchester, New Hampshire

CONCLUSION

Opportunity is limited only by imagination. Most of us can do much of what we want to do, regardless of current job, family responsibilities, and financial constraints. One direction for business educators, particularly at the collegiate level, is to expand our horizons overseas. Feel free to imagine and to contact any of the authors to help you practice your vocation in a non-traditional way.

CHAPTER 15

EXPANDING HORIZONS THROUGH LOCAL AREA NETWORKS

PATSY A. DICKEY-OLSON

Western Illinois University, Macomb, Illinois

A local area network (LAN) is a system of software and hardware that connects computers and allows users to do such things as access common files, share software programs, share hardware, and communicate between computers via electronic mail. LANs can be used in a limited area such as one building or several buildings in close proximity. Most LANs are used to connect devices in about a 2,000-foot radius. They require their own wiring instead of the use of existing telephone wiring. A cable can connect all of the network components. LANs usually transmit at a rate ranging from 256 kilobits per second to over 100 megabits per second. Various models and their cabling can change this rate. LANs can be installed where need is the greatest because they can work independently of a central main frame installation.

The decision to install a network cannot be a swiftly conceived and executed event. Careful planning and considerable thought must precede any decision to install a LAN. A chaotic atmosphere may be the end result if the decision to buy and implement a LAN is made without careful consideration.

The results can also be chaotic if training sessions are not conducted methodically and thoroughly. There are preferred instructional methods for introducing networks and their uses to the employees involved. This chapter introduces numerous guidelines for implementing a local area network and training employees how to use the LAN once it is in place.

PLAN, PLAN, PLAN

Administrators must decide whether or not their department or college really needs a LAN. A formal study conducted by competent personnel should determine definite requirements and needs. The cost of installing a LAN is significant. Once a decision is made to install a LAN, it must remain in place. Costs for maintaining the network and installing future versions of software must be considered. Keep in mind that hidden costs can be expensive.

MANAGEMENT SPONSORSHIP AND SUPPORT

No LAN installation project should be attempted without first having full key management sponsorship and support. Time spent in preparation for the installation of a LAN will be wasted time if management puts a stop to your work when the project is ready to be activated. It is always best to have a champion at the management level.

CHECKLIST OF NEEDS

The first step in the decision process should be to develop a formal study committee to assess the present and future computing needs of the school. The committee should consist of qualified personnel. If there is no information systems department, a knowledgeable computer user from another part of the organization may serve on the committee.

The formal study committee should first address the question, "Why does this school or department need a network?" Every future system user should be interviewed at great length to determine actual needs. The information needs must be discussed and identified. If the users need a mechanism for sharing printers and files, there are less complicated and less costly methods to accomplish this, such as switches, spools, buffers, and boxes. For example, to allow several users access to a laser printer, a simple printer switch may be a more appropriate solution instead of a LAN. Once the definite need for a local area network has been established, the committee can proceed with checklists of what will be needed—the type of LAN, hardware, software, and room layout.

Design of the LAN. There are various options available when designing and building a LAN. Four factors to consider make these options possible. These factors are physical layout or topology, access method or protocol, physical connections or cabling, and network operating system or NOS.

Topology refers to the method by which the information flows on the network. Typical topologies are the bus, ring, star, and distributed star or tree. The terminals or workstations are placed around a hub or master file server in a definite pattern. Merits and demerits of various topologies and what importance they have to the finished network should be discussed. Each has its benefits, and these should be explored.

Bus. A bus system is a simple design with a single length of cable known as the bus or trunk. (See Diagram 1.) Workstations are attached to the trunk like leaves off of a branch. The advantages of the bus are its simplicity and economy. The only consideration in wiring a bus is that the trunk must pass by each networked device. Because all devices share the bus line, the cost of the wiring may be lower than with topologies that require lengths of dedicated wire. A disadvantage is that if there are many users, the network will slow down. Bus networks perform best for such applications as electronic mail, sharing of resources like printers, and file transfers from one machine to another. The most common network for microcomputers is a bus network called Ethernet.

Star. The star topology is arranged like a star (see Diagram 1) with cables radiating from the hub or file server. More cable is required in this style as each workstation has its own dedicated cable. This increases the cost. A star configuration is suitable for larger networks with many workstations that make frequent disk access. Each workstation cable is dedicated solely to the hub, eliminating cable activity which would bottleneck on other topologies.

Diagram 1

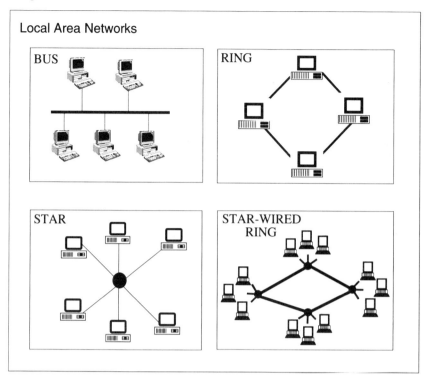

Local Area Networks

Ring. A token ring network is arranged loosely in a ring shape (see Diagram 1). A "token" or signal is passed continually around the network seeking data that any of the workstations might be sending. A workstation must wait until it receives this token in order to send data along the line. An advantage of having a ring system is that it gives the maximum distance between workstations. A disadvantage is that if the cable fails at any point, the entire network will stop. This disadvantage can be overcome by modifying the ring structure into what is called a star ring configuration. This would add to the amount of cable required. The most common ring network is International Business Machine's Token Ring Network.

Distributed Star. The distributed star connects workstations to a central hub. This hub can support several workstations which, in turn, can support other work stations. Distributed star topologies can be easily adapted to the physical arrangement of the installation site. If the site has a high concentration of workstations in a given area, the system can be configured to more closely resemble a star topology. If the terminals are dispersed, the system can use inexpensive hubs with long runs of cables which are shared between hubs. This has a similarity to the bus topology. The distributed star can acquire many of the advantages of either the bus or the star topology.

Access Method. Access methods or protocols are the arrangements used to ensure that each workstation has fair and equal access to the network. The main protocols are contention and token passing.

Contention protocols feature Carrier Sense Multiple Access (CSMA) and Carrier Sense Multiple Access with Collision Detection (CSMA/CD). Access is on a first-come, first-served basis for both methods. The CSMA design is very similar to a CB radio. Stations with data to send listen to the channel and wait until it is clear to transmit data. With the CSMA/CD, if two or more workstations transmit simultaneously, their messages will collide. As soon as a terminal detects a collision, it stops transmission, monitors the network until it hears no traffic, and then retransmits.

Token Passing protocol is an orderly access protocol. Each terminal passes on the opportunity to transmit, or token, to its closest neighbor until a station is found with a message to send. When the token reaches a station with data to send, a part of the token is changed and an indication that it is carrying a message is shown. As the token progresses the message goes with it. As each station checks the token from then on, it is looking for an indication that the message is intended for it. The receiving station reads the message and passes the token on. When the token gets back to the sending station, the message is removed and the token is put back to work going down the line again.

Software Considerations. Whether applications packages will run on a network or whether you will need a new software version should be discussed. There are multiuser software characteristics, such as integrity and security, and requirements which must be resident in the program for it to work properly. Many single-user programs are not suited to network use. Common software packages are word and text processing, spreadsheets, databases, and electronic mail. Graphics, accounting packages, scheduling and calendar programs, and project management programs are also becoming popular. A never-ending parade of software can be obtained. Schools may wish to continue to purchase educational versions of software even though they have limited features. There may be a cost advantage to the educational software.

Software for simultaneous users. Committee members should be aware of the price of multiuser software and the benefits derived from using network vs. stand-alone versions. Planners should consider legal implications involved in installing single-user software on a network. The cost of a site license versus the purchase of multiple copies of a program must be considered. Preplanning consideration should be given to technical problems which occur when the proper form of software is not used. There must be a license on file for each software package used. Specifications for running the software must be determined prior to purchasing the programs. The memory needed to run programs is always listed on the package, as well as the type of printers and monitors which are supported.

Network Operating System Software. Network operating system software is necessary to control the overall operations of the network. Among the functions provided by the NOS are the directory structure for shared hard disk storage devices, interface to the network for applications software, file service for sharing and using data, the means by which the network manager manages the network and its users, communications with other networks, and network security and data protection.

Careful consideration of the various packages on the market will help to ensure satisfaction with the completed network. Once again, the committee members should talk with other people using the product. A determination of what users like and don't like about the product they are using should be made. The ratings the product has received from organizations which administer benchmark tests should be accumulated. This may be as simple as going to the library and reading popular computer magazines.

Hardware. A determination of the location and number of workstations on the network is necessary. An analysis of workflow and what office systems will be included will make this determination more realistic. Careful planning must go into the determination of the number of workstations accessing the network. The number of simultaneous users allowed will be determined by the network operating system (NOS) chosen. LANs usually have less than 20 users per file server. Successful LANs can have as few as 10 stations to a file server. The more work stations attached to one file server, the slower the program processing becomes.

While businesses may be able to function with terminals and no disk drives, it would be best for schools to purchase equipment with two disk drives. There are occasions when a file server goes down or becomes inoperable. If the class is to continue, there must be drives from which the machines can be booted to allow students to continue working. Also, school personnel may wish students to store on floppy disks rather than the network so there is less clean-up work for instructors. There are times when instructors do not wish students to share files or disks. There will be less need for extremely large storage capacity on the file server if student data is stored on personal diskettes.

Plans should be made for the future needs as well as for those of the present. Vendor demonstrations and consultation are necessary prior to making a decision about types of machines which will be purchased. Discussions with other firms in the area which have installed LANs are also of value to the potential LAN user.

The purchase of additional hardware items to be taken into consideration are network cards, cables, hubs, tape backup system, and an alternate source of power.

Wiring. Plenty of thought should be given to wiring *prior* to having the actual room wired. Sound ergonomically-based layout plans for the comfort of employees who will be using the workstations should be implemented, rather than those plans software designers or vendors think are feasible. Once the wiring is in place, the cost to move it may be prohibitive. Vendors usually use coaxial and fiber-optic cable instead of ordinary telephone cable at this time. The increased use of images as well as text calls for the use of these two types of wiring. They are more suited to the faster transmission speeds desired today. Ordinary twisted pair telephone wire tends to allow electronic noise to corrupt the transmissions.

Office and Classroom Layout. Again, plans should be developed for employee or teacher comfort, not to please an engineer's design for functionality. A classroom layout should include attention to the instructor's mobility around the workstations and the direction the monitors face. There should be a specific location in the room where the instructor can see all screens at one time. If there are no breaks in the rows of workstations, the instructor must travel extra steps each day just to go from one side of the room to the other.

Careful planning should be accomplished prior to discussing the network with a vendor. Cables must never be left exposed on the floor just to accommodate a floor plan or workstation arrangement. Old tables and old wiring from old labs should not be used just because they are in the room. Plan ergonomically for future users.

Expansion. Future expansion should be of utmost importance as one plans for the current project. It should be foremost in a planner's mind that this is not the final piece of technology that will be invented.

CONSULTANT SERVICES

It is wise to obtain an expert's advice. Hiring a consultant will prove to be a wise decision if there is no resident expert on the school payroll. A consultant with a proven record in installing LANs will be worth the cost involved. Again, talk to satisfied users who have worked with the consultant before extending a contract to perform the work. Have a full set of questions ready for the consultant or vendor.

The consultant must have the welfare of the client in mind as the work is performed. Optimized information flow should not be the only goal in establishing a LAN. Information customer involvement is just as important. Consideration of the customer's needs as well as the desire to sell the system should be a goal of the vendor. LAN acceptance and success are sure to follow.

INSTALL NETWORK

There are important procedures to follow prior to letting users work with the network. Among these procedures are: hiring a network administrator, finding appropriate interfaces for users, testing the system, and testing the software.

Network Administrator. An individual in the organization should be assigned to administer the network and establish and maintain a stable network environment. It is impossible to allow all users to attempt to settle problems which might occur on the network. There is a need for both a LAN manager and a LAN technician. If there is more than one person assigned to these duties, it is easier to keep the LAN working. One person cannot always be on hand when trouble strikes.

Appropriate interface for users. An appropriate interface must be found for users. Command-driven and menu-driven interfaces are available. Most software companies are developing graphical user interfaces with icons to assist users and afford easy access to programs.

Testing. Each piece of software should be used extensively prior to allowing users to have access to it. Determine, for example, whether the printers will work with a given piece of software. Routine tests should be established for the LAN and the software so that users do not encounter problems. Set a school-wide standard and do not allow privately-owned software to be placed on the network. This is the only method by which you can control the spread of a virus which might destroy your software.

TRAINING

Many companies and educational institutions have formal training programs which meet varying needs of the users in their communities. The information center or group responsible for computer education must provide several avenues for users to learn about computers. Training sessions, workshops, well-prepared documentation, video tapes, and on-line help are different mechanisms for educating the users.

Informal Training Sessions. With the installation of a LAN, it is necessary to hold informal training sessions. Informal training sessions which take place on-site, at the user's desk, or in a central location within the department, are beneficial to first-time users of LANs. The informal and one-on-one setting makes users feel less threatened. Generally, the inexperienced or first-time user will ask more questions when the size of the group is small.

Workshops. Schedule, announce, and hold larger training sessions or workshops in a central location. Care should be taken to schedule workshops for times when the majority of users are less busy or are more able to attend. Users need easy access for sign-up or to register for the classes. Inexperienced users should not be mixed with knowledgeable users. Using prerequisite knowledge as requirements for workshops, you can more easily differentiate contrasting levels of users. Announce training sessions well in advance so users can plan to attend the sessions.

Documentation. Users should have informative and easy-to-read documentation available at all times. Long and involved manuals should be within reach of the users; however, the materials they use everyday should be quick and to-the-point. For basic local area network information (i.e., how to log on, how to send output to a network printer, how to change your password) documents should contain information which is brief and to the point. At the same time, the materials should explain fully the steps to be taken in using the software. Once beginners have mastered the material, advanced lessons should be available which contain detailed information and documentation.

Careful attention should be paid to the appearance of any documentation. There should never be too much information on a page. The same documenting conventions should be used for every document produced. The date should be placed on every document. Always let the user know where additional information can be found.

Video Tapes. Video tape training is one way to reach the user who cannot attend live training sessions. Video training may also be the preferred method for teaching complex or advanced concepts. Several companies produce professional quality video tapes and complimentary materials. Such companies offer tapes on specific software such as the most popular word processing, spreadsheets, and programming languages. Because there are few companies that work with network instruction, there is also the possibility that a school will wish to prepare its own video tapes.

On-line Help. On-line help systems provide users with instant answers to questions. Companies which produce network operating systems software usually ship such on-line help systems with their product as an added service. These new information retrieval systems use character-based interfaces which ease navigation. Additional information can be added to the system as needed.

The information center personnel responsible for computer training should anticipate users' questions and needs. "No question is too simple" is the best attitude one can convey. Beginners should be encouraged and tutored so that their initial enthusiasm is not lost to discouragement.

REVISE ORIGINAL PLANS

Scrap or continue to update documentation that doesn't work. Let users provide feedback when sessions are completed in order to improve the quality of workshops.

As advanced lessons are presented, the instructors should think in terms of implementation of enhanced versions of software which become available. Plan ahead in scheduling for time to prepare the needed documentation for instructional sessions.

SUMMARY

Each step in the installation of a LAN is important to the well-being of the networked environment of a school. If one of the steps is eliminated or given insufficient attention, chaos may result.

The importance of planning the over-all project cannot be over-stressed. Sufficient lead time should go into the planning process to ensure that the job is done well.

The importance of a stable network environment is also important to the users who have to work in the firm.

The importance of properly conducted training sessions will need to be given high priority as the employees convert from stand-alone or mainframe use to the network. There will be numerous questions which must be answered many times.

The importance of documentation formats which will be common to all users as files are shared must be made known in instruction sessions.

The importance of assistance to the active users and those who are "non-users" must be recognized as all users come on-line. Those users who merely get their feet wet are as important to the total success of the LAN as the employees who use the LAN daily.

The importance of frequent revision of plans as environments and users change must be a part of the original planning process because technology never stops changing.

BIBLIOGRAPHY

Dickey-Olson, P. A. (1988, Fall). Installing a local area network: Guidelines for teachers. *Data Base.* South-Western Publishing Company. *7* (1), pp. 11-12.

Judson, M. (1980, January). How to use folio on netware. *Lantimes,* p. 91.

Lederer, Y. (1986, November). Planning, user needs determine final shape of local area networks. *Data Management,* pp. 10-14.

Paznik, M. J. (1987, October). The automated office. *Administrative Management. XLVIII* (10), p. 45.

Pope, B. (1990). Selecting a small business lan. *Proceedings of the Office Automation Society International,* p. 75.

Shorter, J. D., and Groneman, N. J. Local area networks: A comparison of trends with implications for the business classroom. *The Journal of Computer Information Systems,* p. 72.

Stouder, L. D. (1987, October). Lans are the wave of the future, but beware the undertow. *Administrative Management,* p. 45.

Van Kirk, D. (1989, May). Four ways to share. *PC/Computing,* pp. 76-77.

CHAPTER 16

EXPANDING HORIZONS THROUGH DISTANCE LEARNING

CYNTHIA DENTON

Distance Learning Services, Hobson, Montana

Distance learning provides a means of communicating with educators and students in different physical locations. This process allows students who are place-bound to benefit from the knowledge and expertise of a teacher in another school, college, or place of business. The use of one or a combination of several of the technical media to provide two-way communication is at the heart of distance learning. Innovative technology continues to provide new possibilities every day.

With the amazing speed of improvements and advancements in technology, it is very difficult to keep current with the needs of business education. Compounding this difficulty is the fact that business and industry are changing at an alarming pace. Not only is the business world changing technologically, but ideologically as well. Business is no longer transacted simply within the boundaries of one's own city, state, region, or nation. Global interaction is becoming the basis of continuing business success. Additionally, going to work no longer necessarily means going to an office to perform a standard set of tasks. It can mean working at home while fulfilling the needs of a particular business.

These factors place increased responsibilities upon the business educator. If students are to be prepared to successfully function in the business sector, they must have experiences and skills which will allow them to communicate globally and enter the job market with the skills required at the present time rather than those required last year.

BENEFITS OF DISTANCE LEARNING

Distance learning can aid educators in the training of their students for today and tomorrow. Using distance-learning technology, middle school or high school business educators are able to bring into the classroom a unit or series of units on any number of topics which they themselves may be unprepared to present. A teacher with special expertise can teach students in more than one school. Students with special needs or special talents can also be prepared to their full potential through distance learning classes. Distance learning not only has the capability to benefit the students, but can also play a prominent role in helping business educators to keep current in their field of expertise. Finding time to leave home or work to learn new skills and gain additional knowledge is becoming more and more difficult. However, through distance learning techniques, continuing education is possible wherever and whenever the need arises. Technology can provide ways for sharing to take place.

The time for education and learning to become lifetime activities has arrived. For schools and business teachers to flourish, the K-100 concept could be very helpful. There is the need to educate those who have been outside the traditional student categories. Distance learning can greatly assist in retraining efforts. Not only would the professional resources be fully utilized, but the community would have ownership and a personal interest in the process.

The business educator can teach students the needed subject matter as well as teaching other educators the skills and techniques by which they could also be reaching the expanded "student body." Many of the skills which are central to the business education curriculum are imbedded in many of the distance learning techniques. Becoming the provider of distance learning techniques for both students and educators alike is definitely within the grasp of business educators. However, others will take these responsibilities if business educators fail to act quickly.

DISTANCE LEARNING OPTIONS

Distance learning does not refer to one particular set of circumstances. There is a wide variety of successful models from which to learn. A few of the options include: several teachers, the students in one school with a distant teacher, the students in several locations with the teacher in yet another location, or the students in one school with a teacher in the same school but a different physical location. There is no perfect model. The most workable model will be derived from the particular circumstances and resources at each site. When determining which distance learning technology would be appropriate, the resources available and the expenses involved will certainly be decisive in making the final decision.

Likewise, there is not a single perfect mode of delivery of distance learning. Some of the options available are: full-motion video, two-way video, compressed video, audio-only, text-based computer-modem. For the most part these opportunities are provided via fiber optics, satellite, microwave, and telephone lines. One delivery option is not necessarily better than any of the others. It is a matter of what needs are to be met and the resources available to meet them. Distance learning technologies are not without problems. There are equipment problems, scheduling problems, and resistance of teachers and administrators to accept the opportunities available.

The use of satellite transmission for distance learning programs requires large numbers of students to justify the expense and use. At the present time there are a limited number of satellites available, which leads to competition for their use and subsequent expense. The advantage is that satellites are available 24 hours a day and can serve very different audiences at diverse locations. Programs offered via the use of satellite are quite often one-way, full-motion video. The student-instructor interaction can be accomplished via a two-way audio line.

Land-based digital telephone lines are much more common in today's communities. The various possibilities for distance learning are fiber optic cable, T1, T3, 64 and 56-kilobyte connections. T1 telephone lines are perhaps the most available and affordable for the largest number of communities at the present time. Depending upon the size of your community, school district, or university, one of these options may already be available making the expense of developing distance learning courses quite feasible. Some of these options, however, can be quite expensive. For example, offering a course using two-way, full-motion video over fiber-optic lines can be cost prohibitive. However, two-way compressed video over fiber-optic or copper lines is currently more reasonable and accomplishable. This option would be appropriate for courses which have limited enrollment.

Normal voice telephone lines already connect practically every school. These can be used for distance learning courses and projects. Voice and data are usually the methods of transmission, but some video is now becoming possible. This is a much less expensive method of transferring information.

One of the methods of instruction using voice telephone lines is audiographics. This most often consists of two-way audio combined with compressed still images which are sent on a second line. The option also exists to send these images in advance of the class time. This could be in the form of a video, computer disk, or CD-ROM. When this is the practice, only the signal or prompt to have the image called up is sent over the line.

Audiographics is a viable alternative for many situations. It would allow a course to be shared among schools which have too few students to offer the class or to provide an in-house instructor for it. It would allow, in an affordable manner, the opportunity for teachers with differing expertise to team-teach classes from different schools and locations.

Online computer-modem communication offers another option for distance learning projects. This method uses computers, modems, and voice telephone lines. Many people from quite different locations and time availability can participate in common efforts. Discussions can be held among many individuals as well as privately between individuals. This type of course delivery is somewhat different from the traditional teacher-to-student one-way exchange. The student must be actively involved in written responses, and each student has the opportunity for equal participation. The student who is nonparticipatory becomes quite obvious in this method of distance learning. However, limited presentation techniques and use of media exist with this option.

As with all distance learning options, new developments are continually improving the opportunities and effectiveness of computer-modem education. The resources for online text-based communication are generally available and affordable.

IMPLEMENTATION AND EVALUATION OF DISTANCE LEARNING PROJECTS

In order to facilitate the acceleration of distance learning, the awareness of society as a whole must be heightened as to the benefits of this technology.

Additionally, if distance learning is to be successful, there must be an increased training effort for teachers and others to use the technology.

Unless the users of the technology accept distance learning, success will be limited. Care must be made to make the technology easy to use and reliable. Ongoing support for the instructors and students is essential for the growth and effective use of distance learning. Many behavioral changes will need to be made on the part of distance learning instructors, students, classroom teachers, and facilitators. School districts and universities that are experienced in these fields could assist in making the transition successful.

Distance learning may very well open up possibilities for universities, armed services, business communities, and schools to integrate their expertise for the benefit of all students. These situations would benefit the instructor who is new at using the technology as a teaching tool, the distance learning teacher who has students at many sites, or the students who can benefit from the assistance their instructors are receiving.

The colleges and universities could potentially provide a great deal of training for the continuing education of teachers and for the instruction of the advanced-level students in our secondary schools. Those institutions with studios and satellite uplink/downlink facilities could be leading the way in training educators and communities in how these new technologies can be used to bring educational opportunities that would otherwise be unavailable. Many teachers have specialties which benefit their students. Through the distance learning technologies, these specialties could benefit all students in their district, state, region, country, or the world.

When instituting distance learning courses, evaluation should be quite comprehensive. Every element of a distance learning course should be evaluated from virtually every aspect. The content, presentation, facilities, transmission quality and effectiveness, feedback methods, and interaction are just a few of the items which should be evaluated. Also, the timing of the evaluations will be important. Immediate evaluations, followed by mid-course evaluations and end-of-term evaluations are all needed. Each class should be evaluated, not only to find if the course content is being delivered and received toward the desired objective, but also to see if the technology is performing in the manner intended.

ADAPTATION TO DISTANCE LEARNING

Recently, there has been a great deal of discussion about the ability of grades K-12 to benefit from the advanced resources available. With the availability of established networks, schools do not have to remain isolated from the rest of the real world. These networks provide vast resources for information technology and allow individuals to work and study from remote locations.

In the past a new worker went to the place of business and worked there to learn the new trade and gain experience. Today, that can be very reasonably reversed. The expert could come to the students either in person, or more reasonably, through network access. Businesses want trained employees, and in some states they are currently having to train these individuals themselves. The technology and opportunity for distance learning could offer the workplace the training assistance it needs and the school educators the expertise they need to complete the students' course of study.

Isolation of the educational community is a very serious problem when trying to learn and work with new technologies. Educators generally feel uncomfortable teaching in areas where they lack expertise. Access to the various distance learning modes and available networks can assist the individual instructor to offer a current, viable course of study which will prepare the student for successful employment and further study.

We have already networked many schools with computers, telephone lines, and satellites. It may now be time to combine the use of these distance learning technologies with business expertise. Through distance learning and the various networks, educators can resolve some of the equity issues existing between schools by sharing the knowledge and talents of those in the workforce. This can be done without detracting from current programs.

Through distance learning programs, students gain knowledge from their remote classmates that would otherwise not be available. Specialized programs can be provided by the in-house instructor, by remote instructors, or by business-partner instructors via several methods including printed, recorded, and broadcast materials. These programs could also be supplemented by the various interactive and computer-aided distance learning technologies.

SUMMARY

Distance learning programs have been developed in almost every way possible. The options are many; the resources are usually few; and the needs of schools, school districts, and universities are all quite varied. The key to success is in researching the resources available in your area, the funding sources available, the needs of the students, and the potential distance learning classes in question. Excellent distance learning projects can be established and students needs met using all levels of technology.

Some projects are national in direction; others are regional, state-wide, city-wide, school-district wide. Many of the existing projects are in their infancy and are often varied in approach. Very often the states or the universities or a combination of both are responsible for the projects. However, some school districts have initiated their own programs. It is hoped that those who have successful programs will find ways to share them with the outlying areas of their states and regions. The minds and futures of many students are at stake. With the sharing of the distance learning expertise and resources, productivity and success of the students, regardless of their physical location, will be greatly enhanced by the addition of courses and expertise not available to them or to their in-house classroom teacher.

RESOURCES

Lewis, C. T., Hedegaard, T. (1993, April). Online education: Issues and some answers. *T.H.E. JOURNAL* 20:9.

Ostendorf, V. A. (1989). *What every principal, teacher and school board member should know about distance education.* Littleton, CO: Virginia A. Ostendorf, Inc.

Roberts, N., et al. (1990). *Integrating telecommunications into education,* Englewood Cliffs, New Jersey: Prentice Hall.

Schrum, L. (1991). *Distance education, a primer for administrators.* Eugene, Oregon: Oregon School Study Council.

Shaeffer, J. M., and Farr, C. W. (1993, April). Evaluation: A key piece in distance education puzzle. *T.H.E. JOURNAL* 20:9.

Wess, R. G. (1993, April). Distance learning options available in western Nebraska. *T.H.E. JOURNAL* 20:9.

Part IV

EXPANDING HORIZONS IN BUSINESS EDUCATION: MEETING THE CHALLENGE

CHAPTER 17

PROFESSIONAL PIZAZZ: USE IT OR LOSE IT!

JANET SCAGLIONE
University of South Florida, Tampa, Florida

It's a challenging time to be in education. Department of Labor reports give evidence of an increasing mismatch between the skills required for employment and the skills of our workforce. The Secretaries Commission on Achieving Necessary Skills (SCANS) reinforces the demands of the 21st century and offers a challenging new list of workplace competencies. Our nation's economic status is being threatened by competition from around the globe, and we are frequently reminded of how poorly United States graduates fare when compared with students in other countries. One might select from any number of reports, editorials, and exposés that suggest a rule-laden educational bureaucracy, lack of professionalism, inadequate resources, and an underqualified, isolated, unmotivated, tenure bound population of teachers as one mediating factor for the ills of society.

Yet while some in education moan and groan about the complexity of the issues and the helplessness of it all, others simply thrive. While some work to refocus the blame, others work to inspire the cure. While some sit back, relax, and teach just enough, others challenge students and themselves to reach just a little bit higher. And while some dodge the dynamics of technology (and its potential to change our entire curriculum), others plunge ahead and ride the wave into the future.

Why do some of us survive in spite of the flawed system we work in? What prompts the teachers at a rural school in Florida, with a predominantly migrant population, to ignore the odds and create an environment where students join vocational career clubs to enthusiastically explore options and possibilities?

Why do some business education programs continue to lose ground— while a typical high school in Venice, Florida, offers five sections of Business Law/Management?

How is it that while one veteran teacher coasts into retirement by teaching the same lessons for the sixth year straight, another seasoned professional jumps at the chance to install a new computer network?

This chapter will offer some thoughts, suggestions, and over-the-years accumulations related to the art of motivating oneself at work—a subject that might be referred to as professional pizazz!

WHAT IS PROFESSIONAL PIZAZZ?

Though it may be considered slang, Webster (1993) defines pizazz as energy, vigor, vitality, and spirit. It is also defined as style, sparkle, flair, and flash.

The notion of professional pizazz, then, might be defined as the energy and vitality that one demonstrates within the realm of a profession. It is, if you will, a concept that may be demonstrated through a unique array of talents, mannerisms, and behaviors. One key characteristic that remains common is an unwavering, positive vision of education and an unrelenting resiliency to try and try again.

WHY IS PROFESSIONAL PIZAZZ IMPORTANT?

It's difficult to imagine any profession surviving without a highly motivated, full-of-pizazz membership. Business education is certainly no different. Our field is affected by the varying levels of professional pizazz that are demonstrated by teachers and administrators, and the significance of pizazz is obvious —especially when one considers the typical business education classroom.

A casual observer might easily select the classroom that's home to pizazz. In some significant way, the classroom has been changed to conform to the individual's ideals and inspirations. What's more, on any given day, during most any period, one might easily select the classroom led by a professional with pizazz. Students have a way of mirroring what they see. The professional who approaches each task with an enthusiastic zeal will communicate a similar love of learning to the students fortunate enough to be there. In fact, one might even suggest that the students' level of pizazz is directly proportionate to the teacher's level of pizazz. In other words, the more interest demonstrated by a teacher, the more interest returned by the students. And while exceptions to that simplified ratio abound, one might rightly consider the following:

Is it fair to ask students to be attentive and eager to learn if the teacher does not model the same?

Is it right to expect attention to detail or extra effort if an instructor gets away with less?

Can we actually coax students to "take pride" in their work if we aren't proud of what we do?

Professional pizazz is imperative to the future of business education if we are to maintain enrollments, move to the forefront of technology, integrate the curriculum, and attend to the myriad of challenges that lie ahead.

WHAT HAPPENS TO PIZAZZ?

The importance of professional pizazz—the energy and zeal demonstrated in one's teaching career—is obvious. Dealing successfully with the dynamics of a changing curriculum, fluctuating enrollments, and increasing challenges requires high levels of motivation. Indeed, dealing with just the traditional challenges of teaching requires high levels of motivation. The seasoned professional is encouraged to recall the energy, flair, and determination that characterized initial years in the classroom. Typically, the novice teacher, filled with enthusiasm and inspired to make a difference, approaches each new day with renewed vigor. Challenged to meet high ideals and prepared to validate theories discussed in the university classroom, the typical novice loves the profession, enjoys students, and relentlessly seeks solutions to problems when they arise. Frequently ignoring the well-intentioned advice from more experienced faculty, new teachers envision what "could be" and engage in "what if" strategies.

Why then is that image frequently so different five or 10 years later? What happens to the energy and ambition? How is it that the dreamer and the idealist is so quickly replaced by the skeptic and the realist? When does the teacher who was once determined to walk around the room coaching, praising, and correcting students in the process of learning become content to sit behind the desk with a red pen in hand, thereby limiting the personal interaction to the return of a graded paper? When are expectations lowered, failures accepted as commonplace, and the cover-the-curriculum mentality deemed acceptable? And at what point does the vision of hope and positive outcome give way to the sort of frustration, despair, and critical defensiveness frequently found in a teachers' lounge?

An outsider might easily conclude that the teaching profession is hazardous. It's hazardous to one's self-esteem, motivation, and positive outlook.

Some years ago, an ambitious young teacher was approached by her principal on the way to the parking lot after an exhausting day of entertaining students, challenging intellects, and massaging behavior into manageable episodes. As the teacher literally dragged herself to the parking lot, lugging home a ton of papers and a half-completed test, the observant principal queried, "What on earth is the matter?" Apparently a defiant student in sixth period, a quitter in fourth, and a power failure during a thunderstorm had left a telltale sign on the weary young professional. She sighed, "Another exciting day in the classroom, and I'm exhausted."

The wise administrator shook her head, smiled slyly, and said, "If you're going home tired at the end of the day—you're not doing your job right."

One day, about three years later, after repeated attempts to interest a group of I-dare-you-to challenge-me-in-May-seniors, the weary teacher simply gave up. She no longer cared whether "they" succeeded or not. She was tired of spending her evenings grading papers, her weekends on lesson plans, and every bit of her energy devoted to "those kids." Her professional pizazz had slipped away and her energy was gone.

Education is filled with obstacles that chip away at a teacher's motivation. Bureaucratic red tape, administrators who are afraid to make waves, lack of public respect, isolation and despair. Teachers complain of too much to cover, too little time, top-down mandates that make no sense, and students who tune out, turn off, and defy change.

In the midst of this professional dilemma the teacher remembered the words of her wise administrator. "If you're going home tired at the end of the day, you're not doing your job right." Determined not to throw in the towel, she decided on a minor philosophical twist instead, and with renewed vigor opted to "take" from the students and to "take" from the system. She began a pizazz improvement program. The older professional still goes home tired, but each and every day she remembers that the most important person in the classroom is the teacher, and she is ever mindful of how students, coworkers, and the system can meet her needs.

HOW DO YOU KEEP PROFESSIONAL PIZAZZ?

The fate of business education depends on many things, but one element is certainly the motivation and pizazz level of our existing membership. Based on numerous interactions with groups of business educators and the collective reflection of hundreds of years in public education, the following pizazz-building initiatives are offered for consideration:

Identify your talents. . . and share them. Amidst the rigid curriculum, top-down bureaucracy, and mandated paper trails, teachers frequently neglect to share their personal and professional talents. In fact, many times a busy professional is inclined to forget just what those talents are. We begin to approach the tasks at hand and ignore anything extraneous to that charge. How sad it is when we overlook the unique talents that individuals bring to education. How unfortunate if we allow school routines that reinforce uniformity and procedure to become the priority.

Consider what it is that you do best. What special gifts do you bring to the teaching profession? Are you a reflective listener or an activist willing to try something new? Think about the things that you do best and share your talents openly. If you sing—do so for students. If you write poetry, make it part of your curriculum. And if you are secretly a stand up comic or a sit down counselor—build it into your daily classroom routine. It is amazing that so many of us are so modest about what we do best. Apparently, in junior high school we internalized the notion that to share talents and exceptional qualities openly was considered inappropriate behavior. We've replaced the joyous celebration of talents that is evident in any preschooler—with a socially acceptable devaluing of what makes us special. Just recall the last time someone paid you a compliment and the many ways you tried to squirm your way out of it. By doing so, however, you not only trivialize your unique gifts, but you reinforce the notion that others should do the same. The next time you feel good about one of the many unique talents you have—find a way to tell the world. Such a positive expression will only add to your pizazz, and theirs.

Accentuate the positive. Sometimes in the midst of progress reports, reduced budgets, and spiraling obstacles, teachers lose sight of the positive side of the profession. It's easier to join the multitudes of doomsayers than to walk into the teacher's lounge with a smile and a glimmer of enthusiasm. Though problems are real and solutions may be few, a negative attitude is not one of them. One inexpensive alternative for a school environment is simply a positive outlook.

When's the last time you openly shared with your colleagues something special that you did in class? Imagine the atmosphere in the teachers' lounge if more of us spent the time discussing what we feel good about instead of what we cannot change. Your open proclamation of what you do best and how it works in your classroom may allow others the confidence to openly discuss the same. Look for what's right instead of what's wrong. Imagine a teachers' haven where we learn about practices that work, lessons that inspire, projects that engage learners. Such a place might be created in teachers' lounge USA if we focus on the good news and share it.

One group of innovative faculty members, who were determined to turn the teachers' lounge around, initiated a novel idea appropriately referred to as the "Fun File." They collected one great idea from each teacher, organized them (ice breakers, games, grouping activities, etc.), and set up a file cabinet next to the copier in the teachers' lounge. With such a unique sharing system in place, "stealing" good ideas has become the main reason for entering the faculty lounge, and you can imagine the positive change of climate.

Invite interaction. When asked to identify reasons for becoming a teacher, many allude to the fact that they like working with people and were drawn to such a people profession. It's far too easy, however, to totally separate oneself from students as evidenced by the traditional classroom scene where students are seated at their desks and the teacher is grading papers and attending to other noninteractions. The desk, the lectern, and the computer can serve as physical barriers between teacher and student. The old "off seat . . . on feet" concept is a first step toward interaction.

Equally limiting to real student/teacher interaction is the classic post instruction retort, "Are there any questions?" The conditioned silence that follows can be eliminated, however, by a conscious effort to question more—and lecture less. If you find yourself telling and selling simply try the following:

- Lead into every lesson with a question.
- Ask students to write down one idea they remember from yesterday.
- Feign forgetfulness and invite students to bring you up-to-date.
- Frequently ask the reporter questions; who, what, when, where, and especially, why?
- Make it a habit of answering every question with another question.

Though in business education we typically pride ourselves on the fact that we engage students in hands-on learning, two-way interaction is frequently limited by our helpfulness. When working one-on-one, be sure to ask what the next step might be, or try the reflective, "Hmm, what do you think?" To remind you to ask instead of tell, keep a big question mark in front of you at all times to reinforce the critical importance of listening rather than lecturing.

By getting out from behind the podium or desk, and into the rows and clusters, you are more approachable and identifiable as "on our side." When you lecture less, students are free to experience more, and you remain in touch with their interests, personalities, aptitudes, and energies. These connections are critical to your pizazz.

Remember your youth . . . make learning relevant. Nothing erodes a teacher's motivation and pizazz more than apathetic, uninterested students. Unfortunately, textbooks, simulations, and traditional learning materials may not spark that critical interest—we must do that. Unfortunately, increasing years in the system may put us at a disadvantage. We don't speak their language, don't like their music, and don't remember what it was like to be 16. Yet, making lessons relevant is the key to maintaining student interest.

How can we tap into the energy and interest that abounds in the hallways and lunchrooms? What can we do to excite that interest in the classroom? The first rule of public speaking is to know your audience, and the same applies to the classroom. Instead of the routine business letter on page 109, let them write a letter to their favorite DJ or a letter to the editor of the local newspaper about what's right with teenagers. And replace those interest problems on a 30-year mortgage with the interest paid on the car of their choice. Relevance can be found in their television idols or the upcoming school dance. It's up to you to provide creative options to the text.

Some of the most relevant examples arise from everyday problems. How to get a date with the person you want, what to say to convince your mother to buy you a car, teenagers' rights and responsibilities, and how to endure peer pressure. Many relevant topics can be integrated into the traditional curriculum, and providing feedback on assignments becomes a bit more interesting if you vary the content. If you're really running short on creativity and feeling suddenly brave, let the students decide how to spice up the curriculum. You'll be amazed at the competence they can demonstrate when given the corresponding responsibility. A resurgence of student interest can provide a real boost to teacher pizazz.

Give fewer grades . . . but more feedback. Apparently, in our quest for accountability we have overemphasized the importance of grading. We have conditioned ourselves and our students to believe that the grade provides the reason for completing an activity or assignment. While a teacher's evaluation may provide the necessary incentive or reward for some, others need relevance, a sense of accomplishment, peer support, and the intrinsic motivation that goes with the task itself.

Alternative evaluation systems might incorporate student centered feedback, self and peer evaluation, and portfolio assessment. These assessment options require students to take a more active role in evaluating their work. This more active role is similar to the kind of self-evaluation required in the workplace. Even more importantly, however, when the teacher is relieved of the traditional grading burden, he or she is free to monitor a more important element of learning—the process. To get started one might:

- Implement a check mark system instead of a grading system to provide essential feedback (10 out of 10 checks is easily converted to 100 percent if you're still compelled to provide a grade).

- Recognize that you do not have to review everything (especially when the growing stack of papers appears to be more important than the individuals sitting before you).

- Review performance and provide feedback during class by moving from desk to desk.

- Assign a student office manager to check, reinforce, and direct remediation.

There are many methods for reducing the grading burden. Unfortunately, years of traditional pen-in-hand conditioning are difficult to break. Changing your evaluation patterns has the potential to dramatically increase your pizazz level, so what have you got to lose?

Celebrate success. Remember the well-intentioned advice you were offered as a new teacher. "You can't be their friend," and "Don't smile until Christmas." Such austere practices severely limit the potential for celebration. In a system that frequently sets us up for failure, however, it's important to find creative reasons to celebrate. Some creative accomplishments that might be celebrated include: The entire class is present one day; each person completes an assignment on time; each student brought a book to class; it's someone's birthday; it's your teaching anniversary; a new relationship has begun, or perhaps it's Monday. It's easy to find something to celebrate if you're of a mind to, but by now you're probably asking, how? Consider these creative options:

- Lead the class through five minutes of positive imaging.
- Pat each other on the back.
- Create a student-initiated recognition program whereby students reward peers for positive behavior, personal accomplishments, or staying awake in class.
- Lead the class in song.
- Pass out candy or other coveted rewards.
- Cancel the quiz or homework.
- Have a pizza, donut, or Coke party.
- Create a winner's bulletin board and modify the winning criteria according to your weekly goals.

Energy and enthusiasm may reflect an upward momentum if the right behaviors are recognized, and we all know that enthusiasm is contagious.

Dare to be different . . . plan for some fun. A sense of humor may be one of God's greatest gifts. Indeed, given the ongoing challenges facing today's business educator, an element of fun is essential to maintaining pizazz. Laughter is commonplace in an upbeat, motivated group. It's a sign of comfort, caring, and collaboration. In an elective discipline where marketing programs are critical to next year's enrollment, a comfortable classroom climate becomes a powerful marketing tool. Happy students will spread the good news without even being asked. Here are some fun filled options:

- Keep a mirror in class so you can see the positive difference a smile makes, especially when it's on your face.
- Frequently incorporate popular games into your lessons (*Jeopardy, Family Feud,* and *Wheel of Fortune* are great).
- Conduct some friendly intra- or interclass competition.
- Explore role play and other theatrics as a vehicle for learning.
- Post political cartoons and your favorite comic strips daily, and make time for sharing.
- Invite students to write captions to funny pictures or cartoons.
- Encourage students to develop a sense of humor by writing about embarrassing moments, setting up a data base of jokes, or solving the riddle at the end of the quiz for extra credit.
- Lighten up, and be prepared to laugh at yourself.
- Explore the potential humor in office situations by playing "A funny thing happened on the way to the office."
- Play charades to reinforce the power of body language and facial expressions.

Some of your colleagues may not agree that learning should be fun, but given the potential for increased energy and enrollments, it's certainly worth a try.

Create a pizazz portfolio. Today's business educator faces an uncertain future. The brick walls and bureaucratic red tape can sometimes overwhelm even the brightest spirits. That's why a pizazz portfolio is so important. To start yours, decorate a brightly colored folder with markers, glitter, or a collage of your favorite things. List at least 10 of your talents on a sheet of paper and carefully place it in your pizazz portfolio. What you choose to save in your folder depends on what makes you feel good about yourself and your profession. Many people include:

- Cherished thank you notes and cards from students, parents, and peers.
- Inspirational sayings and phrases.
- Pictures that represent what you love about your job.
- A list of students you've enjoyed or inspired.
- A homework assignment that was finally turned in, or an A paper from the one you thought would never succeed.
- Student responses to "What I like best about this class."
- A list of winners from local, state, or national competition.
- Report cards and other evaluative papers.
- Letters of recommendation from previous employers.

Keep your pizazz portfolio within reach. The next time you discover that your batteries are running low you'll have at your fingertips just the boost you need.

It's a challenging time to be in business education. Surviving in the information age requires an unrelenting spirit. This information explosion is forcing dramatic changes in our curriculum, and the dynamics of technology confirm that what we teach today may be obsolete tomorrow. We must rethink routines, reinforce flexibility, and develop a comfortable acceptance of constant change. We can choose to view these challenges as overwhelming . . . or inspiring. Either choice requires energy and enthusiasm. Professional pizazz is essential to our future. Use it before it gets lost along the way.

FIFTY POINTS FOR PIZAZZ

1. Begin each day by asking students, "What do you feel good about?"
2. If you have to sit—sit beside a student.
3. Position yourself in the back of the room one day a week, or move your desk there permanently.
4. Get out of your classroom on your lunch break.
5. Let students do more while you do less.
6. Share the good news with students and parents, routinely.
7. Wear seasonal clothing—costumes on Halloween, snowflakes in winter, and sunshine in spring.
8. While standing in the hallway between classes, say hello to a student you've never met.
9. Greet each student personally as they enter your classroom. Tell them you're happy to see them.

10. Don't talk until everyone's listening.

11. Allow students to establish and monitor classroom rules.

12. Take your class outside at least once each grading period.

13. Survey students regarding their favorite TV shows and radio stations. Watch what they watch and listen to their music (remember to keep the volume low).

14. Share one of your most embarrassing moments with students, and by all means tell them up front—you don't know all the answers.

15. Tell one of your colleagues what was great about today—and why.

16. Applaud achievements. Make a joyful noise of celebration.

17. Lighten up . . . remember your sense of humor. Share a joke each day.

18. Always read the comic section of the newspaper, and use it in class frequently.

19. Post your lesson plans so that everyone can see the exciting things planned for your students.

20. Enter the teachers' lounge with a smile and ask the first person you see, "What do you feel good about?"

21. Tell everyone your good ideas and encourage borrowing.

22. Observe another teacher at least once each grading period.

23. Dress according to school tradition for pep rallies and spirit days.

24. Invite administrators and counselors to your room and "show off" what your students are doing.

25. Eat lunch with a different group of teachers, preferably from a different department, once a month.

26. Have lunch with students at least once each month.

27. Complete 95 percent of your work at school. When you take it home you usually end up feeling guilty.

28. Teach at least one new prep each year.

29. Throw out last year's lesson plans, except for the exceptional ones.

30. Learn a computer recordkeeping system and use it.

31. Read your professional journals. Better yet, write a helpful hint for teachers and submit it.

32. Elect a class photographer and create a picture bulletin board.

33. Offer to conduct an in-service for your faculty on something you're good at, or something you've been meaning to learn.

34. Share your hobby with students and, where possible, make it part of the curriculum.

35. Keep a bulletin board for success stories—anything that students feel successful about.

36. Start each department meeting with at least five minutes of positive sharing or creative brainstorming.

37. Trade places with a teacher in your department once a month.

38. Research your employment options and interview for another job at least once a year.

39. Buy some fun stamps and stickers to decorate student papers.

40. Put up a positive suggestion box and routinely share the ideas with the class.

41. Go on a fun field trip with your students.

42. Join your school improvement team or other faculty group.

43. Treat yourself and your students to five minutes of sustained, silent reading. Gradually increase the time frame as they succeed.

44. Celebrate failures—and be prepared to learn from them.

45. Attend a class reunion for your former students.

46. Identify a positive mentor and converse with him or her frequently.

47. Write your administrator a memo on the positive things you've done in class this week.

48. Write your students a thank-you note when they've done something exceptionally well.

49. Invite a clown, magician, or juggler as your next guest speaker.

50. Decorate your room with helium balloons for special occasions.

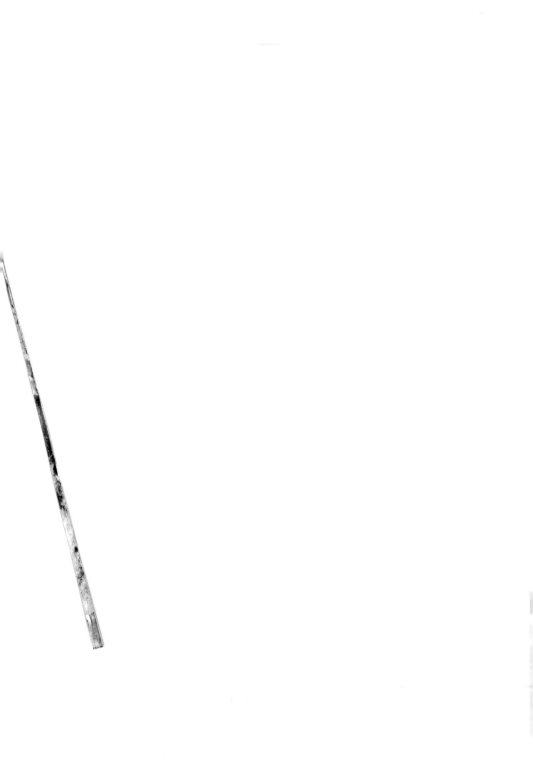